Isabel of Burgundy

Isabel of Burgundy

The Duchess Who Played Politics in the Age of Joan of Arc, 1397–1471

Aline S. Taylor

Madison Books
Lanham • New York • Oxford

First Madison Books Edition 2001

This hardcover edition of *Isabel of Burgundy* is an original publication. It is published by arrangement with the author.

Published by Madison Books
4720 Boston Way
Lanham, Maryland 20706

12 Hid's Copse Road
Cumnor Hill, Oxford OX2 9JJ, England

Distributed by National Book Network

Library of Congress Cataloging-in-Publication Data

Taylor, Aline S.
Isabel of Burgundy : the duchess who played politics in the age of Joan of Arc, 1397-1471 / Aline S. Taylor.
p. cm.
Includes bibliographical references and index.
ISBN 1-56833-227-0 (cloth : alk. paper)
1. Isabelle de Portugal, duchesse de Bourgogne, 1397-1471 2. Burgundy (France)—Kings and rulers—Biography. 3. Burgundy (France)—History—House of Valois, 1363-1477. I. Title.

DC611.B78 T39 2001
944'.41025'092—dc21
[B] 2001034561

∞™ The paper used in this publication meets the minimum requirements of American National Standard for Information Sciences—Permanence of Paper for Printed Library Materials, ANSI/NISO Z39.48–1992.
Manufactured in the United States of America.

For those who helped me bring Isabel back to life:
my husband, Allen, whose photographs called her back to us,
and Clifford and Leslie, whose support joined his and never wavered

Contents

	Illustrations, Maps, and Genealogical Tables	ix
	Preface	xi
One	Flashpoint: Isabel in Jeopardy: 1457	1
Two	The Renaissance Princess, the Medieval Bride, 1397–1431	23
Three	A Diplomatic Education, 1432–1435	47
Four	The Duchess at the Negotiating Table at Home and Abroad, 1435–1445	72
Five	Dual Challenges from France and England, 1446–1453	103
Six	The Eclipse of Isabel, 1454–1456	125
Seven	Retreat, Reconciliation, and Renewed Challenge, 1457–1460	145
Eight	The Changing Cast of Royal Players, 1461–1466	165
Nine	Madame La Grande, 1467–1470	187
Ten	The Death of Isabel: Danger for Burgundy, 1471	207

Epilogue 219
Index 224
About the Author 232

Illustrations, Maps, and Genealogical Tables

1. *Isabel of Portugal,* by Jan van Eyck xvii
2. *Inauguration of the Order of the Golden Fleece at the Marriage of Philip the Good and Isabel of Portugal,* January 10, 1430 xviii
3 *Philip the Good,* by Roger Van der Weyden (?) xix
4. *Charles the Bold,* by Roger Van der Weyden (?) xx
5. *Isabel, Duchess of Burgundy,* by Roger Van der Weyden xxi
6. *Isabel of Portugal Kneeling* xxii
7. *Philip the Good Entering into Ghent* xxiii
8. *Charles the Bold with Marie, his daughter and heiress* xxiv
9. Map of Europe around 1450 xv
10. Map of Burgundy and France xvi
11. Map of Burgundy under Philip the Good 21
12. Genealogy of the Dukes of Burgundy 22
13. Genealogy of the English Connections of Isabel of Burgundy 102

Preface

THIS ACCOUNT OF ISABEL, princess of Portugal and duchess of Burgundy, rescues her from the dusty recesses of history's closet. She has remained hidden in those shadows for four hundred and fifty years, during which time next to nothing has been published about her remarkable life and achievements. In part, it seems, history has chosen to ignore Isabel because she does not fit neatly into one of the few, narrow categories traditionally assigned to women. Yet, it is precisely because she cannot be easily categorized that she deserves our attention. In an age in which public life was a stage reserved for men, Isabel earned a reputation as a formidable diplomatic, political, and financial player. The variety of roles she performed and the breadth of her interests demonstrated that one did not need to be a man to take advantage of the opportunities presented by the Renaissance.

Although virtually none of Isabel's own papers have survived, a wide array of extant sources—royal and ducal records, chronicles, letters, diaries, and journals—attest to the imprint she made on great affairs of state from her marriage to Duke Philip the Good in 1429 until her death in 1471. She wove economic alliances with England that sustained Burgundy's independence. She negotiated territorial claims with the French king that gave her husband the opportunity to assert Burgundy's wealth and power. For twenty-five years she persuaded, cajoled, and strong-armed merchants and nobles into parting with the money needed to keep her husband's armies in the field. She supervised shipbuilding and helped to organize the Burgundian navy. In the face of powerful, pro-French enemies at her husband's court, she promoted her own policy of a close alliance with England, a policy that triumphed in 1468 with the marriage of her son, Charles, to the sister of the English king.

To navigate successfully through the treacherous currents of fifteenth-century diplomacy, warfare, and court intrigues required a blend of self-belief, determination, ruthlessness, and exact judgment that few men possessed. To do so as a woman demanded even more exceptional qualities. Determined to prove her worth in a world ruled by and for men, Isabel learned quickly that she must rely on no one but herself. Forever regarded as a "foreigner" in her husband's duchy, alone and isolated from her own family, she understood that she must keep her own counsel even as she sought to ensure Burgundy's very survival.

Conscious of her vulnerability, the duchess was desperate to achieve financial independence. She invested in property, developed forest land, and obtained salt and copper mines, building a fortune that provided her a rare degree of freedom. Her wealth not only brought some security but also allowed her to satisfy her piety. Isabel's Portuguese upbringing had instilled an abiding faith, and she spent much of her money and her energy on the establishment of a new order of nursing nuns and the reform of mendicant orders.

Her Portuguese background also left her unprepared for the sumptuous decadence of the Burgundian court. She was thirty-two when she married Philip—virtually an old maid by the standards of medieval royalty, which typically pictured its brides to be a nubile twelve or so. Isabel was Philip's third wife, and her first and most important responsibility was to produce an heir. Over the first four years of their marriage, as she journeyed from palace to palace, along contested borders and through rebellious towns, she gave birth to three children. Two died in their first months, but the third, Charles, survived. Thereafter, the conservative, rather dowdy duchess suffered through the many flirtations and affairs of her husband, earning a reputation as a suspicious, jealous, and vindictive spouse.

As the distance between Philip and Isabel grew, so the closer she drew Charles to herself and the more she immersed herself in her ducal responsibilities, financial dealings, and spiritual concerns. Yet, even as she grew old, she never entirely abandoned her husband's court. Though many older aristocratic women pursued a cloistered existence, Isabel kept abreast of events from her estate at La Motte-au-Bois and continued to exert an influence on their outcomes.

This book portrays the many different facets of this remarkable woman. It presents both her public and her private lives, her cool analytical mind and her passionate pride, her piety and her cruelty, her disasters as well as her triumphs. The picture that emerges is of a woman whose tact, intellect, and tenacity brought her influence and independence in an age when women were regarded as politically insignificant and personally dependent. It is hard not to admire Isabel for her courage, her strength of will, and the example she set in an age dominated by men of a woman determined to control her own destiny.

This book and its author owe a debt to several people. My editor, Dr. Nigel Quinney, helped bring the story of Isabel to life with his patience, professionalism, and gentle perseverance. Susan Green, editor of the Huntington Library Press, gave generously of her expertise, care, and time in developing the text. Dr. Carl Christensen, professor of Renaissance and Reformation History at the University of Colorado, guided my first research into Isabel's political importance. Virginia Renner, Readers Services Librarian at the Huntington Library, kindly used her influence to open the door to the archives in Lille, France, where the staff helped me in discovering the latest research on Isabel. I am also deeply appreciative for the contributions made by staff at Madison Books, and in particular for the support and careful attention shown by Alyssa Theodore, Michael Dorr, and Christine Ambrose.

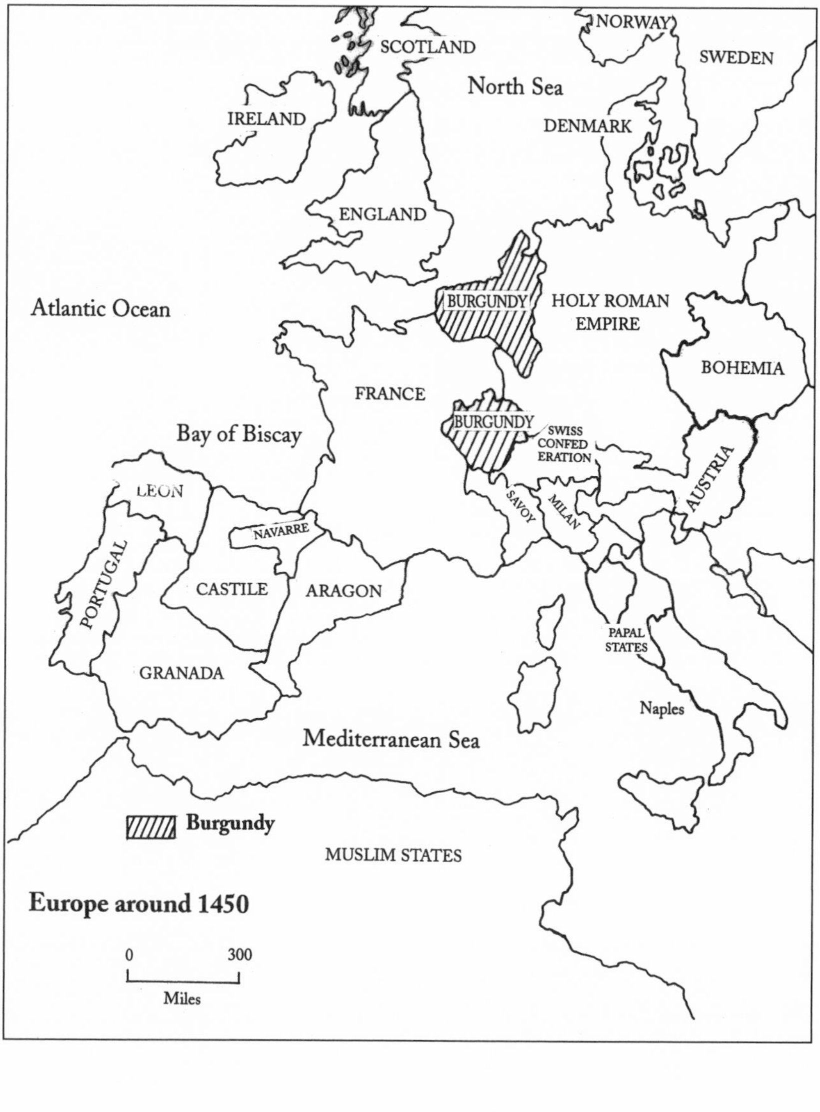
NORWAY
SCOTLAND
SWEDEN
North Sea
IRELAND
DENMARK
ENGLAND
BURGUNDY
HOLY ROMAN
EMPIRE
Atlantic Ocean
BOHEMIA
FRANCE
BURGUNDY
SWISS
CONFED
ERATION
Bay of Biscay
LEON
SAVOY
MILAN
AUSTRIA
NAVARRE
PORTUGAL
CASTILE
ARAGON
PAPAL
STATES
GRANADA
Naples
Mediterranean Sea
Burgundy
MUSLIM STATES
Europe around 1450
0
300
Miles

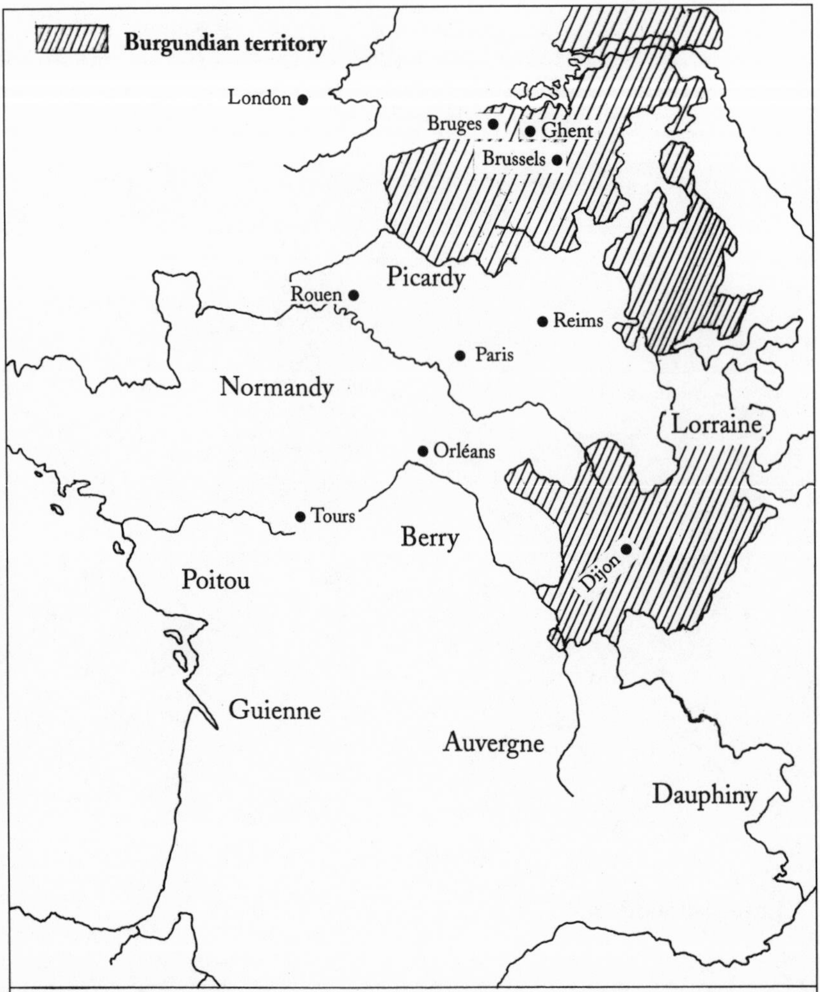

Burgundy and France

Isabel of Portugal, by Jan van Eyck. At the Louvre.

Thought to be the portrait of Isabel prepared by van Eyck for Philip the Good's approval of their betrothal. Isabel would have been thirty-two at the sitting in Lisbon.

Inauguration of the Order of the Golden Fleece at the Marriage of Philip the Good and Isabel of Portugal, January 10, 1430. Wall painting in the Council Chambers of the Town Hall in Bruges.

Philip the Good, by Roger Van der Weyden (?). At the Dijon Museum.

Thought to be painted by Van der Weyden in the mid-1450s, at the same time as the artist was commissioned to portray Isabel and Charles.

Charles the Bold, by Roger Van der Weyden (?). At the Dijon Museum.

Thought to be painted by Van der Weyden in the mid-1450s, when Charles would have been in his early twenties.

Isabel, Duchess of Burgundy, by Roger Van der Weyden. At the Getty Museum, Malibu, California.

Portrait assumed to be of the mature duchess, painted in the 1450s, when the duchess would have been in her fifties.

Isabel of Portugal Kneeling. Courtesy Hulton Getty / Archive Photos.

Philip the Good Entering into Ghent. Courtesy Hulton Getty / Archive Photos.

Charles the Bold with Marie, his daughter and heiress. Courtesy Hulton Getty / Archive Photos.

Chapter One

Flashpoint: Isabel in Jeopardy, 1457

THE DUCHESS ISABEL OF BURGUNDY walked purposefully beside her husband, Philip the Good, as they left the private chapel of the ducal palace in Brussels. Dressed in black as was his custom, the duke appeared to be weighed down by more than the heavy gold chain and pendant of golden fleece shimmering on his chest. His step was firm but more rushed than regal, and he leaned forward as if in agitated debate with his own thoughts. Isabel glanced up toward the man to whom she had been married for twenty-seven years, then quickly looked at their twenty-three-year-old son, Charles, who had accompanied them to mass that morning of January 17, 1457.

As they entered the chapel's oratory, Philip could barely contain his simmering anger. He stopped abruptly and turned to confront Charles. The son, darker and more solidly built than his father, stood unflinching before Philip's furious glare. While the torchlight flickered against the walls of the chamber in these early hours after dawn, the tiny duchess quickly stepped between father and son. Philip, the "Great Duke of the West," was not accustomed to resistance, and his determination to install the nephew of Anthony de Croy, his court favorite, as chamberlain of his own son's household increased with Charles's opposition. The issue was of great practical importance—for the chamberlain's power extended over all matters of household affairs, including its expenses—and of great symbolic significance in the long-standing struggle by Charles to assert his independence. It was also an issue with substantial political ramifications: Anthony de Croy was the man most opposed to the pro-English policies of the duchess Isabel, and Charles was deeply influenced by his mother's views.

Charles was no less furious than his father. Philip had given Charles permission to choose his own chamberlain, and Charles had made an apparently wise choice, selecting the son of Nicolas Rolin, the man whom Philip had retained as the chancellor of Burgundy since 1422. But now Philip had withdrawn his permission and was insisting on de Croy's nephew, Philippe de Croy, lord of Sempy. Charles handed Philip the household registers that the duke had told his son to bring to mass that morning. Charles pointed out how carefully he had kept his accounts, accounts that clearly showed Charles could himself fund the position of chamberlain without any additional financial help from his father. As father and son faced one another, each determined to master the other, their faces reddened in anger. Philip waved his arms wildly, shouting that Charles must agree to accept the lord of Sempy and must do so immediately. Both men stood their ground, haughty and uncompromising.

This nasty drama brought to a boil their family's long-simmering conflict over the power the duke lavished on the de Croy family, trusted advisers from his youth. As the duke's fury mounted, Isabel bent her head and whispered a hint of caution to Charles. Her conical hat and veil cast a striking shadow along the fire-lit walls of the oratory as she moved from father to son and back again.

"My lord, I beg you to keep your promise," Charles insisted repeatedly.

"My God!" his father replied. "Let us have no more talk of promises. It is my privilege to give and to take away. And it is my will that the Lord Sempy be settled in the office."

Charles shouted angrily, "My lord, I beg you, pardon me. I hold by what you have promised me. I see it well—it is the lord of Croy who has cooked up this plot."

Philip stiffened and his face turned deep crimson. Charles straightened his back, legs planted firmly before the apoplectic duke, resolved not to lose another argument with his father, and continued to refuse to accept his command.

The duke raged on, "You dare cross my will, boy? Get out of my sight!" Philip threw his son's household registers into the fire—and then Isabel saw the duke lift the dagger from his waist. The knife in Philip's hand came up swiftly and plunged downward. But neither the duchess nor Charles was there to receive the blow, for Isabel pushed her son back and hustled him through a narrow passage away from the chapel and Philip's fury.[1]

At sixty, the duke seemed an old man, rigid in the exercise of his authority and often a victim of his own willfulness. Isabel was only one year younger than her husband, but age had not robbed her of her ability to reason coolly and act decisively when her will was threatened. She had already invested many years disciplining her desires and honing her diplomatic skills. She did not lose sight of her goals by blundering ahead oblivious to obstacles; instead, she found ways to turn obstructions into advantages. This family argument, however, was to test that skill to the utmost.

As Isabel and Charles fled into the passageway outside the oratory, they encountered the clerk of the chapel, Caron, who had rushed to the scene, alarmed at the raised voices of the duke and his son. Isabel pleaded with the clerk to give her the keys to the door of an ascending stairway. But in fear for his own life, Caron refused to assist their escape.

"Go back," he cried. " You know how easily the duke can be swayed with gentleness. And you, monseigneur," he chastised Charles, "you have no right to contradict your father in anything. I beg of you, in God's honor, humble yourself before your father and you will find him forgiving."

Faced with Caron's refusal to help her, and recognizing the logic of his plea, Isabel wavered. She and Philip had argued often, and now that her panic was subsiding, she remembered that unless she approached her husband to soften his anger soon after a quarrel, the resentment between them would grow. And now that his fury involved their son as well, Isabel decided that she must convince Charles to return to his father and beg forgiveness. Turning to Charles, Isabel tried to persuade her proud, obdurate son to return to the oratory and make peace with Philip.

"Dear madame," Charles cried loudly, "my father has forbid me to come before him and I am justified after this command not to return into his presence."

On the other side of the half-open oratory door, the duke clearly heard Charles's impudent words. Thrown into an uncontrollable rage, Philip shouted at his wife and son with such violence that Isabel panicked once more and begged the clerk, "My friend, quick, quick, open the door, it is time to escape or we will be dead."[2]

As Caron gave in to her plea, Isabel thrust Charles before her, and they both entered the winding stairwell that led to the chamber of the future king of France, the dauphin Louis. Like Charles, Louis too had run from his own father's anger—he had done so the year before, fleeing on horseback across the French border and into Burgundy, where he found protection at the court of his uncle, the Great Duke of the West. Philip had provided this splendid apartment for Louis at the ducal court in Brussels several months earlier, when on October 15, 1456, he had welcomed his nephew with great pomp and ceremony.

Startled by the abrupt entry of the duchess and her son, Louis quickly dismissed his visitors to comfort Isabel and Charles in privacy. On learning the reason for their sudden and fearful appearance, the dauphin acceded to Isabel's request that he talk with the duke immediately to subdue Philip's anger and bring some understanding between him and his son. Louis left mother and son in his rooms, ran down the stairs, and, after knocking on its door, entered the chapel.

Philip stood facing the doorway as Louis approached. The duke was deathly pale, the veins standing out purple on his forehead, his hand still by his waist where he had returned the knife to its scabbard. In spite of his reluctance to become involved in the intimate matters of this passionate family, and uncomfortably aware that Burgundian angers and resentments could easily spill over and threaten his own position in the duchy, Louis pleaded with Philip: "My dearest uncle, my dear aunt just came to my room in the greatest distress because of the quarrel between you and your son, Charles. I beg you, if you love me, please pardon my dear brother and excuse his mistake on his youth with which he still struggles." Louis plunged on, appealing to the greatness of the duke, to his stature as the beloved ruler of his people, and assuring him that Charles was eager once again to pay his father the honor he justly commanded. As Louis continued to plead the case for Charles and for Isabel, however, he could see the duke's face darken. In trying to bring peace to this family, Louis realized, he was courting his own alienation from it.

The duke, who had always treated his royal guest with the formality and respect that a subject owed his sovereign, tried to hold his tongue as his nephew begged his forgiveness for the repentant Charles and Isabel. But the duke was beside himself with the defiance of mother and son, and his fury exploded at Louis: "Enough, my lord, pardon me—I beg you to make no such request—I will show Charles that I am his father—that I can appoint a little valet if I please! And better would it have been for his mother, instead of burdening you with her woes, to have slept a long sleep."

Philip was clearly in no mood to be persuaded of his family's penitence. Louis quickly left the oratory.[3]

Philip turned, sent word to the de Croy brothers to meet him at the nearby castle of Hals, and stormed from the chapel. Indignant at Charles's rebellion, confused by the flight of his wife and son, and blinded by pride, the duke sought the company of friends he trusted, and none were closer to him than the de Croys. Without mantelet or wrap of any kind, the aging duke left his castle at Brussels that wintry afternoon and rode his horse alone into the surrounding woodland of Soignes, heading for Hals.

When Louis told Isabel and Charles of his failure to soften the duke's anger and obtain some forgiveness for them, Isabel fled to her rooms in tears. Charles stomped from the dauphin's room and rode directly to his estate at Termonde. Charles, who had heard the rumors that his father was considering transferring his son's inheritance to Anthony's nephew, was overheard muttering darkly against the imposition of the de Croys into his affairs. He was determined that the land and income his father provided him would not come under the control of the de Croys, and he swore that "anyone who takes a foot of my land will bring an evil hour upon himself."

In the ominous quiet of his apartment after Isabel and Charles had departed, Louis thought again of his uncle's threat, hurled at him as he rushed from Philip in the chapel: "If you have this business of Charles so much at heart and want me to pardon him," Philip had vowed, "you can watch over him and take care of him. But as long as you live and as long as I live, you will never again behold me with your eyes."

Now, Louis too felt jeopardized by his uncle's anger. He did not sleep that night, and instead spent those long dark hours in the saddle searching the town, inquiring if anyone had seen "an elderly man" riding toward the city gates, and combing the neighboring villages, stopping those abroad on the highways to ask if they had seen such a traveler. Returning in failure to the castle at Brussels, Louis learned that the search parties sent into the forest to find the duke had also failed to find him. And now a snowstorm had begun to lash the forest. In great distress at the news, he joined the tearful Isabel and then paced his rooms, crying out loudly enough to be overheard by his servants that he was "the most unfortunate king's son ever born."

That night the survival of one of the most powerful princes in western Europe was in grave danger—and the prince's future sovereign was convinced he shared a similarly dismal fate.[4]

On leaving the castle at Brussels, Philip rode through the winter afternoon and into the early dark of that tempestuous night, his resentment and indignation blinding him to the hazards around him. His horse slipped on the icy ground as the wind blew the snow between the trees and covered the trail to Hals. The duke must have wished for the cloak he had left behind, as gusts of sleet slipped icy fingers down his back. He was cold, hungry, and, for all his pride, surely frightened. But as the gloom descended, the thickening fog lifted just enough to reveal the flickering of a small light ahead of him.

The light belonged to a woodsman's cottage in a small glen. As he reached it, Philip cried out for help. Inside, the woodsman, terrified of the roving bands of thieves that filled the woods bordering France and Flanders, yelled back, "Go away! By St. Matthieu, I am going to do nothing. It is nearly midnight. Let me sleep."

The richest and most powerful duke in the west begged the poor man, "My friend, in the name of God, get up! I mean you no harm: I am a man who has been lost all night in the forest and dying of cold and misery. I beg you, get up and help me; you will be part of an adventure that will live long in memory."

The frightened woodsman and his wife then hesitantly opened the door to their small, earthen-floored room, and Philip followed an icy sweep of wind and snow as he fell into the astonished man's home. One suspects that few men can have regarded dying fire embers so fondly as did Philip the Good on that January night in 1457. And even though, as he later recalled, Philip was "forced to break bread with his own good hands and without a trench squire," one can imagine that no bread and cheese ever tasted so good as that which the forester set before him by that fire.[5]

Refreshed and grateful for his deliverance, Philip set out the next morning for a nearby chapel to give thanks for his life. He then rode on to his castle in the nearby town of Genappe. Meanwhile, that same Monday morning, desperate to locate the duke, Louis persuaded Isabel to send Philippe Pot, a knight whose renowned humor and wit might best placate the duke's offended pride, to search for her husband. Mid-morning Tuesday, the engaging young envoy located the duke reclining in his own bed at Genappe as his wounded leg was being tended. Philip had fallen with his horse, which had slipped several times on the icy forest pathways, and the duke's leg had been cut by his sword. The knight wisely took a light tone with the duke. "Good day, my lord," said Pot. "What is all this? Are you acting King Arthur now or Sir Lancelot? As I can see, you have not been without adventures."[6] The duke laughed and bandied jokes with the young knight as he retold the story of his night in the forest and his rescue by the woodsman.

For the next several days, Isabel reminded those who attempted to help her make peace with her husband that she was all too aware of Philip's prowess as a fighting knight. She described how often she had witnessed his ardor in battle and his skill with weapons, and she declared that she had been afraid that he would wound their son in his fury in the oratory. It was, she said, because of this fear, and not because of any disrespect toward the duke, that she had pushed Charles from the chapel and followed him to Louis's apartment. About a week later, she approached her husband directly and begged "her worthy lord" to forgive her, explaining to him that she had acted out of panic. She had always felt herself a stranger in Burgundy—if she were in any danger, there was no one to help her except her own son, whom she cherished, as she knew Philip did as well. These attempts to bring peace between herself and the duke were to continue for a long time; in the meantime, Isabel remained secluded in the rooms of her nearby private castle of La Motte-au-Bois, waiting for her husband to summon her back to court.[7]

The Duchess Isabel

The explosive anger in the oratory was only the latest in a series of bitter quarrels that had shattered the relationship between Isabel and her husband. Duke Philip had chosen Isabel, the only surviving daughter of John I of Portugal, as his bride in 1429 to profit from her family's close ties with the English; Philip wanted to flaunt such an alliance before the throne of France, which he blamed for the assassination of his father ten years before. Yet, to Isabel's dismay, soon after this marriage, he turned his back on England to pursue an alliance with France and, as a member of the Valois ruling dynasty and as cousin to the king, to enjoy the privileges of his rank as a great peer of the French realm.

Isabel had grown up in a court that appreciated the value of English friendship: the Portuguese had profited from English merchant trade, from English help in defending Portugal's borders against Castilian attacks, and from cooperative ventures in conquest and exploration. Her father, indeed, could not have secured the throne of Portugal in 1385 without the help of John of Gaunt, the duke of Lancaster; the bond between these two men was made yet stronger the following year when the Portuguese king married the English duke's daughter Philippa. Isabel held firmly to the idea that an English alliance would secure Burgundy's economic future. Philip, however, increasingly saw himself first as a

French prince and only second as a ruler independent of both France and the Holy Roman Empire (that vast but loosely organized empire in which Philip held, in allegiance with the emperor, the largest and richest territory). Their opposed political leanings on this crucial issue added to the personal differences that began in the 1430s to divide them; by the 1450s, the barriers between them had become virtually insurmountable.

This was also a period of great tension in England. Isabel's nephew, the hesitant and weak-willed Lancastrian, Henry VI, struggled to maintain his crown. The resurgence in French morale inspired by the meteoric career of Joan of Arc had helped the French to take back almost all of their land from the English and to reclaim from Henry of England the crown of France for Charles VII. Alongside the image of his father, the warrior king Henry V who in 1415 at Agincourt had won the double crown of France and England, Henry VI now appeared fragile indeed. Poor Henry surfaced only occasionally from bouts of nervous disability to attend to affairs of state, and even then he relied heavily on his wife, Margaret of Anjou, to represent him with the great lords of the realm and secure their support against the challenge to Henry's remaining authority posed by his uncle, the duke of York. In 1446, the duchess set to one side her relationship with the red rose of Lancaster and instead sought to ally herself with the white rose of York, which she believed was more likely to triumph in the struggle for the English crown. In May 1455, this struggle between the Yorkists and the Lancastrians exploded at the battle of St. Albans. As the nobles fought one another from the south of England to the north and back again. Isabel hedged her bets on the victor, courting first one side, then the other. (Ultimately, she was to ally herself firmly with the house of York with the marriage of her son, Charles, to Margaret of York in 1468.)

By the mid-1450s, as the Wars of the Roses began their thirty-year bloodbath in England, Isabel had already spent more than twenty years laboring in Burgundy to counter Philip's association with the French interests and his opposition to English alliances and English trade. She had manipulated negotiations with English merchants and Burgundian guilds to accommodate the needs of Flemish looms for English wool. She had urged Philip to lift his prohibitions against the trade caravans that crossed his lands, so that Burgundy could harvest the profits resulting from the exchanges in English cloth and merchandise. She had employed her own network of informers to monitor the intricate course of the struggle between the English factions. The stakes of her wager on the outcome of this contest for the English crown were personal as well as diplomatic: were she to back the winner, Philip would regard her with new respect and perhaps regain some of his earlier appreciation for the value of their marriage; and were her marriage thus secured, so too would be a rich inheritance for her son.

While Philip sought to bring Burgundy into an alliance with France, Charles VII of France had rather different ambitions. He was less concerned about negotiating with the wealthy duchy than absorbing it into his own kingdom. Aware of Charles's goals—goals that continual French military and economic incursions into Burgundy's borderlands made clear to all save the purblind Philip—Isabel pressed for an alliance that would help to keep the French at a distance. But Philip was so determined to forge a closer tie with France that he had delayed his son's marriage (arranged by Isabel) to the duke of York's eldest daughter, Anne, for eight years—until he could arrange a French match between his son and his niece, Isabel of Bourbon. Recognizing his wife's opposition to him in this affair, Philip even refused to leave his duchy until the French marriage was consummated.

Isabel continued, however, to lead embassies of peace and trade to both France and England; Philip still relied on her proven negotiating skills and her kinship with their royal houses to conclude beneficial agreements for Burgundy. But by late 1456, Philip had begun seriously to question his wife's willingness to comply with his wishes. Indeed, Philip had become so concerned that she would pursue her own designs on these embassies that he enlisted the de Croys to observe, to report on, and when necessary to counter the activities of the duchess. Furthermore, Philip saw that Isabel was instilling her own opinions in their son. As Isabel prepared Charles to take his place beside her in pending negotiations with France and England over damages to their merchant fleets, the letters passing between mother and son showed that Charles was thoroughly influenced by Isabel to favor the English interests.

In mid-January 1457, Isabel was struggling to maintain her position as Philip's preferred diplomatic emissary. To do so, she had to triumph over the vicious factionalism that swirled around the Burgundian court in the competition for her husband's favor. She could keep her power at the bargaining table only by maintaining ascendancy over her opposition at court—and only with this power could she knit the alliance with Yorkist England that she believed was essential to Burgundy's survival.

Duke Philip the Good

Two goals, both of them pursued with passion and persistence, formed the basis of Philip's state policy. First, he wanted to enjoy the privileges due him as a prince of the ruling dynasty of France, the House of Valois. His grandfather, Philip the Bold, the first Valois duke of Burgundy, had been a brother of King Charles V of France. And even though Philip the Good's father, John the Fearless, had been murdered in 1419 by the man who now reigned as Charles VII, Philip longed to be recognized not only as a loyal subject of France but also as one of its most important pillars of support, and thus to have greater say in counseling the French king on the affairs of state. Second, he wanted a crown from the Holy Roman Emperor for the Burgundian lands he held within the empire.[8] Philip's territories, within the empire and outside, were indeed fit for a king. In 1457, his northern possessions included Holland, Hainault, Zeeland, Luxembourg, Flanders, Brabant, and Artois. His southern lands, separated from his northern lands by the French county of Champagne and the duchy of Lorraine, included the duchy of Burgundy and Charolais and the county of Burgundy.

Philip's continuing eagerness to be accepted as a valuable supporter of the French king was remarkable in light of the years of provocation and abuse to which France had subjected Burgundy. After Joan of Arc's campaign reestablished Charles VII on the French throne, the king encouraged French piracy along the Flemish coastal waters and sent French troops on border raids into Hainault. Well into the late 1440s and early 1450s, Charles VII subsidized the incursions of fierce bandits *(écorcheurs)* into the Somme Valley areas that divided Burgundy from northeastern France—an area the king was determined to reclaim from Duke Philip as quickly as possible. And more threatening still, each spring from 1445 onward the king held court at Nancy, in that portion of Lorraine held by France that separated Philip's northern territories from his southern lands (see the map on page 21). From Nancy, Charles could directly threaten Burgundian control of the cities of Metz, Toul, Verdun, and Basel. According to Philip's nephew, the bishop of Lisieux, Charles's strategy was to bring down the house of Burgundy by "consistently undermining it all around as one does who wants to remove the massive bulk of an ancient tree with its huge trunk and extensive roots buried far in the earth, start to by digging a deep trench round it so that he can drag it down with ropes."[9] From the mid-1450s, the French crown forged alliances with many of Philip's enemies: with the king of Denmark (in 1456); with England (1454)—more particularly with Queen Margaret of Anjou, whose father was a prisoner of the duke of Burgundy; with a union of the Swiss cantons (1453); with the duke of Savoy (1452); and with a number of princes and electors of the Holy Roman Empire. In 1458, the year after Philip's violent argument with his wife and son, the French, with the encouragement of King Ladislas of Bohemia, were to take possession of Luxembourg.

Still, Philip obstinately refused to believe that Charles VII was planning his destruction. Instead, the duke chose to believe that the king's councillors were behind all these aggressive moves.[10] Philip might, perhaps, have been wiser to suspect councillors closer to home—his own close advisors, the chancellor Rolin and his intimates the de Croys, were rumored by chroniclers such as Georges Chastellain and Olivier de la Marche to have profited handsomely by serving the French king's cause in Burgundy since 1435.[11]

Impervious to Isabel's warnings, the duke maintained an attitude of cautious rectitude toward the French king, forgiving if he did not forget Charles VII's role in the death of John the Fearless. And toward the king's son, whom he had harbored since the summer of 1456 in a type of protective custody, Philip practiced a deference that bordered on servility, an attitude that caused the down-to-earth Louis great discomfort. Philip hoped that with the dauphin under his protection, Charles VII would be reluctant to send his forces against Burgundy. But the longer that Philip maintained Louis, free of his father's control, the greater grew Charles VII's anger toward the duke, and the greater became the king's rewards to the French faction at the duke of Burgundy's court for information about the wayward dauphin. Isabel tried to alert her husband to the dangerous intimacy between the de Croys and the French, but once again her warnings fell on deaf ears. This time, however, Philip's inattention was not confined to warnings against French machinations but extended to all matters of state. Instead of concerning himself with the details of politics and wars, Philip turned to petty pastimes and pretty mistresses. The duke, it seems, had become either extremely irresponsible or a little mad.

This uncharacteristic lapse in Philip's active involvement in the political life of the duchy began in 1456. It was encouraged by Anthony de Croy, who recognized an opportunity to acquire more authority by keeping the duke busy with a wide variety of pastimes and handicrafts. Both in his private apartments and during public audiences, the Great Duke of the West was to be seen threading needles, making clogs, soldering broken knives, and repairing broken glasses. De Croy catered to the duke's sensual nature as well, and filled his nights with an array of mistresses and other entertainments, encouraging the duke to relax his courtly etiquette among such company and to exchange crude jokes with his ministers.

Soon, the de Croys were not only manipulating the administrative machinery of Burgundy to suit their own best interests, but also fighting their own wars against neighboring provinces and duchies without any approval from the duke. Thus, it was virtually inevitable that the duke would accede to the suggestion from Anthony de Croy that his nephew, Philippe, be placed on the staff of the duke's son, Charles, and assume the role of his household chamberlain.

What had prompted this sudden change in Philip's personality? Although the duke's advancing age might have contributed to it, a more likely explanation is to be found in events that occurred a few years earlier.

Since 1443, when he absorbed Luxembourg into the duchy of Burgundy, Philip had enjoyed considerable success in creating a formidable Burgundian power center within the Holy Roman Empire. The ambassadors he sent to attend the regular meetings of the emperor's congress—the Reichstag—carried more weight than did any other of the imperial representatives—the "electors"—on matters dealing with the levying of troops, foreign policy, trade, taxes, and church policy. To reflect his power, Philip wanted a crown. First, a scheme was put forward to create a kingdom of his possessions of Frisa or of Brabant. Then, when this plan was abandoned, Philip suggested to Emperor Frederick III that a new kingdom, independent of the empire, be created from all the duke's imperial possessions. This would have created a "middle kingdom" reminiscent of Charlemagne's grandson Lothair's old crown lands. Understandably, Frederick III was reluctant to approve the creation of so powerful a kingdom, and all discussions of such a crown ended in 1448 without resolution. Talks resumed again in 1452 when arrangements began for a marriage between the emperor and Eleanor of Portugal, niece of Philip's wife. Finally, in 1454 the duke made a long and dangerous journey eastward to Regensberg, where he was to meet with Frederick and secure his long-sought crown, while also inspiring enthusiasm for a crusade. Frederick, however, was either unwilling or unable to meet with Philip, who thus failed in both his objectives. The blow to the duke's pride was great—so great, indeed, that it seems to have temporarily unhinged, if not his sanity, then at least his interest in affairs of state.

Charles the Bold, Count of Charolais

In 1457 the twenty-four-year-old Charles was frustrated by his father's refusal to grant him the power and prestige he felt he deserved as the duke's heir. He was also receptive to his mother's influence, resentful of the de Croy family's leverage at court, and full of admiration for his father's guest, the dauphin Louis, who had successfully rebelled against his own father's control. Charles was drawn ever closer to the dauphin's household at the castle of Genappe, near Brussels, which Duke Philip had provided to the fugitive prince along with servants and a handsome annual allowance. The young Louis was eager to play a leading role in the governance of his father's kingdom of France; Louis was, indeed, eager to become king himself, and he maintained a network of spies to keep constantly apprised of his father's affairs. Pleased with his growing international reputation for leadership and effective government in his own province of Dauphiny—in the nine years between his arrival in and flight from Dauphiny, Louis had formed a parliament and provincial councils, established an efficient litigation system, and set up the first governmental postal service in Europe—he had also welcomed the development of his own small court at Genappe into a center of European influence. There was much about the dauphin that attracted the count of Charolais.

Charles and Louis were alike in some ways but different in others. The dauphin's appetite for hunting in the magnificent woodlands surrounding his Flemish estate was matched by a similar enthusiasm in Charles, and the two young men spent many days riding to hounds together. The duke's athletic, well-built heir was a man of action who loved life in the saddle and delighted in triumphing over opponents in tournaments and in the field. He formulated grandiose plans and sweeping strategies but paid little attention to their practicality. The dauphin, by contrast, most enjoyed the challenges of psychological combat presented by diplomacy and negotiations. His schemes tended to be simple, leaving no room for self-deception. Charles must have noted to himself that in any such contest Louis, his senior by ten years, would be a dangerous adversary.

As this relationship between the future king of France and the heir to Burgundy strengthened, so did Charles's resistance to the influence the de Croys exerted over his father. At the same time, Philip's jealousy of the attention the future king of France was lavishing on his son increased in the same measure as his determination to support the de Croys against his son.

Physically and temperamentally dissimilar, father and son could find no meeting ground. Impatient and quick to anger, suspicious like his mother and restless to exert his authority, Charles showed little interest in personal relationships and generally ignored his wife, Isabel of Bourbon, who in

January 1457 was eight months pregnant. Charles preferred to keep his councillors and the control of his finances close by, but his wife at a distance from his household at Termonde. This austere and ambitious young count did not, however, have control over his own territory of Charolais (Philip insisted on maintaining his own authority there), and he was provided with only a small allowance, the exact amount of which depended on his father's whim and the state of Burgundy's budget. Otherwise, Charles had to depend on income from a scattering of some of the duke's other holdings that Philip allowed Charles to oversee. That the de Croy brothers, Anthony and Jehanne, enjoyed positions governing Luxembourg, Namur, Boulogne, and Hainault—and that yet another de Croy, Philippe de Croy, lord of Sempy, the son of Jehanne, was now about to be given power over the household at Termonde—was more than Charles could bear.

By 1457, therefore, the court of Philip the Good was a ferment of spies, a confusion of plots and counterplots, and a cauldron of fearful partisan jealousies. As Louis sought to profit from this situation by mining the contending factions for information, cultivating the de Croy family, and comforting in turn the irascible duke and his stiff-necked son, the dauphin noted with dismay that his uncle the duke was a most important prince who had always had his own way. He had never known of anyone whom Duke Philip had knowingly allowed to hold sway over him—and because of this, Louis declared to his councillors, he did not find his uncle too clever. Instead, he found Philip easily manipulated by pride and, in his increasingly isolated old age, too willing to follow those who flattered him and obsessed with the need to force his will on those who resisted his command.[12] In January 1457, therefore, Louis was not much surprised by the family drama that erupted in the oratory of the chapel in Brussels.

Several days passed between the duke's precipitous departure from Brussels and the return of Philippe Pot with the news that he had found the duke in the safety of the castle at Genappe. Pot also reported that the duke had made clear that he would return to Brussels only if sufficiently convinced that he would not be badgered by pleas for forgiveness. On hearing this,

Louis sprang into action. He ordered his scribe to draw up documents by which Louis and Charles would guarantee the conditions the duke required for his return—namely, that he not be badgered for forgiveness by either Charles or the duchess Isabel. Many trips followed between Brussels and Termonde to negotiate the terms to which the dauphin and the duke's son and wife would sign their names, and to assure Philip that Charles had beaten down his pride and was appropriately penitent.

Philip appears to have wanted no more angry scenes that would publicly reveal his family's discord. He was ready to play his part in a scene of reconciliation staged by his future sovereign in which he, the duke, as an act of submission to the royal will rather than as a personal commitment, would forgive his errant son. After receiving the assurances he demanded, the duke returned to Brussels within a few days to participate in the show of family peace that Louis was to stage manage.

Well aware of the bristling pride and tension between father and son, Louis wisely entered the presence of the duke only with Philip's daughter-in-law, Isabel, countess of Charolais. She had not required much schooling in the scene that was required, for she had grown up in the Burgundian court of her uncle Philip. She was sincerely distraught over the estrangement between her husband and his father and—with her first child nearly full term—was distressed at the thought of disinheritance and banishment from Burgundy. Having been led into her uncle's presence by the hand of the dauphin, the pregnant countess fell to her knees and covered Philip's feet with her tears and kisses. Joining this favorite of Philip, Louis fell to his knees before the duke as well, and acting as the advocate of her husband, began to describe Charles's great sorrow for his act of rebellion against his father. As both countess and dauphin played their parts, the dauphin noticed how Philip's face began to soften. Seizing this opportunity to bring Charles into his father's presence, Louis called to the count, who had been thoroughly rehearsed for his part by the dauphin and was waiting in an antechamber.

Louis implored the duke, "Truthfully, dearest uncle, you promised me earlier that you would pardon [your son] and I pray that you do so now for he is thoroughly penitent for his mistake."

"My lord," Charles immediately added, "I very humbly pray in God's passion, that if I have said or done anything to displease you, that you will find it in your grace to forgive me and that you will accept me in your grace and mercy for I am heartily sorry for what I have done and such will never happen again in all the days of my life."

Once more in control of the drama, the duke Philip was happy to play his part as a man overcome by humility and reluctant to pursue such an embarrassing domestic contest of wills before the future sovereign. "My lord, your prayers are my commands," the duke protested as he let himself be persuaded to forgive his son, "I will do what it pleases you to order."

With what must have been a great sigh of relief, the exhausted dauphin bowed, "Very well, then," he told the duke, "since you wish it that way, I command you to forgive your son."

Thus, peace of some kind was restored between father and son.[13]

For the de Croy brothers, however, the renewed accord between father and son was most unwelcome. Domestic harmony within Philip's family would work against their goal of isolating the duke and steering him away from Isabel's pro-English policy and toward a French alliance that would increase their own wealth and power. They thus sought to exploit their relationship with the duke as his intimate friends and trusted advisers. They threatened to leave him alone in his court and to retire to their own estates in Luxembourg and Hainault. Such a sad step, they noted, would deprive them of the pleasure of serving the duke, but it was necessary because of the animosity that the count of Charolais bore toward them. "My God," the duke exclaimed, "do not make more of my son than of me. I am his father and his master, and never think I would abandon a trusted servant to his will." Increasingly suspicious of his wife's political aims, and offended by his disobedient son, Philip was quick to restore the preeminence of his boyhood friends, the de Croys, vowing to protect Anthony, Jehanne, and their sons.[14]

The duke then extracted a price for his forgiveness of Charles. He demanded the discharge of two of his son's favorites while immediately installing Sempy as the chamberlain of Charles's household. The de Croy family now had a unique vantage point from which to spy on, and perhaps also to influence, the heir to Burgundian power. And Isabel would face even greater opposition to her plans to tie English trade to Burgundian markets. She would never relent in her efforts to forge a duchy that was wealthy and secure enough to stand independent of France and the Holy Roman Empire, but she recognized that she must remain quiet for a time and retire from court. Isabel prepared herself to wait out the simmering factionalism at court, hoping to influence Burgundian policy indirectly through Charles while waiting for her husband to call her back to his side. Little did she suspect that that call was never to come, and that from this moment until her husband's death she would have to battle the influence of the de Croys from a distance.

Notes

All quotations in the text are taken from reliable contemporary sources and have been translated into English either by this author or by other historians whose works are cited below. The quoted material is entirely faithful to the original except that, on occasion, a few words or phrases have been omitted so as to make the text more readable. This author has taken great pains to ensure that the omissions do not in any way alter the tenor or meaning of the quoted material.

1. For an eyewitness account (by Caron, clerk of the chapel) of the events in the oratory on January 17, 1457, see *Oeuvres de Chastellain*, ed. M. Le Baron Kervyn de Lettenhove, 4 vols. (Brussels: R. Heussner, 1864), 2:232–57.
2. *Oeuvres de Chastellain*, 2:233–34.
3. For the direct quotation of the dauphin's words, as well as those of Duke Philip, see *Oeuvres de Chastellain*, 2:235. For a paraphrased version of the interchange between the dauphin and the duke, see Paul Murray Kendall, *Louis XI* (New York: W. W. Norton, 1971), 401.
3. For Duke Philip's threat to the dauphin, see *Oeuvres de Chastellain*, 2:288.
5. *Oeuvres de Chastellain*, 2:288.
6. For the report of Sir Philippe Pot, see *Oeuvres de Chastellain*, 2:279; for an interpretation of the meeting of the knight and the duke at Genappe, see Kendall, *Louis XI,* 402.

7. For Isabel's attempts to explain her precarious position, see Richard Vaughan, *Philip the Good: The Apogee of Burgundy* (New York: Barnes and Noble, 1970), 339.
8. For a discussion of the dual nature of Philip's allegiance to France and the Holy Roman Empire, see Olivier de La Marche, *Mémoires,* ed. E. D. Beaune and J. d'Arbaumont, 4 vols. (Paris: Société d'Histoire de France, 1883–88), 2:418–19.
9. The quotation is from G. du Fresne de Beaucourt, *Histoire de Charles VII,* 6 vols. (Paris: Libraire de la Socitété Bibliographique, 1881–91), 2:246.
10. For a detailed description of French aggression against Burgundy—including those incidents that appeared on the lists of complaints presented to Charles VII by Isabel and Philip from 1440 onward—see G. du Fresne de Beaucourt, *Charles VII,* 6 vols. (Paris: n.p., 1885–92): 4:112–41.
11. For an examination of the French faction in Philip's court—among them men of very high rank—see Marie Rose Thielemans, "Les Croys, conseillers des ducs de Bourgogne," *Bulletin de la Commission de l'Histoire* 142 (1959): 1-145. Among those who are listed as having received rewards from Charles VII for helping persuade the duke of Burgundy to ally with the French as early as 1435 are Nicolas Rolin, chancellor of Burgundy; Anthony de Croy, captain-general and Bailiff of Hainault; Pierre de Bauffremont, captain-general (former) and husband of Marie of Burgundy (Philip's natural daughter); Guy Guilbaut, treasurer of Burgundy and second only to the chancellor; Jacques, Seigneur de Crevecoeur; and Jean Brimeu, Seigneur d'Humbercourt.

    Richard Vaughan, in *Philip the Good* (352), writes that "Anthony de Croy and his relatives . . . [with the aid of] Nicolas Rolin had maintained secret contacts with and enjoyed favours from the French king at least until the mid-fifties." Discussion of these accusations can be found in J. Bartier, *Légistes et gens de finances au XVe siecle: Les conseillers des ducs de Bourgogne* (Brussels: Mémoires se l'Academie royale de Beligique, Letters, 1952), 257; and G. Valat, "Nicolas Rolin, Chancelier de Bourgogne," *Memoire de la Société Eduenne* 42 (1914): 53–58.
12. See Vaughan, *Philip the Good,* 369 n. 3, citing B. De Mandrot and C. Sanaran, eds., *Dépêche des ambassadeurs milanais en France sur Louis XI et François Sforza,* 4 vols. (Paris: SHF, 1916–23), 1:361.
13. For an eyewitness description, see *Oeuvres de Chastellain*, 282–86.
14. The ability of the de Croys to manipulate the duke of Burgundy is highlighted in *Oeuvres de Chastellain*, 286–87.

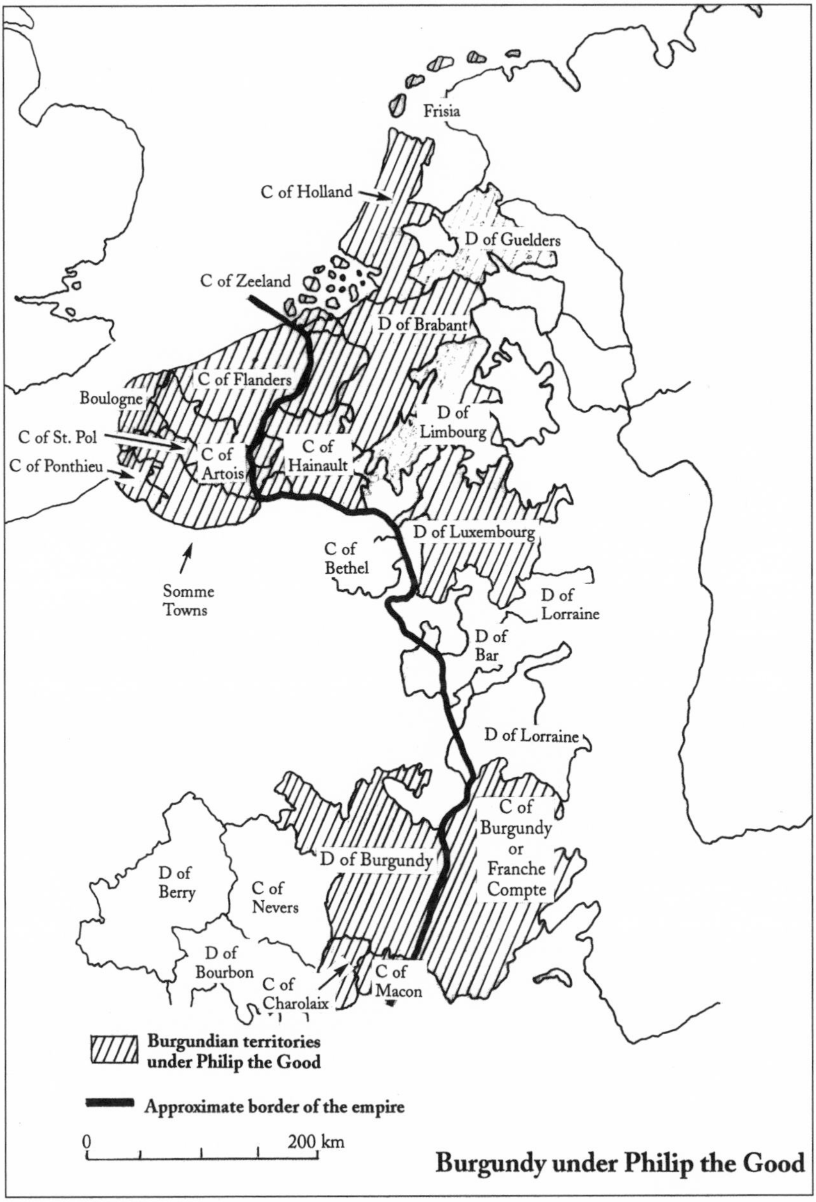
Frisia
C of Holland
D of Guelders
C of Zeeland
D of Brabant
C of Flanders
Boulogne
D of Limbourg
C of St. Pol
C of Artois
C of Hainault
C of Ponthieu
D of Luxembourg
C of Bethel
Somme Towns
D of Lorraine
D of Bar
D of Lorraine
C of Burgundy or Franche Compte
D of Burgundy
D of Berry
C of Nevers
D of Bourbon
C of Charolaix
C of Macon
Burgundian territories under Philip the Good
Approximate border of the empire
0
200 km

Burgundy under Philip the Good

GENEALOGY OF THE DUKES OF BURGUNDY

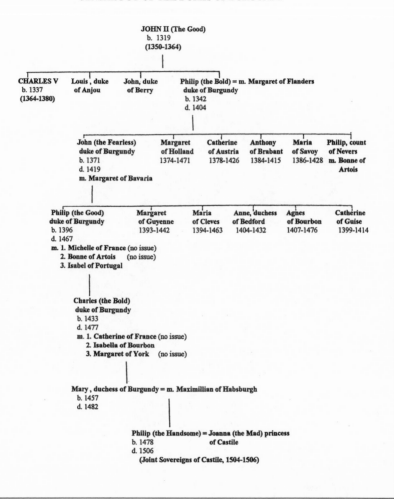

JOHN II (The Good)
b. 1319
(1350-1364)

CHARLES V
b. 1337
(1364-1380)

Louis, duke of Anjou

John, duke of Berry

Philip (the Bold) = m. Margaret of Flanders
duke of Burgundy
b. 1342
d. 1404

John (the Fearless) duke of Burgundy
b. 1371
d. 1419
m. Margaret of Bavaria

Margaret of Holland
1374-1471

Catherine of Austria
1378-1426

Anthony of Brabant
1384-1415

Maria of Savoy
1386-1428

Philip, count of Nevers
m. Bonne of Artois

Philip (the Good) duke of Burgundy
b. 1396
d. 1467
m. 1. Michelle of France (no issue)
2. Bonne of Artois (no issue)
3. Isabel of Portugal

Margaret of Guyenne
1393-1442

Maria of Cleves
1394-1463

Anne, duchess of Bedford
1404-1432

Agnes of Bourbon
1407-1476

Catherine of Guise
1399-1414

Charles (the Bold) duke of Burgundy
b. 1433
d. 1477
m. 1. Catherine of France (no issue)
2. Isabella of Bourbon
3. Margaret of York (no issue)

Mary, duchess of Burgundy = m. Maximillian of Habsburgh
b. 1457
d. 1482

Philip (the Handsome) = Joanna (the Mad) princess of Castile
b. 1478
d. 1506
(Joint Sovereigns of Castile, 1504-1506)

Chapter Two

The Renaissance Princess, the Medieval Bride, 1397–1431

An Offer of Marriage

ON DECEMBER 18, 1428, a second serious offer for Isabel's hand in marriage was made to her father, King John I of Portugal. The first offer had been made thirteen years before, in 1415, when an English king had considered a union with the Portuguese. Then eighteen, and already a little old for a first-time bride, Isabel must have watched with curiosity and some excitement as the negotiations proceeded between King John and the stern warrior king, Henry V, victor at Agincourt and destroyer of more than half the chivalry of France. Although the negotiations ultimately led nowhere, the young Isabel does not seem to have mourned the failure. Now, at the age of thirty-one, as she observed the efforts of this splendid embassy from Philip of Burgundy, the most powerful duke on the continent, she most likely was torn between her duty to marry and secure a profitable alliance for Portugal and the freedom of her father's court.

Philip the Good's delegation had left the Burgundian port of Sluis on two Venetian galleys on October 19. It had made a port of call in England at Sandwich, where it was joined by two other ships. The small fleet had then sailed from England on December 2, and had arrived at Lisbon on December 16. However, the Burgundian embassy led by the Seigneur de Roubaix—chief counselor and first chamberlain to Duke Philip the Good—was forced to wait a full month at nearby Cascais before it was allowed to present the formal request for Isabel's hand. In the meantime, King John, who always involved all of his sons in decisions about important matters of state, called them to join him at his court at Aviz, one hundred miles east of Lisbon at the headwaters of the Sorraia River. Finally, on January 19, Duke Baudoin de Lannoy, governor of Lille and a man who was to become Isabel's fast friend, joined Roubaix and the well-traveled and experienced Burgundian ambassador André de Chalonja in the formal negotiations for the duke of Burgundy's marriage to Isabel. As Isabel waited the outcome of their discussions, which lasted four weeks longer, a valet named Jan van Eyck who traveled with the Burgundian embassy distracted her by painting her miniature, which Duke Philip wished to see before giving his final assent to the match.

Philip's desire for a union with Portugal was prompted by both political and economic considerations. His two previous wives had been French; a Portuguese bride would bring with her the weight of an English alliance with which to balance a Burgundian strategy that aimed at maintaining peaceful relations with both England and France. A marriage to a Portuguese princess would also bolster the financial ties between the merchants of Flanders and those of Portugal that had been forged in the twelfth century.[1] The idea of marrying Isabel had probably been suggested to Philip during visits to Burgundy by her older brother Peter in 1424–25. As for Isabel, marriage to the most powerful prince in Christendom next to the king of France would have presented an attractive challenge. She may also have felt a sense of victory over her sister-in-law as she recalled the embassy Philip had sent with an offer of marriage to Eleanor of Aragon between 1425 and 1427, an offer that was turned down because Eleanor had already accepted the offer of Prince Edward, heir to the Portuguese throne and Isabel's other older brother.[2]

No complications arose in the discussions at Aviz, and on February 2 four messengers were hurried on their way to Philip with the good news. The two who went by sea, Pierre de Vaudrey and the special courier Renty, were the first to return from Philip's court in Burgundy with the duke's response. When they arrived in Lisbon on June 4, they carried with them the notarized acceptance of the duke of Burgundy, signed on May 5 in the Church of St. Sauveur in Bruges. The Burgundian delegation had not been idle while awaiting the couriers' return. Not only had they become better acquainted with Isabel, whom they found both interesting and charming, but also they had traveled to other Iberian courts to foster enthusiasm for the crusade Duke Philip was planning against the Turks. When the delegation returned to Lisbon, they were received by Eleanor of Aragon, who was about to deliver her firstborn.

The Seigneur de Roubaix presented the marriage contract to John I at Cintra on June 11. He informed the king of how pleased Philip had been with Isabel's miniature. Aware of the duke's eye for women—he had a reputation for maintaining a bevy of mistresses during his two previous marriages—Roubaix was hopeful that Isabel would monopolize Philip's lustful appetites long enough to produce a much-needed heir for Burgundy.[3] While waiting first for the return of the couriers, and then for her father's final approval of the agreement with Philip the Good, Isabel might have swayed between the challenge of her new life and fears of another possible rejection. Any doubts about her destiny, however, were swept away when the king sealed the notarized marriage contract, which was presented to the Burgundian ambassador on July 23. Philip had not wanted to delay the union with Portugal until Isabel could reach Burgundian shores, and so—as was customary in royal houses at the time—he had already given Roubaix the authority to stand in for him as the groom in a marriage ceremony. The next day, therefore, on July 24, the princess Isabel of Portugal became the third duchess of Burgundy.

The following eight weeks were filled with activities held under skies that alternated between sunny weather and heavy storms, and that must have mirrored Isabel's trepidations about her imminent sea voyage to Burgundy and ambivalence about her future life as Philip's wife. Her concerns, though, were overwhelmed by days filled with feasts and tournaments, morality plays, and village celebrations, as the Portuguese prepared to say good-bye to their only princess. The king equipped about twenty ships for his daughter's journey, and on September 30, 1429, he led the flotilla with his sons, daughter-in-law, ambassadors from Flanders, and lords and knights and their ladies from Lisbon to Oporto, where Isabel boarded. The full convoy left the harbor on October 19 and headed for Sluis with nearly two thousand Portuguese on board to accompany their princess. The ships of the Portuguese and Flemish fleets were square-rigged and ponderous, but fit for carrying heavy merchant cargo. This fleet also included several caravels of more than a thousand tons each, ships that were considered to be unsinkable. Sadly, this reputation proved to be ill founded, for a dreadful toll was taken on Isabel's convoy by storms that autumn.

The fleet was pummeled by high winds and waves in its passage through the Bay of Biscay, and then, as the convoy hugged the coastline between England and France, the remaining ships met the increasing force of heavy, wintry squalls. Several caravels were lost at sea, and two of them reached Flanders a full month before Isabel herself arrived; six others were forced into shelter at Southampton to wait out the storms. Tossed about by rough seas for most of her voyage, Isabel remained sealed tightly in her cabin beneath the bridge, longing for a chance to breathe fresh air again. For eleven weeks, Isabel saw little sun, fought fear and illness, and witnessed most of her trousseau torn from crates and scattered on the sea. The trials of this wedding journey were difficult to bear, even for a princess from a land of merchant seafarers. At last, at noon on Christmas Day, the gray, foggy port of Sluis—a crescent, sliced from the Flemish coastal beds, and very different from sunny Portuguese harbors—came in to view. It must have been a welcome sight for the exhausted Isabel and the remainder of her convoy.

Tired, ill, and apprehensive at meeting her new husband, Isabel needed to rest a day before leaving her ship. When she did disembark, to the sound of trumpets, so many people had gathered to greet the new duchess that she could barely make her way through the town on the carpeted pathway that led to her lodging. Although prepared to consummate her marriage—which she did a fortnight later after a formal religious ceremony with Philip on January 7 at Sluis—she must have paused before stepping into that new world to remember the life she had just left behind. In Portugal, she had been part of a large, close-knit family; now she was isolated in a strange, stormy land that was swept up in the final phases of the Hundred Years War. She would hold close the comfort of her memories of Portugal.

The Renaissance Princess

Isabel grew up with five robust brothers. Although she had been protected and indulged as the only daughter of the family, and had been raised within the stiff etiquette of her mother's nursery, she had been allowed to play with her older brothers—Edward, Peter, and Henry—and to help look after her younger brothers—John and Fernando. All six children were encouraged to develop their minds as well as their bodies, and were tutored to read several languages, experiment in the sciences, and hone their mathematical skills. Isabel was often allowed to accompany her brothers when they met with their father to be instructed in affairs of state. And although she did not participate in the governing councils of the realm as did her brothers as they grew older, she was nonetheless well schooled in the vagaries of politics and the intricacies of diplomatic negotiations.

Her mother and father were opposite in temperament but marvelously well fitted to producing heirs of strength, intelligence, and character. Isabel's father, John of Aviz, had successfully competed with other contenders for the crown when the established Portuguese dynasty of Burgundy—formed in the eleventh century by Henry of Burgundy as he carved out the country of Portugal from Moslem occupation—weakened at the end of the fourteenth century. John had organized and led an armed resistance against Portugal's land-hungry neighbor, Castile, which had seen this weakness of central authority in Portugal as an opportunity to extend its own territory westward to the Atlantic. In three wars against Castilian aggression between 1369 and 1385, and with the help of the forces of John of Gaunt, duke of Lancaster, John of Aviz had established

Portuguese independence. The people of Portugal had rewarded him with the crown of the realm on April 6, 1385. The following year, on May 9, John of Aviz and John of Gaunt—the former looking to secure his new crown, the latter to expand his power on the Iberian peninsula—signed the Treaty of Windsor to settle the amount of men, horses, and weapons they required to formalize their alliance. John I is described by historians as not exceedingly bright—though we should note that his courage, knowledge of men, and charisma made him an effective leader—but his common sense led him to seize the opportunity to marry into the royal house of England. He asked for and was given the hand of the duke's daughter, Philippa, cousin to the English king, Henry IV. John of Gaunt relinquished any claim he harbored toward Portugal as the future king of Castile, and instead married his other daughter, Constance, to that kingdom's heir, the future Henry III. Philippa and King John's marriage was sealed and celebrated in February 1387. Considering the differences in their personalities, theirs was a happy union.

Isabel's father was a dreamer as well as a warrior, and he considered himself cut from the same cloth as King Arthur of legend. Although he suffered from a bothersome inability to make timely decisions, he had the good sense to choose wise counselors—among whom he placed his sons—and to listen to them with care. His court was in transition during Isabel's youth, with power shifting from an amalgam of older knights who had served in battle with John—his confidants of the "Round Table"—to a newer order of younger lords from the ranks of the status- and money-hungry "middle aristocracy." As the new king set about bolstering his authority, he did so with the support of the younger lords but at the expense of the clergy and the upper ranks of the nobility, who resented their loss of feudal powers and rights. Philippa attempted to impose some order on the chaos of a court whose older and wealthier families were being forced to relinquish their positions and power to the hands of those they considered of lesser quality.

Queen Philippa was tall, slim, sharp-tongued, and, like others in her family line, quite able to produce a large and healthy family. Philippa and John's oldest son and the future king, Prince Edward, was born in 1391.

The next child, also a boy, the future regent Peter, duke of Coimbra, was born in 1392. The next oldest son—and the most famous within Europe, then as now—was Henry, duke of Viseu, born in 1394. Records indicate that Isabel was born to Philippa in 1397, and that two other children, possibly girls, died at birth. Philippa then presented her husband with two more sons—John, born in 1400, and Fernando, born in 1402.

The conservative Philippa stands out as an austere figure against the colorful background of the court of Portugal, animated by the spirit of adventure and embroiled in aristocratic struggles for power. She was always a pragmatic woman, a realist amid her husband's dreams of Camelot. But although John was a romantic, he also maintained a tight hold over the kingdom. He announced repeatedly that he had absolute power to give, approve, grant, and confirm all privileges, liberties, charters, and customs of the kingdom. In John's kingdom there was place for only one ruler; in his family, however, Philippa occupied a central role, establishing a firm and consistent discipline, instilling a strong religious faith, and inculcating a stern sense of royal duty and the belief that the key to fulfilling such duty was learning.

The queen carried her sense of duty even to her deathbed. She called her five sons to her and gave them her final instructions and permission to secure armaments and provisions for their imminent campaign against the Moroccan port city of Ceuta, on the Straits of Gibraltar. The eighteen-year-old Isabel was devastated by her mother's death. Philippa's only daughter had tried to model herself on her mother, and it seems the two had shared a close and affectionate relationship. The loss of her mother—her confidante, guide, and exemplar—led Isabel to withdraw for a while into a quieter life. She sought out the comforting company of her ladies-in-waiting, among whom she became more adept at distinguishing gossip from fact, flattery from sincerity; if she grew a little more suspicious of the world, she also grew better able to survive the world's deceits and fictions.

Despite this temporary retreat, during which she practiced such "feminine" arts as needlework and song, Isabel retained her interests in books and in politics, which was exceptional for a woman, even a princess, of the time. In most other courts of Europe, few women, whatever their rank, could aspire to an active role in diplomacy or politics; nor were women encouraged to pursue the "new learning" that stressed the study of contemporary as well as classical languages, of vernacular as well as religious literature, and of financial skills, such as double-entry bookkeeping. Isabel, however, not only rode and hunted with her older brothers but also observed their training for active participation in the government of Portugal and joined them in their academic work, becoming agile in Latin, French, English, and Italian. The wide range of visitors that came to her father's court in this kingdom of international merchants gave her ample opportunity to hone her skills and to follow her mother's practice of observing personalities and guessing motives and missions. These lessons sharpened Isabel's wit, political perceptiveness, and natural diplomatic talents.

As Isabel embraced the Renaissance spirit of her father's court, her brothers took an active role in the expansion of Portugal after 1415. The three older princes of Portugal took their knighthood seriously, and nothing less than conquest would give them the satisfaction of proving their courage and worth. Eager to experience real combat, they had chafed earlier at the suggestion by King John and Queen Philippa of a tourney, and they mourned the fact they had been born too late to take part in their nation's wars of independence. At the age of twenty-six, Isabel's oldest brother, Edward, was eager to sail to North Africa and attack the port of Ceuta. And six days after Philippa's death, the Portuguese fleet left Tagus, on July 25, 1415. As a leader, however, Edward had his shortcomings. Although intelligent and scholarly, he was inclined to his father's lack of decisiveness—and was consequently vulnerable to the influence of strong counselors—and his mother's overly pious nature—which encouraged introspection instead of forceful action. These traits, though perhaps desirable in an older brother, were ill suited to a young king who would have to exercise a firm hand with an old aristocracy that had lost its prestige and clamored for recognition, and with a virile new wave of young knights eager for conquest and glory.

Isabel's more adventurous brother Peter, next in line to the throne, always stayed close to Edward, recognizing his brother's need for moral support and guidance. Peter, duke of Coimbra, was a man of action who tempered his forcefulness with a self-discipline that enhanced his strength as a leader. Like his mother, he was practical in nature, and he wisely advised his brother Edward that he must wait before making decisions "about things that do not clearly appear good and reasoned," and that he should "neither grant nor decide them at once; and those that certainly do not appear bad and unreasoned, do not deny, but put them off so as later, with more repose and less fatigue, to determine them as you ought."[4] This was sage advice from a brother who most likely adopted the role of family arbiter and who might have made a great king—but who, unfortunately, when he served as regent to Edward's son, attracted such resentment from the factions surrounding the throne that he was rendered powerless.

Isabel may have been most drawn to the enigmatic scientist of the family, her third brother, Henry, duke of Viseu. Cool and aloof, he projected a self-confidence and strength that would have both attracted and challenged a sister seeking solace and security amid the passion and turmoil of the Portuguese court after her mother's death. Henry's firm determination not to give up Ceuta—won in 1415—in exchange for his youngest brother, Fernando, who had been captured and taken hostage at Tangiers by the Moors, suggests the harshness of a warrior whose coldness would eventually discourage a young girl in need of a brother's advice. Henry, best known to us today as "the Navigator" for his support of exploration, established a laboratory for the study of geography in Sagres, in the bay of Lagos. From this base, Henry pursued his bold ambitions: to explore the African coast beyond the Canary Islands; to search for Christians in Africa with whom Portugal could trade; to determine the extent of the land and power of the Moslems; to search for yet another Christian kingdom to help in the crusade against the Moslems; and to extend Christianity. Reigning princes, merchants, scholars, and explorers from Europe and the Middle East closely followed his experiments in navigation, instrumentation, and cartography.

Equipped with the drive to succeed and iron discipline, Henry was well suited to the rigors of scientific inquiry. But these same qualities worked to his disadvantage. Henry was too cool to others' needs to remain engaged in court politics, and he repeatedly abandoned the details and obligations of government for the excitement of Sagres, returning to court only when called on to consult on pressing state concerns. Isabel would have had few occasions for intimate conversations with this distant brother.

Her younger brothers, John and Fernando, seem often to have been overlooked in the bustle of their older siblings' affairs. John was a private person, retiring and too content with the peace he created for himself in his circumspect and restricted world to become involved in the stress of government and the niggling affairs of the court. Fernando, younger still, adored his brother Henry and was inspired by Henry's colorful cast of collaborators from around the known world to dream of adventures for himself. He was fascinated by the visiting Jews, Italians, Moors, and Negroes who brought to Sagres accounts of their own countries and of those through which they had traveled.

Isabel was no such dreamer. Certainly, she had sentimental attachments, but she would not be ruled by these alone. For example, she was predisposed to view England favorably because it was the land of her mother's birth, but she also recognized the political, military, and economic advantages to be gained from a close relationship with that country. By 1430, the thirty-three-year-old Infante Isabel was a fully formed woman—and an ideal bride for the duke of Burgundy. She was shrewd, proud, skillful, self-contained, and could keep her own counsel. She also had the physical stamina to produce heirs. And—although Philip may have come to consider it a defect rather than a virtue in a wife—she had the emotional strength, intellectual fortitude, and sustaining courage to advance and adhere to her views in the face of very powerful opposition.

The Medieval Bride

According to a Venetian merchant in Bruges in the winter of 1429, Duke Philip was all but pacing the walls of the castle of Princehof, waiting "hour by hour" for Isabel's ship to arrive. He had made great preparations for their wedding, and the aristocrats and wealthy merchants of his duchy were acting in accordance with those plans even while they prayed silently for Isabel's safety. A great convoy of four hundred carts rolled northward from Philip's southern capital of Dijon, joining others from Lille, all creaking with the raw materials for court entertainments. They clattered into Bruges in November and joined the masses of people and supplies crowding the small city that seemed to hold its communal breath in the suspense of Isabel's arrival. Kitchens were stocked with game; fruit and wines were unloaded and stored in cellars; herbs and spices were carefully collected for the coming feasting. Outside, street merchants loudly hawked their wares in the gray, misty streets of the coastal city, and inns and hostels overflowed with eager celebrants. Philip ordered his fifteen cartloads of tapestries, one hundred wagons of Burgundian wines, fifteen cartloads of arms and armor for tournaments, and fifty cartloads of furnishings and jewels to be unloaded. The duke, his court, his guests, and all of the city of Bruges prepared to welcome the new duchess. Everyone waited for Isabel's convoy to arrive at Sluis—which at last it did, on December 25, 1429—and then for the duke and Isabel to be joined in a formal wedding ceremony—which they were, on January 7, 1430.

When Isabel made her formal entry into Bruges on January 8, the celebrations began immediately. She entered the city on a golden litter carried by two white chargers. Her brother Fernando and the Seigneur de Roubaix rode on each side of her litter, keeping close hold of the reigns of the horses. A great assembly of lords and ladies followed her on foot, the nobility of Flanders as well as those who had accompanied her from Portugal. Knights in armor, trumpeters, heralds, and minstrels followed close behind, their music resonating on the walls of the city. Isabel wound her way toward Philip through streets that were draped in rich, red Flemish cloth. Her train took two hours to bring her through the cheering crowd of fifty thousand.

The duke had transformed his residence in Bruges to accommodate the wedding festivities. He ordered that the entire castle courtyard be filled with a temporary wooden construction to house kitchens, larders, and a magnificent banquet hall. There were three great kitchens, each with its own huge oven. Six large storehouses were filled separately with soups, boiled meats, jellies, roast meats, pastries, and fruit. In the middle stood the banquet hall, one hundred fifty feet long. Those who had not been invited to join the banquet within the palace could drink wine that poured into a basin from the paw of an exquisitely painted lion on an exterior facade of the duke's residence. Those privileged to enter the courtyard during the ceremonies could drink spicy hippocras wine and rose water from a similar device within the palace walls. Sixty heralds occupied a gallery above the banquet hall and joined the minstrels, trumpeters, and musicians who entertained at the feasting. In one of the corners of this great hall stood a golden tree that bore on each of its branches the coats of arms of the duke's lands and of his gentry—territory through which Isabel would soon travel in a procession to announce her arrival to all the citizens of Burgundy.

At the banquet on January 8, Isabel watched in wonder the parade of tableaux that accompanied the presentation of each dish. In some of these elaborate scenes, women swept into the hall leading "unicorns" (goats dressed with a single horn) and holding pennons (triangular banners) bearing ducal arms. In other tableaux, men were dressed as soothsayers, angels, and spirits, or as savages and wild beasts; in one scene, men made up to look like wild animals came "riding" into the hall on roasted pigs. The pièce de résistance, however, was a huge pie that contained not only a man dressed as a savage but also live sheep dyed blue with gilded horns.[5]

The end of this banquet did not mean the end of the wedding festivities. In fact, celebrations continued for several days, culminating in an event that, for the groom especially, was of more political than nuptial significance. Philip saw his wedding as an opportunity to announce to the world that no one—be he prince, king, or emperor—was above the duke of Burgundy. He was, after all, not only the duke of Burgundy and premier peer of France, but also a sovereign duke of Brabant and Limburg (to which he was to add Luxembourg in 1443), count of Flanders, Artois, and Franche Compte (the southern possession that bordered the French Alps of the Dauphine), Hainault, Holland, Zeeland, Namur, and Charolais, marquess of the Holy Roman Empire, and lord of Friesland. He was also wealthier than any other European monarch.

Looking to unite this sprawling group of territories—separated not only by geography but also by language and political and economic history—the duke enlisted the symbolism of Christian chivalry, the code of honor found in the legends of King Arthur. At the final banquet in the festivities of Bruges, Philip established his own chivalric order: the Order of the Golden Fleece. The order was patterned after the English Order of the Garter, which, for political reasons, Philip had refused a short time before. The statutes of the Golden Fleece provided for a membership of thirty-one knights, including the sovereign of Burgundy, who would always be the master of the order. Although the statutes of the order declared its purpose to be a reverence of God and a maintenance of the Christian faith,[6] at its foundation the order was said to have been inspired by the story of Jason and his quest to obtain the golden fleece from the dragon serpent and bull on the island of Colchis. However, because Jason abandoned his wife, Medea, after she had helped him win the crown, both his lack of chivalry and the paganism of the legend caused problems with the Catholic Church—but not the knights! Thereafter, frequent mention was made not of Jason but of the biblical character Gideon, the hero who was decked with the golden fleece and who, with God's help, overcame the Philistines. Philip's main goal was to bind the order's noble members tightly to Burgundy's welfare. Soon, or so Philip hoped, the flower of chivalry from Italy, England, Germany, and Spain would gather around the Burgundian court, eager to pledge their lives to the purpose of the Golden Fleece. Isabel, who was to preside at each of the banquets that succeeded the order's annual meetings, must have found cause for comfort—but perhaps also for some dismay—in discovering that Burgundy was touched by some of the unrealistic ideals of the Camelot she had left behind in Lisbon.

The gown of the order was a bright scarlet velvet lined with ermine, covered by a mantle laced with gold and a long-banded hood. The name of the order and its badge—a pendant of sheep's fleece made of gold—was a new device for the House of Burgundy, and a fitting one considering that the weaving of wool was the economic foundation of the Low Countries. Twenty-eight fired-steel links, each formed in the letter *B* for Burgundy, alternated with pairs of golden finger rings to form the collar from which the golden fleece was suspended. The central filigreed symbol of *B* bore two mottoes: on the surface was engraved in Latin, "Not a bad reward for labor"; the obverse carried Philip's own promise, "I will have no other"—an appropriate promise for a new groom, and one that would have given Isabel much peace had Philip abided by it.

After a full week of celebrations, the duke and duchess began their formal progress through Philip's territories. Their long supply trains of carts creaked and slid through the narrow, frequently icy winter roadways toward Ghent, where they arrived on January 16. They made their way through Courtrai on February 13 and arrived at Lille the next day. They then traveled to Brussels, Arras, Peronne, Malines, and finally to Noyon. The pageantry of parades with caparisoned horses, attending aristocrats, blaring trumpets, and streets decorated with tapestries was repeated in every town through which her convoy passed. Isabel's route took her along the border area separating the duke's lands from the territory of France—an area that, notwithstanding the sumptuousness of the welcome it presented to the duke and his bride, was in turmoil. In mid-March, the newly pregnant Isabel chose Noyon, northeast of Compiègne, for a welcome rest from the rigors of her travels. She was to remain there for most of the spring of 1430.

Jeanne de Harcourt, countess of Namur, accompanied Duchess Isabel in her travels through Burgundy, instructing her in every detail of the customs of the Burgundian court and schooling her in the demeanor of her exalted rank. No doubt, Jeanne de Harcourt would also have told Isabel about Joan of Arc, the French maid from Lorraine who dressed in armor like a mounted knight and had inspired French forces to retake from the English the towns of Orléans, Jargeau, Beaugency, and Patay the previous spring and who was chiefly responsible for the coronation of Charles VII in Reims, where French kings had for centuries been crowned and anointed. Philip, too, would no doubt have told his new bride about Joan, and of his frustration at her successes against his English allies. These reports of Joan's exploits presumably disturbed the new duchess of Burgundy, but the fact that a woman of such humble origins could accomplish so much must also have surprised her, perhaps even excited a reluctant admiration. Since the pageantry of the coronation at Reims on July 16, 1429, however, the only news of Joan had been of her failure to retake Paris, and the English and Burgundians hoped that Joan had returned home to the village of Domrémy in Lorraine.

In fact, Joan was now refocusing her efforts on Compiègne, only thirty miles from Noyon, where Isabel was resting. Charles VII and Philip, too, were turning their attention toward this key city that was a gateway to Paris. From 1425 until 1430, the duchy of Burgundy had been protected by a system of local truces, which France (which was busy fighting the English in the north) had largely honored. As stipulated in one of these truces, Charles VII had ordered that the city of Compiègne open its gates to the Burgundians; Compiègne's French citizens, however, were aware that Joan was in the field again and on her way to their city, and instead of opening the city gates, they reinforced the city walls against a possible Anglo-Burgundian attack.[7] In the second week of May, Philip the Good left Isabel at the castle of Noyon in the company of her ten-year-old-nephew, John of Cleves, and the countess of Namur, then rode to the neighboring town of Mondidier to raise troops. He then proceeded to the northern outskirts of Compiègne to organize an attack against the city.

The Challenge of the Maid of Orléans

The seventeen-year-old Joan had traveled a long way from her hamlet of Domrémy, her home in eastern France wedged between Champagne and Lorraine, to meet with Charles VII at Chinon on the River Loire in the early months of 1429—at the same time that messengers were speeding toward Philip the Good with news of the acceptance of his offer of marriage. The villages of Joan's childhood, strung along the winding Meuse River, claimed allegiance either to the Holy Roman Empire to the east or to the French king to the west. To the north and the south, however, lay Burgundian territory. Like two giant pincers, Philip's northern lowland provinces and his southern highland territories gripped Lorraine.

Joan believed herself to be on a divine mission to save France, and claimed she was guided by the "voices" of saints directed by God. (Not surprisingly, her enemies considered these voices to be either hallucinations or fabrications of an unstable, attention-seeking young girl.) She had twice asked for help in her sacred mission from the captain-general and governor of Vaucouleurs, Robert Baudricourt, who commanded the military defenses of the duchy of Bar, which lay just to the north of Lorraine. The first time that she asked Baudricourt to dispatch her to her king to help him secure his crown, she had been refused. The second time, in February 1429, she was successful. Baudricourt was by then desperate for any help he could muster: France was now much more vulnerable to English power than it had been just a few months previously; Orléans had been under siege since October 1428; and Baudricourt's own lord and ally, Rene, duke of Bar, was trying to fend off the attempts of the duke of Bedford (who was both the commander of the English forces in France and regent to the orphaned Henry VI) to march into Bar and force him to become a vassal of the English king. Although most of Baudricourt's forces greeted Joan with derision, a few officers were struck by the intensity of her belief in her mission and her straightforward approach to fulfilling it. Baudricourt was persuaded to provide her with a letter of introduction to the king at Chinon and a small escort of five men, including the hardened soldiers Jean de Metz and Bertrand de Poulegny. He then washed his hands of her safety and her mission, which began from the gates of Vaucouleurs on February 23.

Accompanied by her escorts and by the king's messenger, Colet de Vienne, Joan rode under the cover of darkness across contested land swept by English and Burgundian patrols. On the first night of their journey, Joan and her party reached the Marne River, and for the next eleven days they continued to advance with great caution. So as not to advertise their presence, they carried their swords across their saddles to prevent them clinking, muffled their horses' hooves in rags to deaden the noise, and weighted their horses' tails to prevent the animals from neighing. At length, they reached the township of Fièrbois on the Loire River on March 6, 1429, 325 miles from Domrémy and only 15 miles from the dauphin's retreat at Chinon.

Meanwhile, Charles quivered with indecision about whether to stay in the recesses of his castles in southern France—thus allowing the English and their Burgundian allies to roam freely across his northern kingdom—

or to make a dash for the safety of Spain—thus relinquishing the entire kingdom to the hands of Henry VI. Whereas Charles had once dressed in the red, white, and blue of France to lead his troops against the English, he was now a hesitant and insecure man; he had put his symbol of the mailed fist holding a naked sword aside, and now he cowered in the protection of his itinerant court in the Loire Valley, resigned to his title, "King of Bourges" (Bourges being the name given to a region of southern France where Charles spent much of his time). In 1421, he had suffered two great defeats: he had shamefully withdrawn from the field of battle against Henry V, and his parents had repudiated him as the legitimate heir to the French crown. These twin blows had shattered his self-confidence and made him a virtual recluse. The mission of the seventeen-year-old peasant girl, Joan of Arc, was to inspire this broken man to lead his people as their rightful king, to see him crowned at Reims, and to prod him to expel the English from France.

At Fièrbois, Joan was hesitant to proceed farther without permission for an audience from Charles. She dictated to Colet de Vienne a letter for the king in which she declared that she had traveled so far to aid him in ridding France of the English, that she would recognize him in any crowd of courtiers, and that she sought his permission to meet with him. While waiting for his reply, she gave thanks for her safe journey in the town's chapel dedicated to Saint Catherine, Joan's patron saint. The inside walls of the chapel were adorned with crutches and braces of those cripples who had been miraculously cured through prayer. Just outside the chapel was buried the sword of Charles Martel—the grandfather of Charlemagne and the man who had defeated the Moors at Tours in 732, thereby eliminating the Moslem challenge to France. Martel had requested that his sword be left in the chapel in gratitude for his victory over the Saracens. Joan soon had occasion to remember that chapel, the sword, and the monks who cared for it.[8]

Colet de Vienne delivered two letters to the king at Chinon on March 7, one from Baudricourt, the other from Joan. "Why not hear what the girl has to say, and then decide?" the king asked his closest counselor, Georges de la Trémoille. His reply reached Joan at Fièrbois within two days, on

March 9. Still dressed as a man, Joan hurried the next day to meet Charles, who was in disguise in the midst of his courtiers, in a clumsy attempt to test Joan's self-proclaimed ability to recognize him even though she had never before seen him. She identified him at once, bowed low, then knelt and embraced his knees, saying "God give you a happy life, sweet King!" Continuing his charade, Charles responded, "I am not the king! That," he said, pointing to a courtier, "is the King." But Joan was not to be put off, and she said firmly, "In God's name, sweet prince, it is you and none other who are the king." Startled, Charles replied "And who are you?"

Standing then, and looking at Charles directly—calling him "dauphin" from that moment until he was crowned as king of France four months later—she said, "Gentle Dauphin, my name is Joan the Maid. I have been sent here by God to bring help to you and to your kingdom. Through me the King of Heaven sends this message, that you shall be crowned and anointed in the city of Reims, and shall be His lieutenant, who is the King of Heaven and of France."[9] Charles then took Joan aside and both entered into a side chapel where they exchanged words in private. Witnesses at Joan's retrial in 1456 claimed that during this interview Joan revealed to Charles that she knew his innermost wishes, desires that he had never voiced to any man or woman and had articulated only in silent prayer. Whatever did or did not pass between them, the fact is that the private interview seems to have awakened in Charles a certainty of manner that was obvious to all of his court. The change in Charles was so startling that the courtiers' own attitudes toward Joan changed immediately to match their king's.

The king provided Joan with a horse and clear "white" armor (so described because there were no etchings or decorations of any kind). She ordered that a great blue-and-white banner be made and inscribed with "Jesus, Maria"; this she would carry into battle. She also requested the sword of Charles Martel to carry by her side—marked by five carved crucifixes along the blade, the sword was unearthed from behind the chapel at Fièrbois. Her first test was to escort provisions into the starving city of Orléans, a task she readily accepted, declaring that "in God's name, we will put it into Orléans as we will, nor is there an

Englishman that will make sortie against us, nor any show of preventing us in our action." She proved as good as her word, and took the opportunity of her twenty-four-hour stay within the city walls to assess how best to raise the English siege. On May 23, the French finally relieved Orléans. Her June campaigns to retake the cities of Jargeau on the 12th, Beaugency on the 17th, and Patay on the 18th were equally successful. The other small cities that lay between Joan and her goal to have Charles crowned fell one by one into French hands as she and Charles moved eastward into the province of Champagne, evicting the occupying English and Burgundian forces as they went. Their goal was the city of Reims, whose cathedral held the ampule of oils that, according to legend, had descended from heaven in the care of angels to be used to anoint the rightful kings of France.

On July 1, Charles and Joan arrived within the diocese of Reims. The king was still terrified of defeat at the hands of the English and of rejection from the citizens of Reims, but Joan assuaged his fears: "Advance boldly, and be not anxious, for if you will but play a man's part, you shall have all your kingdom." The morning after their arrival on July 1, she wrote to the duke of Burgundy to remind him that she had notified him of the coming coronation ceremony three weeks earlier and had not received his reply. Philip had indeed not replied, for he was reluctant to give any indication of whether he supported the royal claims of Charles VII or of Henry VI. In the event, he decided to send deputies to the coronations of both men!

At nine o'clock on the morning of July 16, Charles VII entered the cathedral of Reims to be anointed by the oil from the sacred ampule. In full armor and bearing her standard, Joan stood next to the king. When he was anointed, she knelt, weeping, and whispered, "Gentle king, now has God's pleasure been accomplished." The ceremony lasted until two o'clock.

Reverberations from the coronation echoed all through France as distant towns sent notice of welcome to the king; even the people of Picardy in the Somme—the control of which was fiercely contested between France and Burgundy—assured Charles that the gates of their cities would open widely for his troops. Charles VII had suddenly become a powerful king, while Philip had quickly become vulnerable to French attacks on both his territory and his independence. The English responded by crowning Henry VI as king of both England and France on November 5, 1429, at Westminster Abbey. The duke of Bedford realized, however, that Henry VI also needed the added prestige of a coronation *in France* to counter the rousing effect that Charles's coronation had had on French morale. Thus, on April 23, 1430, the nine-year-old king was brought to Calais, and then to Rouen—where he was to remain while Joan, then a prisoner of the English in that city, was tried, convicted, and executed as a heretic. Eventually, on January 19, 1432, Henry was to be crowned king of France at the cathedral of Notre Dame in Paris.

In late 1429, however, Joan was still very much alive, and was urging the newly anointed Charles to press forward with attacks on the northeastern towns held by the English and the Burgundians. Joan insisted that peace with the Burgundians would come only at the point of a lance, and she opposed the truces that Charles had agreed with Philip the Good.[10] Charles, though, calculated that those truces would free him to concentrate his forces against the English, and he resisted Joan's counsel. To quiet Joan's insistence, and as a reward for her services to France, the king issued her a patent of nobility. She quietly rode to Jargeau, twenty-five miles east of Orléans, for Christmas Day, and then rode on to Orléans, where in mid-January of the new year the city celebrated her return with presents of fifty-two pints of wine, six capons, nine partridges, thirteen rabbits, a pheasant, and a doublet for her brother.

On March 16—at the same time as Isabel arrived at Noyon—Joan rode into the village of Sully, where she dispatched a number of letters to her friends at Reims expressing her continuing distrust for the Burgundian word of honor and in particular for the recently signed truce between Philip and Charles that promised to return Paris into the king's hands. Joan told her friends that she would soon have a plan to counter the expected fickleness of Philip the Good.

With the approach of Easter, Joan donned her armor again and, holding tightly to her banner, rode hard with her handful of men toward Lagny on the Marne River, to the east of Paris and well inside the Burgundian area of control in Champagne. As rumor spread that Joan was back in the field, Burgundian-held French villages in the northeastern provinces from Champagne to Picardy rose up against their Burgundian lords. Joan, however, was beginning to anticipate the end of her sacred mission. That Easter, while she was walking the walls of Melun, a little town south of Paris that had recently thrown off Burgundian control by opening its gates to the French, the "voices" that had guided her mission from its beginning warned her that she would soon be captured and must not be afraid as God would be with her.[11]

The encounter at Lagny soon after Easter was brief but decisive, and Joan's small band succeeded in bringing Langy back into French hands. However, Joan's reputation was somewhat tarnished by this campaign. For once, Joan was not carrying Martel's sword—it was said that she had broken it over the back of a camp follower—and instead had in hand a Burgundian one she had picked up on the battlefield, saying that "the sword was a good one, a proper sword with which to give good blows and buffets." In previous campaigns, Joan had carried her weapon for defense, holding her banner and standard high in the midst of battle; at Lagny, however, she had wielded her sword. Upon hearing of Joan's efforts at combat, Charles—who, since his coronation, had started to see the belligerent Joan as something of a menace to his plans—remarked that "it would have been better if she had carried a stick instead."[12]

Despite Charles's diminishing respect for Joan's advice and conduct, none doubted that she could exert a powerful influence over the king, his plans, and his people. And as Joan rested her men at Senlis, twenty-five miles northeast of Paris, the English and the Burgundians both recognized that, if left unchecked, her influence might well spell their own defeat.

In early May, undaunted by her king's lack of enthusiasm for aggression against the enemy, and ignoring the warnings of her voices that her own capture was imminent, Joan turned her attention to Compiègne—the city that was refusing to obey Charles VII's orders to open its gates to the forces of Philip the Good. Upon hearing that Joan and her small force were approaching Compiègne, Philip marched his main force that had gathered at Montdidier toward Noyon to guard the river crossing at Pont L'Évéque.

Isabel had only a few days to organize her household and leave the peaceful retreat that was soon to become an armed encampment.

Meanwhile, the English, conscious of the strategic importance of Compiègne for the safety of their hold on Paris, sent a large force from the capital to help Philip's men take the city. As a result, Joan's forces lost all the bridges surrounding Compiègne on May 14, 16, 17, and 18, and her small army was even turned away from the French-held town of Soissons, twenty miles upstream. During the night of May 22–23, Joan rode the fifteen miles from Crépy, south of Compiègne, in the dark of a night that chroniclers report was starless "and had a moon that was a slip only one day old." She entered Compiègne without encountering resistance. She emerged at five o'clock that afternoon to attack the English encampment at Margny, opposite the city gate.

But her troops were outnumbered, scattered, and in a poor strategic position to battle the combined Burgundian and English forces that swept in from the north and the east to surprise them. Alarmed at the heavy odds against them, French soldiers pleaded with Joan to join them in retreat. As more and more of them clattered across the drawbridge, Joan shouted, "Shut up! Their discomfiture depends only on you. Think only of falling upon them." But she could not rally them, and they poured back across the bridge into the city gates. As Joan tried desperately to defend their rear, the captain of the town panicked and lowered the portcullis and pulled up the drawbridge. Joan, left on the wrong side of the closed gate, was ridden down by the Burgundian forces of Jean de Luxembourg, count of Ligny, whose captain tore at her gold cape and dragged her from her horse. At nearby Coudun, just north of Compiègne, Philip was notified at once that Joan of Arc was captured.

Notes

1. Claudine LeMaire and Michèle Henry, *Isabelle de Portugal, duchesse de Bourgogne, 1397–1471* (Brussels: Biblioteque Royale Albert Ier, 1991), 27. Portugal and Burgundy were bound by genealogy, diplomacy, economics, and art;. matri-

monial alliances and commercial treaties between these kingdom had been established at the end of the twelfth century. In 1147, the Flemish and Brabantines had joined the Portuguese of Lisbon in the conquest of their enemies, the Mauritians. By 1386, the Portuguese community installed in Bruges received special trade privileges from the first Valois duke of Burgundy, Philip the Bold, Philip the Good's grandfather. In 1411, Philip the Good's father, John the Fearless, had granted the Portuguese in his duchy a charter extending these privileges.

2. LeMaire and Henry, *Isabelle de Portugal,* 27.
3. L. Gilliodts-Van Severen, *Inventaires des Archives de la Ville de Bruges, section 1: Inventaire des chartes, series 1* (Brussels: Le Planche, 1876), 4:517–19.
4. Quoted in H. V. Livermore, *History of Portugal* (Cambridge: Cambridge University Press, 1947), 194.
5. Jean LeFevre de Saint-Remy, *Chronique, 1400–1444*, ed. Fr. Morand (Paris: Société d'Histoire de France,1876–81), 2:162–65. LeFevre was an eyewitness at the banquet and was named the "king-of-arms" of the new Order of the Golden Fleece.
6. Otto Cartellieri, *The Court of Burgundy* (New York and London: Alfred A. Knopf, 1929), 59.
7. Richard Vaughan, *Philip the Good: The Apogee of Burgundy* (New York: Barnes and Noble, 1970), 62–63.
8. M. G. A. Vale, *Charles VII* (Berkeley and Los Angeles: University of California Press, 1974), 34.
9. Jules Quicherat, *Procès de condemanation et de rehabilitation de Jeanne d'Arc* (Paris: Lucien Renouard, 1861), 3:103. Although the witnesses at her Rehabilitation Trial in 1456 offered variations as to Joan's exact words, they were essentially the same. Lucien Favre, *Joan of Arc* (London: Odhams Press, 1954), 113; Vita Sackville-West, *Saint Joan of Arc* (New York: Doubleday, 1964), 115; and Regine Pernoud, *The Retrial of Joan of Arc: Evidence at Her Trial for her Rehabilitation, 1450–1456,* trans. J. M. Cohen (New York: Harcourt, Brace, 1981), 104.
10. See Quicherat, *Procès*, 5:165.
11. Quicherat, *Procès*, 1:115. While on the walls of the town of Melun in April 1430, Joan's voices returned. According to testimony given in her Rehabilitation Trial of 1456, she said that the voices of Saints Catherine and Marguerite announced that she would soon be taken prisoner.

When she asked when this would occur, they refused to tell her. When she begged the voices that she might be killed instead of imprisoned, they told her to take heart because God would be with her.

Andrew Lang, in *The Maid of France* (London: Longmans, Green, 1908), argues that when Joan failed in her campaign to regain Paris for Charles, she sought to save the reputation of her voices for infallibility by blaming the defeat on the half-hearted efforts of French commanders. "She falsely denied," contends Lang, "having received any special command from her voices [regarding an attack on Paris], and falsely reported that the French nobles intended to make no serious attack."

12. Sackville-West, *Saint Joan of Arc*, 241.

Chapter Three

A Diplomatic Education, 1432–1435

"MORE DELIGHTED than if a king had fallen into his hands," Philip the Good raced from his encampment at Coudun to see Joan of Arc for himself at nearby Margny. He ordered her brought into the great hall of the command center where he could interrogate her.[1] Still in battle dress, tired and disheveled, Joan faced the duke of Burgundy, his field commander, the count of Ligny, and an assembly of their officers who crowded about her to take the measure of the young girl who had kept English and Burgundian forces at bay during a full year of campaigns.

Several miles downstream at Noyon, Isabel prepared to move her court away from the dangers of the encroaching Compiègne campaign. Her husband had ordered her to go to Ghent in the north, where she would not only be safe from the battle but might also play a useful part in cooling a threatened rebellion by both the merchants and the artisans of Ghent. Isabel was now entirely occupied by the elaborate preparations for her departure. Her three magnificently painted carts stood by the main entrance to the hotel, and the sturdy horses chosen by Jacques de Villiers, her equerry and cupbearer, waited patiently in their traces for her garments to be loaded into their wagons. Tapestries and the precious chapel items that always traveled with the duchess were placed under lock and key for the duration of the journey. Bocquet de Lattre, her chief kitchen officer, was delighted that the household was returning to his northern homeland, and his bustling orders echoed throughout the village of Noyon as bakers, larder men, and kitchen staff loaded equipment into carts. All told, forty carts drew into alignment for the journey.

Although outwardly Isabel was busy readying her household for the trek northward, inwardly she chafed at her husband's order to quit Noyon. "She hesitates to accept the dismissal," one of the duke's secretary's wrote, "and she insists on following her lord into battle in the rain and wind." The safety of the newly pregnant Isabel and her obligation to shoulder ducal power during her husband's absence in the field were weighed against her own wishes, and her duty took precedence. "There are those in the court who would have wanted the duchess to win her argument and accompany her husband into battle," another secretary slyly noted, "as this would have delayed his actions and given the French forces more opportunity to defeat him."[2]

Indeed, several Burgundian nobles, convinced that Burgundy's brightest future—as well as their own—lay with France, had already made separate truces with Charles VII, involving their own estates. The most prominent of these was Jehan de la Trémoille, a knight of the Golden Fleece and brother of Georges de la Trémoille, the favorite of the French king. Rumors circulated that the duke's own chamberlain, Anthony de Croy, also had French sympathies, which explained his persistence in pressing for peaceful terms with the French king. Even the prince of Orange, Louis de Chalon, spoke of the advantages of changing his alliance from England to their enemy, Charles VII, and talked openly of relinquishing his English Order of the Garter.

First Lessons: Trade and Domestic Conflict in Ghent, 1430

The spring and summer months of 1430 proved a challenging but valuable introduction to Burgundian affairs for the new duchess of Burgundy. From June through September, Isabel found herself in a maelstrom of military and economic turmoil surrounding the populous and industrial city of Ghent. The crises acquainted the duchess with the century-old feuds between Philip's northern cities and with the economic realities of the Burgundian cloth industry and merchant trade. An intelligent woman as well as a quick study of circumstances, the Portuguese princess began in Ghent to hone her negotiating skills—skills that were to prove priceless in the future.

While Isabel was on the road for Ghent, Philip the Good ordered Joan taken from Margny to the count of Ligny's castle at Beaulieu on the Aisne River, and the prisoner's path may well have crossed Isabel's own winding caravan of carts, carriages, and mounted horsemen, bringing the two women as close to each other as they would ever be.

However, the armed men who escorted the duchess made sure that the two women did not meet, for they piloted Isabel's caravan along the trail with great caution, alert not only for the French forces but also for marauding *écorcheurs*—the roaming bands of French deserters who laid waste many of the towns and the countryside of eastern France.

As Isabel approached Ghent in the lacy green of early June, the gray mound of dark stone that was the castle of Ten Waele—family home of the dukes of Flanders for centuries—must have chilled her heart and challenged her new-bride's enthusiasm. Her apprehension was then confirmed by the news that Philip's southern forces near Charolais, which had been operating independently of the duke, had lost their entire infantry to the French.[3] Isabel, however, was soon forced to concern herself with dangers much closer to hand. Only a few days after her arrival at Ten Waele, the threat of war arrived in a letter from the bishop of Liège, John of Heinsberg, who wrote to demand that the duke of Burgundy honor the rights of the citizens of his duchy to reparations for the outrages committed by Burgundian soldiers. Heinsberg promised military action against the duke's towns of Bouvignes and Namur if Philip did not furnish compensation. Philip refused to do so, and so in mid-July the men of Liège and Dinant opened hostilities by laying siege to Namur and Bouvignes. The violence lasted only a few weeks, but three hundred houses, thirty-three fortified places, and seventeen windmills near Ghent were destroyed. When, in early August, Philip assumed the dukedom of

Brabant, the Liègeois were soon cowed by his additional power and accepted a truce on September 1. A payment of 100,000 English golden nobles by Liège ended its war with Burgundy.

But Ghent itself continued in turmoil, with the struggle between its merchants and artisans threatening to shut down its most important industry. Ghent was the capital of Flanders, and the principal industry of Flanders was the manufacture of cloth. Trade in cloth had been increasing steadily since 1419; however, this rise reflected the development of a rural cloth industry that was rapidly leaving the city's looms idle. Isabel's task was multifaceted and difficult: she had to stem the migration into the countryside, prevent the artisans still living in the city from rising in rebellion against the city's rich merchants, and persuade those merchants and Ghent's trade guilds to adopt policies that would defuse the artisans' anger.

Now dressed in loose-fitting garments appropriate for her advancing pregnancy and confined within the somber castle of Ten Waele, which stood in the center of Ghent, Isabel looked for a solution to the city's festering discontent. The duchess accepted the suggestion of her secretary and treasurer, Paul Deschamps, to summon Guillaume de Lalaing, grand bailiff (governor) of Hainault and an ambassador to England. He was a man on whom Isabel would come to depend for his loyalty and sound advice on the Lowlands and the economic challenges presented by England. She listened carefully to Lalaing through the hours of their first afternoon together as he explained the intricacies of the economic problems besetting the Flemish. English cloth was rolling off the cargo ships in Bruges and crossing the flat, open fields of Flanders toward the great fairs held at Antwerp. Although the quality of the English cloth was not as fine as that produced by Flemish looms in Ghent, the price was more attractive to European markets. Furthermore, the weavers in the villages surrounding the large industrial towns of Flanders were mounting a stronger challenge to the English product than were the urban looms that labored under the strictures imposed by Ghent's merchant-controlled guilds. The villages' success was fed by their independence from guild standards and their easy access to raw materials from neighboring regions and from Spain. The artisans of Ghent were numerous and well organized, and they demanded that the guilds relax their standards and that the city's merchants offer them a better price for the cloth they wove.

Although Isabel was sympathetic to the artisans' cause, she needed more information before she could take action to defuse the brewing rebellion. Why, she wondered, were the merchants unable to see that they were going to lose the very industry that spun their wealth? Was English cloth the only danger to Burgundian weavers? What about French, Italian, and German goods? Lalaing told her that all these foreign goods did indeed pose a threat to the Burgundian economy; cloths from Holland, for example, added to the problem of the Ghent weavers, while an emerging linen industry presented serious competition for the wool cloth of Flanders. But he emphasized that perhaps the most serious cause of the artisans' distress was that the guild corporations imposed such strict standards on their members that the artisans could not earn a living wage unless they fled to the less regulated countryside.

Lalaing encouraged Isabel to meet with the representative body of the state, the Four Members of Flanders, and to try to convince its members to relax the guild standards. This powerful body of men representing Ghent, Bruges, Ypres, and the Franc of Bruges (the incorporated hinterland of Bruges) exercised considerable control over Flanders, meeting frequently to deal with taxes, military defense, disputes between their members and foreign merchants, monetary policy, and a wide range of other economic and administrative matters. Most members belonged to the rich merchant oligarchy that controlled the trade of Ghent. Their chief weakness was a tendency to fight among themselves for self-centered commercial interests.[4]

Isabel convoked the Ghent Council, composed of the leading merchants and nobles who controlled the guilds, and warned of the dangers of allowing the Germans, Italians, and French to flood the Antwerp markets each year with their own goods at the expense of the Flemish cities' looms. She also pointed out that the guild standards were spurring the continuing exodus of weavers into the countryside, and emphasized the need for the merchants to lower their standards for the quality of their wool cloth. As it turned out, she had little success in changing the practice of either the merchants or the artisans, but during the summer and fall of

1430 she kept the latter aware of her efforts to establish a dialogue between them and the merchant oligarchy, and so helped to maintain a temporary peace among the contending factions in Ghent.

These four months at Ten Waele not only challenged the negotiating skills of the duchess but also exercised her financial and administrative talents. Isabel's experience at her father's court in arranging charter agreements with foreign merchants at Lisbon had prepared her to deal with the kinds of issues that surrounded guild contracts and charters. Her responsibility for Portugal's international banking, as the administrator of that kingdom's funds in the Medici banks of Florence and Rome, had left her with a refined appreciation for the value of investments. And as she was therefore an able forecaster of the slippery scale of profits and losses in the merchant trade, she was well prepared to assess the current status of Ghent's treasury.

After a short review of that city's account books, she warned the members of Ghent's ruling council that she was in no doubt of their treasury's capabilities to support her husband's summer campaigns against the French. Caught off guard by her financial awareness, they were easily harangued into furnishing Philip with the funds that would allow him to keep his forces in the field both in the south and along his northern borders.

As Isabel approached the seventh month of her first pregnancy surrounded by her own large court at Ten Waele, weary of the challenges presented by the feuding artisans and merchants in Ghent, she must have longed for word about the safety of her duke. She must also have worried about the prospects of the child she was carrying, given the increasing challenge to Burgundy's stability posed by France. Nevertheless, Isabel put her personal concerns aside as September passed into October, and she became more involved in Flemish economic affairs, offering innovative ideas for revised trade contracts between the merchant-controlled guilds and the city's artisans. She continued to press the members of the Four Estates of Flanders to bear down on the uncooperative guild corporations, negotiating better charters for those artisans who demanded a voice in their own economic future. By early fall Isabel had won enough respect as arbiter of the ducal government to have delayed a civil revolt, and to have used that fragile peace to secure funds for her husband's defense of his duchy. She had proved herself clever with both finances and people—a valuable facility for the duke to find in his third wife.

But Philip was not thinking about Isabel or the affairs in Ghent at this time. With his northern forces before Compiègne that summer, he continued to hammer the gates of that stubborn city until they would open for his Burgundian troops. Philip was contemplating ways to refurbish his southern defenses when he learned of the unexpected death on August 4 of Philip St. Pol, duke of Brabant. Philip had long coveted Burgundy's rich neighbor, Brabant, and he did not hesitate to leave the field around Compiègne to the count of Ligny and to ride hard for Brussels, the capital of Brabant.

On arriving in Brussels, just thirty miles from Ghent, he challenged the right of Margaret, Philip St. Pol's widow, to assume the duchy as her husband's legitimate heir. Philip counterclaimed, asserting that he was the only true male heir, having been named by the childless Philip St. Pol as his rightful heir in a formal act of September 4, 1427. With Brabant surrounded by neighbors enmeshed in Burgundian alliances, neighbors who could easily suffocate Brabant's commerce and trade by prohibiting the traffic through Brabant of rich caravan routes that carried imported wool, cloth, leather, metalwork, and jewels, Philip found it relatively easy to persuade the governing council of the Brabantine Estates into accepting his claim. The widowed duchess was duly released into Philip's guardianship. But Brabant's leaders were not as willing to agree to Philip's demands to alter their form of government to one he could more easily dominate. They continued to be wary of Philip's plans to bring Brabant wholly under his personal rule. Two months later, in October 1430, Holy Roman Emperor Sigismund ruled that at the death of Philip St. Pol, the Brabantine territory would revert to him. Sigismund had warned both the Estates of Brabant and Philip the Good to withdraw from the contest for control as the area now belonged to the empire. The members of the Estates of Brabant now used this threat of imperial force to resolve their negotiations with Philip. They acknowledged Philip the Good as Brabant's overlord while retaining nothing less than their own accustomed system of self-rule, keeping control over their coinage and monetary policy, maintaining their vote on economic matters, and settling their own disputes within the estates and with foreign merchants.

Philip moved quickly into his new capital on October 5 and summoned Isabel to join him in Brussels. No doubt pleased to be called from the grim castle of Ten Waele that seemed forever washed in rain and echoing with the chicanery of Ghent's politics, the duchess left Ghent within a few days. On October 8, three days after the Estates of Brabant recognized Philip as their new duke, Brabant's new duchess made her "Joyeuse Entrée" into Brussels. Isabel rode through the narrow streets of Brussels on her white palfrey, following the scarlet carpet the citizens had placed along her route. Great banners were suspended from the buildings that lined her progress toward the castle of Coudenberg, which Philip was refurbishing at the city's charge. Gifts of cup and plate in gold and silver, crates of the best imported wines, and beautiful tapestries were piled high for Isabel's treasury. The celebrations lasted several days.

While Philip congratulated himself on acquiring Brabant without having to field an army, and while Isabel collected her treasures at Coudenberg, a lighter and airier castle that promised happier days with a growing family, Joan of Arc simmered in despair within her new prison. She had been moved from the pleasant castle of Beaulieu in late summer to the more secure castle of Beaurevoir, which lay within Luxembourg, about sixty miles from Ghent. She remained there through early December 1430 in the care of two women who proved to be her most compassionate jailers: Jeanne de Bethune, wife of the count of Ligny, and the count's seventy-seven-year-old aunt, Jeanne, known to those in his territory as the "Lady of Luxembourg," who controlled the rich inheritance of the duchy.

The days that followed Joan's arrival at Beaurevoir were filled with bitter quarreling between aunt and nephew. The count, who badly needed funds to maintain Luxembourg's services to the duke of Burgundy, planned to sell Joan to the English, but his aunt declared that to do so would be to sell one's soul. The tension between the count and his aunt ended on

September 10, when she signed her will in her nephew's favor with the provision that he not sell Joan to the English. As a consequence, although the Estates of Normandy had already allotted the money with which the English could buy Joan, she was not sold while the count's aunt lived.

During this reprieve, the aunt spent many hours with Joan, walking the sixty-foot-high walls of her donjon prison discussing the existence of God and the mission the Maid of Orléans believed she had been given to fulfill. In spite of the aunt's company, however, Joan's isolation became so severe a burden for her that by October she begged her voices to let her escape from Beaurevoir by jumping from her tower.[5] Then, in the depths of her torment, came the news that Compiègne had fallen. "How could God allow all the good people of Compiegne to die when they had been so loyal to their lord [Charles VII]?" she cried when she heard that all of the town's citizens had been put to death by Philip's forces. Desperate and confused, she fell from the high wall of the donjon to the ground below.[6] She survived, but lay unconscious for nearly a week. At the same time, her jailer and protector fell mortally ill. The Lady of Luxembourg died on November 13, 1430.

Joan no longer had any powerful friends. The French king, who in Joan's absence had always been eager to avoid confrontation, entertained no thought of rescuing the Maid of Orléans, arguing that her capture was proof she was no longer in God's favor. Philip the Good—who had once valued Joan as a possible bartering chip with the French or the English, who now threatened his economy—had gladly turned her over to Ligny. The English threatened not to buy Flemish wool if Philip did not release Joan into their hands—and when Philip's Flemish weavers began to grumble about their economic straits, Philip gave in to the English request. As for Jean de Luxembourg, with his aunt dead he saw little reason to refuse the money offered him by the English through their emissary, Pierre Cauchon, the ambitious bishop of Beauvais. Furthermore, by the custom of France, any prisoner could be bought—even a king—for the sum of ten thousand francs, and Jean de Luxembourg was more than happy to follow such a custom. Unlike Charles and Philip, Henry VI of England did want Joan—indeed, in July Henry VI demanded that "this woman must be sent forthwith to the King, who will deliver her to the Church that it may put her upon her trial, she having been accused of crimes against the Faith, for which reason she cannot be regarded as a prisoner of war."[7] This distinction between a prisoner of war and a heretic was important, for according to the existing code of war, if she remained a prisoner of war she could not be sold to her enemies and instead must be held for ransom. On November 21, 1430, Jean de Luxembourg sold Joan to Bishop Cauchon. He then joined his brother Louis—chancellor to the English government in Paris—and Cauchon on England's payroll, receiving his first payment of five hundred francs from Isabel's uncle, Henry Beaufort, the cardinal of Winchester, on December 2. Within days of her sale, Joan and her English captors began to make the journey northward toward her last imprisonment in Normandy. She reached Rouen on Christmas Day.

While Joan was en route to Normandy, Bishop Cauchon was busy positioning himself to become the judge at her trial. On the day of the sale, he obtained letters from the University of Paris faculty—who wanted her trial to be held in Paris—ruling that Joan must be placed under Bishop Cauchon's jurisdiction to answer charges made by the Catholic Church. On December 28, three days after Joan's arrival in Rouen (the bishopric of which was, conveniently for Cauchon's purposes, vacant), Cauchon obtained permission from the Cathedral Chapter to have her trial held in that city instead of Paris, where security, so he argued, could not be as easily ensured. On January 3, 1431, the English king stated that "in as much as we [act] to honor God, to protect and exalt the Holy Church and the Catholic Faith, we do hereby . . . give order that the said Joan be given to the Reverend Father in God Cauchon, that by him she may be set upon her trial."[8]

Cauchon had done well for his English masters. By securing the money for Joan's purchase from the French Estates of Normandy, and by obtaining an indictment from the University of Paris that her trial should be held for the "edification of all Christian people," Cauchon had ensured that the trial would be a religious, not a political, one, and moreover a trial staged by Frenchmen, not Englishmen. Yet, while the English were happy to appear as mere observers in the affair, the duke of Bedford added a provision to the process of Joan's trial that revealed the depth of the English determination to see Joan removed from the scene one way or another: "It is our intention, should the said Joan not be found guilty or attainted of the aforesaid charge, or of others affecting our Faith, to have her examined a second time, and brought to justice."[9]

Second Lesson: Family and Financial Crises in the Lowlands, 1431–1432

As she and Philip waited for the birth of their first child in the security of Coudenberg that winter, Isabel tried valiantly to join in the festivities of the Burgundian court. The court was famous for its color and fashion: men sauntered through the halls of Coudenberg in absurdly short, padded *pourpoints*—jackets in velvet or silk—their shirts flashing in and out of the slashes in their leg-of-mutton sleeves; ladies-in-waiting wore elegantly embroidered bodices that flared their holiday gowns down to tiny jewel-shod feet, while veils waved like butterfly wings from the peaks of their pointed hennin headdresses.

Isabel had recently learned that the Burgundian embassy that negotiated her marriage contract the previous year had remarked to Philip how much like a nun she had appeared to them when they first met her in Lisbon.[10] Faced with the fashionable court at Coudenberg, Isabel must have promised herself that after the birth of her child she would have her wardrobe master pack away the flat, over-panels that now concealed her gown beneath. The panels were a perfect solution to her present girth, but not one to please a husband who admired rich beauty and gaiety, and who demanded that the women about him flaunt these same qualities.

Since their marriage, and especially since Isabel had become pregnant, Philip had showered her with splendid gifts. She always traveled with the sumptuous golden cup—encrusted with a giant ruby surrounded with seven large and perfect pearls—that Philip had given her their first New Year together. And though it was somewhat tight on her now swollen finger, she wore the magnificent double diamond ring he presented when he learned of her pregnancy. One can almost feel the mounting dismay of the thirty-five-year-old, conservatively brought-up Catholic princess—whose greatest talents lay in finance and whose dearest desire was to inaugurate a crusade to the Holy Land—as she became increasingly aware of the competition for her husband's eye and affections. Philip did not conceal his enjoyment of the beautiful young women with whom he surrounded himself—and whom he on occasion would place on the pummel of his saddle during his ceremonial progresses—but Isabel knew that these women were not her chief rivals. Before her marriage she had heard that Philip was not like other French princes who had a succession of favorites at court. She had come to realize that Philip kept not one but several mistresses concurrently, each one residing in a different and usually distant corner of his duchy. Although she never met any of these women, she was only too aware of the large number of his illegitimate children who gathered about him and whom he showered with honors. Isabel learned of their mothers, who lived in all the far-flung reaches of her husband's scattered possessions, and she thus found herself growing more suspicious of his activities during frequent absences from court.

Anthony arrived on December 30 and was baptized on January 16. He was a tiny baby with a weak cry and a listless appetite, but his three godfathers befitted a powerful prince: Henry Beaufort, cardinal of Winchester and Isabel's uncle; John of Heinsberg, bishop of Liège, who had just been beaten in battle by Philip; and the count of Ulrich, brother of the empress of the Holy Roman Empire. Anthony's godmothers were Marie of Burgundy, duchess of Cleves and sister of the duke, and Jeanne de Harcourt, countess of Namur and Isabel's lady-in-waiting. With such a splendid array of godparents, neither the duke nor the duchess saw any need to fret about Anthony's well-being while both parents were away. Although they maintained their court at Coudenberg for an exceptionally long period after Anthony's birth, they made frequent short trips, together and apart, to bolster or establish ducal authority in the military and economic affairs of the duchy.

This relatively stable time at Coudenberg provided Isabel with an opportunity to become better acquainted with Philip's views on the vagaries of French politics and the economic power of the English, and with opinions and affairs at her husband's court. She soon discovered that the duke and his courtiers were not always of the same mind, and that among the courtiers mistrust was widespread. Whereas she and Philip agreed that Burgundy must be free of French suzerainty if the duchy were to become a powerful and independent entity (they disagreed on the best strategies to achieve this), Isabel saw that some of Philip's advisers urged him to reunite his duchy with France, encouraging Philip to remain a loyal French prince in the House of Valois. She became aware, too, of the rumors of spies at her husband's court, their allegiances bought by sizable French bribes. Meanwhile, away from court, the truces that the French king had made with Philip rarely lasted long, and a succession of border conflicts kept the duchy unstable and vulnerable.

Not too distant from the Burgundian court at Brussels, the English slammed Joan's prison door shut in Rouen that January of 1431. Although accused of a crime of faith by the University of Paris, Joan was denied the privileges international church law required for religious prisoners—a separate ecclesiastical prison and guards of her own sex—and instead, she was chained to a bed in a cell guarded by *houspilleurs,* or "toughs," the lowest category of soldier, tolerated because they did the most menial work in the camps. An attempted rape, at least, was bound to occur.

Isabel's uncle, Henry Beaufort, realized how important it was to discredit this woman who had secured the French crown for Charles VII. To accomplish this, he and his brother, the duke of Bedford, kept Joan within English control. They realized they must erase any doubt that Joan was a heretic. Bedford and the cardinal hoped that once Joan was eliminated physically and emotionally from their thoughts, the French forces would lose the fervor that the Maid of Orléans had ignited within them. The duke of Bedford was too intelligent to summarily execute his prisoner and thus risk turning her into a martyr, and instead arranged to isolate Joan to frighten her and then force the needed confession. With a confession of heresy, the very person who had secured the French coronation would condemn it. To ensure the bishop's continuing interest in securing the same outcome, the English paid him a generous daily sum until Joan was burned.[11]

The first phase of Joan's trial began on February 21, 1431, with a series of public interrogations, each lasting several hours. Between March 10 and 17 she submitted to nine more interrogations in secret. Altogether, the fifteen interrogations lasted nineteen days. That one-eyed old warrior, Jean de Luxembourg, came to her with the offer of money and the possibility of a ransom if she promised never again to bear arms against English forces. Charging him with mocking her by suggesting a ransom, she exclaimed she knew the English were determined to kill her so they could consume all of France more easily. She declared that even if there were a hundred thousand "Godons" (French slang for the English, who repeatedly swore "Goddamn") in France, they would never have that kingdom for their own.[12]

The formal open trial of Joan of Arc began on March 26 and lasted eight weeks. Then, exhausted from six months of torment in her cell and the terrible stress of her interrogations by the examiners, Joan faced the most critical moment of her trial at the cemetery of St.-Ouen on May 26. Threatened with burning at the stake, she searched for a way out. When presented with a statement of seven or eight lines beginning with "I, Joan," and told that it acknowledged only her submission to God and the pope and that her signature would allow her to be transferred to a prison of the church, the exhausted Joan signed her mark. This confession was never found, but instead there was presented to the court a document with her signature that began "All who have erred," which was a recantation of all her deeds and acts, specifically denying her mission and the legality of the coronation. Two days later, she was told the real substance of her admissions during a visit by Bishop Cauchon and a number of English lords who presented her with her recantation. Joan exclaimed that by attempting to save her own life, she had damned herself, and thus she must retract her confession: "All that I then said, I revoke, as I said it from fear of the fire." The clerk in attendance wrote the words *Responsio mortifera* in the record he kept of these visits—her retraction carried the sentence of death.[13] On that day Joan was formally excommunicated from the church as a "diseased member likely to infect others." On May 30 she was sentenced to be burned at the stake, with her execution to take place that same day in the Old Market of Rouen.

Silence shrouded the market square as one of Bishop Cauchon's men approached Joan and took off her hat. He placed on her head a tall, pointed cone made of a wide strip of curved paper, crudely clipped together, carrying the inscription "Heretic. Relapsed sinner. Apostate idolater." The church had separated itself wholly from Joan, and thus her execution was entrusted to the secular authorities. With some reluctance, a secular judge waited nearby to accept the Maid of Orléans from Bishop Cauchon. The tumbril then carried Joan toward the concrete post that stood heaped on four sides with faggots ready for the flame. After her death, the cardinal of Winchester demanded that Joan's ashes be scattered in the Seine River. But the cardinal's action could not halt Joan's elevation to the status of a martyr, nor could it reverse the reinvigoration of the kingdom of France that Joan had set in motion.

Isabel and Philip were seldom apart in the spring and summer of 1431, and in the autumn it was clear that she was once again pregnant. Their time together ended in early January 1432, when Philip left Coudenberg for Dijon. Ironically, once Joan was dead, the French king had at last followed her advice, voiding the truces he had signed with Burgundy and in the winter launching attacks against Philip's territories. Responding to these challenges along both his northern and southern borders, the duke gathered his troops for the winter campaigns. "You will serve the duchess in her state and office representing me during my absence," he ordered in a January 19 letter to the council he established at Ghent to serve his wife as administrator of the northern territories that winter.[14] Although Anthony had recently become restless and irritable in the care of his wet nurse, neither of his parents felt his condition to be of concern, and Isabel occupied herself with Philip's plans for her to take over ducal authority in the Lowlands. A few days after Philip's departure on January 21, as heavy winter storms pummeled the area, Isabel's cart lurched over the flat, windswept plains away from Coudenberg and from Anthony and toward the challenges waiting for her thirty miles down the road in the council at Ghent.

Isabel traveled with three lords assigned to guide her administration. Several weeks before the duke left Brussels, she had proved her ability to negotiate delicate financial agreements when she arranged terms for the payment of ten thousand guilders to Philip for damages wreaked on Namur earlier in 1431 by the men of Liège. Now, with the cautious respect of Jean de Thoisy, bishop of Liège and president of the ducal council, and in the comforting presence of Jean, lord of Roubaix and ambassador to Portugal, who had acted as proxy for her marriage to Philip two years before, she began to exert her influence on the council.

Only Anthony de Croy, the duke's first chamberlain and his closest friend, gave her pause. He sat quietly at their meetings, offering no advice, but instead appeared to be silently taking her measure, noting her judgments and estimating her growing skills. For her part, Isabel examined de Croy's motives more carefully with each meeting of the council.

But Isabel had much else to concern herself with that January. On the political front, the Lowlands faced a financial crisis that was aggravated by the reticence of the English to transport their trade goods through the Burgundian Lowlands or buy the Flemish wool for their looms. The artisans of the area were again on the verge of revolt. And on the personal front, she was four months pregnant and her son was not well. She had asked that Guillaume de Lalaing travel to Coudenberg immediately after her departure to observe the care given her year-old son, and on January 27 she also dispatched Guillaume le Zedelaire, a member of the Ghent Council, to ride to Brussels and report on the state of Anthony's health. He returned with the discouraging news that the child was fevered and congested and eating little. Isabel sent Lancelot de la Viefville to Coudenberg the next day. But after remaining close by the ailing Anthony's side for the next few days, Viefville returned with the dreadful news that the child had died alone in his nursery on February 5.

Overwhelmed with sorrow, Isabel blamed herself for having left Anthony in his first major illness, even though she realized that she had had no choice but to obey her husband's orders to take over affairs in

Ghent. Isabel wrote daily letters to Philip explaining the tragedy at Coudenberg. Absorbed with his military campaigns, Philip could not return, and instead responded with letters that shared her grief and asked about her progress in the Lowlands. Until Philip's return, Isabel would comfort herself with the thought of the child she carried within her, and yield to her sorrow only in the privacy of her bedroom, where her grief could be shed into a pillow that would be dry by morning.

On February 11 the Ghent Council presented Isabel with the Great Seal of Burgundy, giving her the right and duty to wield princely powers during Philip's absence. With no time allowed her to mourn the death of her little boy, she threw herself into the resolution of the Lowlands' problems. Whether demanding to review the general receipts of Flanders or examining the legal issues of confiscations, her attention to matters both great and minor was impressive.

With the milder weather of spring making travel easier, the duchess journeyed frequently between Ghent and Brussels, concerning herself with her household responsibilities at both castles while maintaining tight control over the affairs in the Ghent Council. The castle at Coudenberg was filled as usual with men sent home from the campaigns against the French. Many were too wounded to move; others shuffled and limped through the castle's rooms and gardens. Isabel also kept an eye on the young noblemen who lived at her court, still too young to engage in battle, but who were preparing themselves for a life of service to the duke.

At the combined courts of Ten Waele and Coudenberg, Isabel was immediately responsible for caring, feeding, and keeping the peace among well over six hundred men and women. And as her pregnancy advanced, the constant travel between these two courts must have drained much of her strength. Nevertheless, for four months the duchess managed her households, oversaw the financial and legal questions that simmered in the Lowlands, forced herself to review the papers involved in each problem, found time to ponder appropriate settlements, and wove her decisions through the complex fabric of contending egos.

On April 23, her second child prepared to make its appearance. Isabel labored all that night in the presence of the men who would legally verify the birth. Between five and six o'clock the following morning, as the sun rose and warmed the rough stonework of Ten Waele, the thin cries of Josse sifted through the passageways of the castle. Once again, Burgundy had an heir. He was taken from Isabel immediately, swathed in the softest silks and wools, and whisked into his own chamber to be nestled in a white and golden cradle. As the lords and ladies who had clustered about Isabel's bed dispersed to carry the news throughout Ten Waele, Isabel fought her exhaustion to demand Josse be returned to her. The duchess refused to place Josse into the care of a wet nurse. She hovered over this second son with a surprising tenacity for a princess who had not shown a great deal of maternal concern over her firstborn. Determined to present Philip with his new son, Isabel left Josse's side only briefly now to review the council's affairs—and then returned to the nursery in the cold and drafty castle of Ghent. His listlessness and weak nursing worried Isabel, and she waited in mounting anxiety for her husband's return from Dijon.

Although the exhausted duchess willed her second son to live, at least until his father's return, little Josse weakened. Finally, realizing that she could not wait for Philip, she sent messengers with letters to all the treasurers of the Burgundian Estates calling them to come to Ten Waele for Josse's baptism on May 6. The counts of Ligny and St. Pol and the bishop of Cambrai were Josse's godfathers, and the duchess of Guelders, La Dame de Ghistelles, and the viscountess of Meeus were his godmothers. In spite of Isabel's care and the attention of the entire Burgundian court, the child died during the early summer months when not yet four months old. Isabel had lost two sons within six months, and she needed the comfort of her husband, who arrived almost immediately to mourn both his sons.

After placing Josse in a small tomb in the Abbey of St. Michael in Ghent and spending a summer on pilgrimages to the Abbey of Ponthier and to the shrines of St. Anthony (a favorite saint of Isabel's) and St. Josse (a popular saint in the Netherlands) in Boulogne, the duke and duchess returned to a hostile Ghent in early August 1432. The rebellious sentiments that had simmered there among the weavers erupted on August 12, as a result of Philip's monetary policies, which placed the weavers at a trade disadvantage with their guilds. Jean, lord of Roubaix, pleaded with the duke to forgive the town of Ghent or "we and the other poor ducal officers living in Ghent will be on the way to total perdition of lives and goods."[15] Fortunately, the duke paid attention to Jean's sound advice, and by the close of the year he pardoned Ghent, but troubles continued to foment in Flanders and to challenge both Philip's and Isabel's administration of the duchy for years to come.

Third Lesson: A New Heir and a Military Defense, Dijon, 1433–1434

The ducal couple spent the winter months of 1432 in Brussels, keeping a close watch on nearby Ghent. And after a splendid Christmas season when court ceremonies and revelries must have alleviated some of their cares, Isabel soon found herself pregnant once more. News from Philip's southern territories through the winter and spring of 1433 gave her cause for concern, however. French military aggression against Burgundy was growing. And a plot (the second in as many years) by Georges de la Trémoille to kidnap the chancellor Nicolas Rolin had only recently been frustrated by an alert ducal government in Dijon. Isabel had reason to be increasingly concerned for the safety of her husband, and she must have dreaded the approach of his summer campaigns.

In mid-June 1433, the duchess, now in the fourth month of her pregnancy, joined Philip for travel to their territories in southern Burgundy. She was eager to follow Philip's order that, while he was in the field, she take over the administration of Dijon, a city she had not yet visited. "First, be aware that your lady duchess demands that you will always be in attendance to her [in the Dijon Estates] advising her in the [business and government] affairs of your lord," she informed Nicolas Rolin that October. "Further, in all the affairs of my lord and his lands, you will consult and advise me, because I desire to use all my ability in the employ [of my lord] and to accomplish all the good that I can."[16]

Philip and his duchess organized their caravans to travel together toward the French positions that threatened Burgundy's southwestern borders. Isabel alternated riding her palfrey with suffering the rattling carriage ride over roads so overgrown or deeply rutted that Philip demanded they be repaired on the spot by the towns and villages along their path. Their caravan continued to snake southward across the Oise, Aisne, Marne, and Aube Rivers until the trail reached the Seine. The baggage carts were loaded onto barges for easier shipment whenever possible and then duke and duchess were able to enjoy more frequent rest stops during a day that regularly covered twenty to thirty miles. Dinner for the traveling court was served in mid-morning and the whole caravan was settled for the evening by early afternoon. At Chatillon-sur-Seine, Philip parted with Isabel, waving her onward toward Dijon. He would remain in the field to fight French attacks along his southern borders until November. These were to be the most serious and longest campaigns of his struggle against Charles VII. And once again the duchess resisted leaving her husband, insisting that she ride with him to face the French. But he soon reminded her that neither he nor his men could make any progress in recapturing the territory lost to the French unless she succeeded in providing him with men, money, and supplies from Dijon.

As Isabel entered the southern territories and approached the capital, she must have been affected by the quiet of the tree-covered countryside and the rich vineyards that filled the rolling fields between vast mountain forests. This was an agricultural land, and a striking contrast to the heavily populated and industrialized north. Isabel looked forward to visiting Beaune, an area famous for its wine, and the small village of Auxonne, where her husband's mints were located. And, of course, she wanted to visit Chalons, the great center for trade fairs in the south.

However, beneath the idyllic, pastoral surface, Dijon was a dangerous place. Great and powerful merchant families dictated the economy of southern Burgundy, and Isabel would have to try to control them. The French troops continued to sharpen their attacks against the duchy, consuming more and more of Philip's lands—and Isabel would have to find the men, the funds, and the armaments to help Philip defend the land that now seemed so blissful, the people so unconcerned with any challenges to their livelihood.

Dijon sat in the embrace of low mountains, a bristle of spires rising from the city of ten thousand souls. And soon after her arrival, Isabel would meet with the powerful families, who together with the mayor and the guilds controlled the flow of merchandise in and out of the Dijonnais (the economically significant hinterland of the capital). She learned that these powerful cliques controlled the guilds of goldsmiths, painters, glaziers, weavers, fullers, saddlers, joiners, locksmiths, cutlers, and others. These trade guilds strictly regulated not only the routes of merchant caravans, but also the quantities, types, and prices of merchandise available at the great southern fairs. At Isabel's arrival in the summer of 1433, butchers, fishmongers, bakers, and mustard makers joined the other artisans in demanding the right to price their wares themselves.

With the help of Nicolas Rolin, whom Philip had ordered to accompany Isabel, she quickly became adept at identifying the leading figures in Dijon's financial, social, and religious lives, the people whose support she would need to raise funds for the duke's military forces. She studied the pattern and practices of Dijon's system of trade and reviewed the city's accounts. And she met with Odot Molain, Philip's official salt merchant, who had lent money to the duke before. He did so on this occasion, too, providing Isabel with a sizable loan for the immediate needs of the duke.

After securing these emergency funds, she called the Estates of Dijon into session. But after she pled her case for funds with which to defend the duchy, the rich merchants of the estates only grudgingly promised the chancellor Rolin four thousand francs for the repair of the city's fortresses—this to be delivered in two payments, the first at Christmas and the second the following June. Not willing to wait so long for their help, she recalled the estates within weeks and persuaded them to provide the whole sum immediately—which they did that November. Determined to exploit every source of men, supplies, and armaments for Philip, she met with the director of his mints, Amiot le Chisseret, whom she pressured into providing one-twentieth of the town's contribution toward Philip's military expenses.

She followed up this success by traveling to other parts of the duchy. From Dole she secured twenty-three thousand francs for her husband's military campaigns. When the recalcitrant town of Mâcon threatened to refuse her written request for funds to support Philip's defense of their territory, she announced that she would demand the funds from the council in person. She then ordered canons from Bruges, and ordered them placed along the earthen mounds that guarded Dijon.

Although pregnant for the third time—and consumed with fear concerning the child's safe delivery—she still traveled to the reluctant town of Chalons to order a convocation of the nobles. Chalons did not want any part of a border war and was not an enthusiastic host to Isabel. Nevertheless, she managed to galvanize that town's fighting forces in early autumn 1433, providing much needed support for Philip's campaigns against French intrusions. She ordered the religious houses in the area to bring their carriages, carts, horses, and drivers to Dijon to transport cannon and other artillery to the field of battle, warning them that "if 'tis not done without delay and without coveting any materials that would diminish the amount due the duke, I shall seize all of the goods of those guilty of such acts."[17]

Isabel's energy was abundant and her ambitions clear: she intended to help Philip build a secure Burgundy; she wanted to provide Burgundy with an heir; and she wanted that heir to rule over a rich and powerful Burgundy that was independent of French control and equal to England in political strength and influence.

On November 21, 1433, her third son, Charles, was born in Dijon. In terror that she would lose yet another child, Isabel consecrated him to the Blessed Sacrament within days of his birth. When Philip arrived later that month to celebrate the baptism, he made his son the count of Charolais and a knight of the Golden Fleece. Charles's eighteen-year-old godfather was Charles of Nevers, a ward of Isabel's court and Philip's adopted son from his second wife (and aunt), Bonne of Artois, who had been the sister of John the Fearless.

The duchess turned fervently to the church as she sought God's help in safeguarding the life of this third son. She lavished gifts on the Charterhouse of Champmole in the mountains above Dijon, and with her husband selected that Cistercian abbey for their family interment. When Philip left them in early spring 1434 for further military campaigns against the French along his western border, Isabel moved with Charles to the mountain fortress of Talant, where they found refuge from the plague that swept southern Burgundy from May to September of that year. She left Talant very rarely, and then only to visit the abbey and dine with the monks.

Even though the duke needed more supplies for his campaigns, Isabel would not return to Dijon while the plague continued to claim victims. Determined to shield her son from danger, she refused to convoke the estates and was forced instead to raise funds for Philip's wars by selling many of the jewels, plate, tapestries, and other treasures she had received as gifts from the towns she had visited. When the dangers of the plague finally passed beyond Dijon, she descended from her mountain retreat to convoke the estates in April 1435, only to notify them that she and Charles would soon leave the city to travel north.

This was a time of change in Isabel's life. She had proved her worth as an administrator and as a wife. With her support, Philip had been successful in his campaign against the French in 1434, and she had at last provided Philip with a healthy heir.[18] But, as Isabel was shortly to discover, a period of yet greater change was in store for Burgundy.

In spring, Philip sent word from Nevers that Isabel was to join him in Paris as soon as she could arrange her household caravan. Eager to rejoin her husband with their robust eighteen-month-old son, the duchess made plans to leave Dijon immediately. Her life had been reclusive in the south and she was ready to involve herself again in the political matters of the duchy. She was particularly curious about why Philip had been holding meetings with representatives of Charles VII at Nevers. On receiving word that English representatives were on their way to join the duke and the French at Arras, Isabel quickly left Dijon. She and her son traveled to Paris, and then with Philip journeyed to Lille, where they arrived on May 5. A month later, on June 4, they entered Coudenberg Castle in Brussels; and after several weeks of rest, they joined Philip at Arras on August 3, where Isabel's uncle, the cardinal of Winchester, represented the English in a discussion with the French and the Burgundians about the future of all three states.

Notes

1. *Oeuvres de Chastellain*, ed. M. Le Baron Kervyn de Lettenhove, 4 vols. (Brussels: R. Heussner, 1864), 2:48.
2. Archives du Nord, series B, no. 17642; a letter written by Jugle Bommaire, secretary of John, duke of Cleves, who lived within the household of Duchess Isabel, which stated that not only did the duchess resist leaving the duke, but also that by his own observation, others in the court were eager for her to remain with him to slow down and damage the duke's efforts against the French.
3. This battle between the French and Burgundians on June 11, 1430, near the border of Dauphiny and the duchy of Burgundy, was so intense that most of Philip's forces in the south were scattered and lost—one armored knight was found in 1672 still wedged within the trunk of a tree in which he had sought shelter.
4. These representative institutions, whose members were chiefly clerics and merchants, had an important if uneven amount of influence within Philip's territories that generally decreased from north to south (where the economy was more agricultural than industrial). In the south, the estates attended mainly to administrative and financial, rather than political, matters and were usually summoned only to vote on taxes and discuss monetary matters. The northern estates had much more of an impact on the ducal economy, however, and were also often convoked, consulted, and cajoled in regard to political issues, both domestic and international.

   The Four Members of Flanders or Four Estates were composed entirely of powerful merchants from the cities of Bruges, Ghent, Ypres, and the Franc of Bruges, who met regularly. The Four Members not only voted on taxes and wielded considerable political power, but also insisted that the duke of Burgundy live among them. The second representative body in Flanders was the Estates, composed of only a few nobles and some clergy.
5. Regine Pernoud, *The Retrial of Joan of Arc: Evidence at Her Trial for Her Rehabilitation, 1450–1456,* trans. J. M. Cohen (New York: Harcourt, Brace, 1981), 167–69.
6. Lucien Fabre, *Joan of Arc,* English translation of 1st ed. (London: Odhams Press, 1954) , 154–57. Many of the following details concerning the trial and execution of Joan of Arc are taken from Fabre, *Joan of Arc,* 252–323.

7. Fabre, *Joan of Arc*, 252–323.
8. Fabre, *Joan of Arc*, 252–323.
9. Fabre, *Joan of Arc*, 252–323.
10. Claudine LeMaire and Michele Henry, *Isabelle de Portugal, duchesse de Bourgogne, 1397–1471* (Brussels: Biblioteque Royale Albert Ier, 1991), 28–30.
11. Fabre, *Joan of Arc*, 249; Pernoud, *The Retrial of Joan of Arc.* 175–99.
12. Fabre, *Joan of Arc*, 267.
13. LeMaire and Henry, *Isabelle de Portugal,* 317 and 322–23.
14. A letter from Philip the Good to his council at Ghent written from Valenciennes on May 8, 1432—and signed upon receipt by Savare, secretary to Duchess Isabel—verifying that "Isabel would wield the full ducal power during his absence from that territory." Cited in Somme, "Isabel de Portugal" (Ph.D. diss., University of Lille, France, 1985), 694.
15. Archives General du Royaume, CC21805, folio 20b, cited in Richard Vaughan, *Philip the Good: The Apogee of Burgndy* (New York: Barnes and Noble, 1970), 86.
16. Somme, "Isabel de Portugal," 696.
17. Archives of the Cote d'Or, series B, no. 11872. Isabel's letter of May 13, 1434, to the equerry or master of the cavalry, detailing the action to be taken if any of the religious houses hesitated to obey her orders: "in the case that they would make any excuses, order them in the name of the duke of Burgundy to come to the finance chambers in Dijon to provide the amount of money to rent other chariots, wagons and carts that they owe us."
18. Philip the Good's first wife was twelve-year-old Michelle of France, daughter of Charles VI. Married in 1409, she died at Ghent on July 8, 1422, though most likely not, as rumored at the time, from poisoning. There were no children from this marriage. Jean LeFevre de Saint-Remy, *Chronique, 1400–1444*, ed. Fr. Morand (Paris: Société d'Histoire de France,1876–81), 4:118–119; *Oeuvres de Chastellaine,* 1:341–44.

    Philip the Good's second wife was his aunt, Bonne of Artois (his father's sister), who was the widow of the count of Nevers, killed at Agincourt in 1415. The required papal dispensation for the marriage allowed Philip to consolidate his hold over Nevers, a territory between his Burgundian lands and France. Bonne died on September 15, 1425, less than a year after the marriage. Philip still had no legal heir. Vaughan, *Philip the Good,* 8.

Chapter Four

The Duchess at the Negotiating Table at Home and Abroad, 1435–1445

Behind the Scenes

IN THE SUMMER MONTHS OF 1435, Arras was a scene of great pomp and bustle as the prancing horses and sumptuous trains of great French, English, and Burgundian lords arrived in the city for the conference that was to begin in early August. The conference held out the promise of a "general peace"—a comprehensive end to the armed conflict between France, England, and Burgundy that had begun in 1337. For Isabel, who in July was still in Coudenberg Castle in Brussels making her preparations for Arras, the conference also promised a welcome change from the quietude of her life in Dijon over the past two years. As a Portuguese princess, Isabel appreciated that the survival of a seagoing land depended on freedom of access to sea lanes, and she was keenly aware of the advantages that would accrue to Burgundy if peaceful merchant traffic with England and France were to be guaranteed. Isabel was eager to help Philip expand his territory and power and create wealth, influence, and prestige equal to those of England and France. Thus, she was pleased that her husband had asked her to play the role of lobbyist that summer, working behind the scenes to sway the English in particular to reach agreement on a general peace.

Full of enthusiasm to bring peace and increased prosperity to the Burgundians, Isabel spoke to them before her departure to rejoin Philip. "My dear friends," she told the gathering of women in Dijon who had come to wish her a safe journey, "this general peace is one of the things in the world that I most desire. I beseech my lord day and night because of the need I see for it, and my lord has a great will to accomplish."[1] Although she learned later that Philip had met at Nevers that January with his French brothers-in-law, the count of Richemont and the duke of Bourbon, to plan ways for him to slip out of the vow of alliance he had pledged the English in 1422 and to join instead with France, Isabel still hoped at this juncture that her own diligent efforts toward a three-party peace would be welcomed by both her husband and Charles VII. She wanted to believe in Philip's desire for the three-party peace that she felt was so important to the duchy. So strong, indeed, was her wish to believe in the possibility of securing a general peace that she chose to ignore her suspicions regarding her husband's true goals and the extent to which he was influenced by the pro-French nobles at court.

Living in the style of the Burgundian court required its nobles to adopt an appearance of unlimited wealth and power. Nicolas Rolin, chancellor of Burgundy, Philip's closest friend Anthony de Croy, and his brother Jehan de Croy, and the lords of Crevecoeur, Brimeu, Humbercourt, and Guilbaut needed money. They competed with one another for the attention and favor of Philip the Good, which in turn brought them additional gratuities and rewards. Isabel herself was trained by her father to turn a profit with investments and was not above joining this company in their relentless quest for money, as long as their goals did not obstruct her larger purposes. She decided early in her marriage that she would not be secure without financial independence, and thus she did not refuse rewards from France, Flanders, or England for her efforts, as long as she was not asked to do something that conflicted with her own goals. Rolin, the de Croys, and the lords of Crevecoeur, Brimeu, Humbercourt, and Guilbaut had been offered not only a healthy sum for swaying Philip toward the French but also an attractive future in the French court if Burgundy weakened. Their cooperation was therefore certain,[2] and this powerful clique sought to manipulate Philip both before and during the conference, while Isabel worked at the conference table to arrive at terms that would be satisfactory to the English as well as to the French crowns. Only after the negotiations were concluded did she receive a reward from Charles VII in recognition of her support of French interests.

The colorful delegations rode into Arras throughout the month of July. The cardinal of Cyprus, ambassador from the Council of Basle and one of the two mediators for the conference, arrived on July 8. The papal legate and second mediator, the cardinal of St. Croix, joined him on July 12. The Burgundian chancellor, Nicolas Rolin, made his entry on July 15 and brought excuses for Philip the Good, who had decided to wait for the presence of the royal ambassadors there before arriving himself. On July 29, Philip the Good made his entry into the town with his brother-in-law the duke of Guelders, his nephew John, duke of Cleves, and a brilliant party of lords dressed in sumptuous robes and embroidered linen doublets that announced his own splendor. A few days later, on the morning of August 3, the duchess Isabel approached Arras in her magnificently ornate litter. She was followed by a gay and richly attired procession of women and maidens on horseback, weary from the journey but excited about the prospect of the coming banquets and possible assignations awaiting them at the gathering. That morning, in spite of earlier indications of Isabel's sympathy for French demands, the English acknowledged her rank by riding out from their town lodgings to meet her. But to the astonishment of the citizens of Arras, the English delegation accompanied Isabel only to the outskirts of the town, where they left her. The French and Burgundian lords who had already prepared to meet their duchess were at that time parading out of the enclosure of St. Vaast, where they were stationed apart from the English; with great display, they escorted her from the edge of Arras back into the abbey at the town gates where she was to be lodged with Philip the Good.

Exhausted from her early rising that morning and from the rigors of her journey from Dijon in late April that had taken her through Paris, Brussels, and Lille, and now preoccupied with the demands of her role at Arras, Isabel would have preferred to rest before her first public appearance. But Philip required her presence that afternoon at spirited games of tennis between the French and the Burgundians. Significantly, the English were absent from the games, just as they were absent, because uninvited, from the long series of entertainments held before and during the conference. Isabel sat quietly beneath the canopy built to protect her from the unrelenting damp heat of August, politely applauding first one team and then the other as the day slipped slowly into twilight. That evening, she sat beside Philip to host a grand banquet in the abbey's great chamber for all of the French and Burgundian delegations, to which the English were again not invited. The French courtship of the Burgundian delegation was so obvious throughout July and August that the English became more and more convinced that the conference was a lost cause for their nation. Suspicion that the French planned to separate the Burgundians from their English alliance, earlier only a rumor, was fast becoming certainty. Not only were the English excluded from social gatherings, but also their ambassadors were kept isolated within their separate cluster of hotels in the town of Arras, quite apart from the Abbey of St. Vaast, where the significant events of the conference took place. The mood of the English soured and their patience thinned.

The conference opened at three o'clock the day after Isabel's arrival, when in a tide of elegant color and sedate mien, the delegates flowed into the second of the three chambers reserved for the assemblies in the abbey. The two mediators—the cardinals of Cyprus and of St. Croix—sat on a curtained dais before the delegates. After the cardinals had ceremoniously greeted the duke of Burgundy, the members of the conference heard Nicolas Rolin officially open the session. There were to be few such general assemblies; each of the three delegations was to meet separately with the mediators to lay out their positions on the issues under discussion: the crown of France; the return of occupied French lands; and the release of the duke of Orléans from English custody. Most of the negotiations occurred at secret nightly meetings in either Burgundian or French quarters.

Isabel devoted most of her time and energy with the English and French delegates before and after these private meetings, trying to persuade each party that its interests would be best served in the three-party peace. While Philip the Good occupied center stage, hosting all the diplomats and the rival ambassadors of France and England, Isabel worked behind the scenes to sway opinion.

Isabel lobbied consistently through August to position Burgundy not only as a third party to this sought-after peace but also as a neutral state with the strength to affect the political strategies of both France and England. But the agenda developed earlier at Nevers contained demands that the English would never meet, and Isabel's efforts were bound to be fruitless. How could she convince the English that their king must relinquish all of his rights to the throne of France before peace talks could continue? The English remained obdurate in their resistance to all of her arguments. Her earnest efforts became no more than a smoke screen for her husband's determination to free himself from his oath of alliance and to join the French.

She visited her husband frequently during these last days of August, and as her hopes waned for the Anglo-French and Burgundian peace, she threw herself at his feet begging him not to stand in the way of that general accord. But Philip, also adamant, held to the position he had adopted that January at Nevers: If Henry VI did not give up his claim to the French throne and allow a general peace, Burgundy would make its own separate peace with France. Philip the Good had been reassured by the French at Nevers that the cardinals of Cyprus and St. Croix would handle the thorny issues of the penance due from Charles VII for the murder in 1419 of Philip's father, John the Fearless, and of Philip's oath of alliance pledged to the English in 1422. Philip ignored not only the pleas of his wife but also the warnings from Hughes de Lannoy that making an enemy of England would bring bloodshed and economic crisis to Burgundy. Instead, he listened to the advice of his courtiers, who would profit handsomely from an alliance with France.

Isabel's uncle, Cardinal Beaufort, arrived on August 23, and his worried niece visited him in his apartments the next day. Isabel convinced Beaufort that his mission must be focused on retaining England's alliance with Burgundy. But at a meeting with the cardinal on August 25, Philip the

Good made it clear that he would break his alliance with England if the English did not accept the terms demanded by the French. Four days later, a discouraged Cardinal Beaufort accompanied the English delegates to a plenary session at St. Vaast, where they described the Franco-Burgundian terms as ridiculous. The cardinal was quick to approach the papal mediator, Cardinal Albergati, and after their discussion Beaufort left for yet another private session with Philip. Philip stood his ground: the English must relinquish all rights to the French crown, accepting only the homage of Normandy in the north and Guienne in the southwest; and they must also release the duke of Orléans. It appeared that there was nothing for the English to do but leave Arras.

On September 1, just before the English departure, Philip the Good and an increasingly harrassed Isabel gave a great banquet in honor of the English cardinal and his companions. But because Isabel had once again encouraged Beaufort to do his utmost to soften Philip the Good's position, the cardinal did not give up completely on his desperate mission to convince Philip to remain loyal to England. And after the banquet, ignoring protocol, the two men held a dramatic two-hour talk within view of the assembly. Isabel joined the other witnesses, who watched in silence as Beaufort pleaded with such passion for Philip to remain true to his oath of alliance with England that gleaming beads of sweat rolled down the cardinal's face. Attendants discreetly brought the men wines and spices to cool their tempers and stop the discussion.

Beaufort realized that this was the end of the English cornerstone policy on the continent. He and the duke of Bedford had relied on their decade-long relationship with Burgundy—and on the links forged by the marriage of Beaufort's niece to Philip the Good—to maintain English economic and political interests there. Insulted by their treatment and furious at Burgundy's betrayal, the English left Arras five days later, in a pelting rainstorm. Each member of the cardinal's retinue dressed in scarlet livery and had the word "honor" embroidered on his sleeve. As they rode through the town of Poperinge on their journey to the coast, however, honor was not served, and several of the English ambassadors were roughly treated by the citizens of the town. In this bitter moment, the cardinal announced that he still had "two million nobles" in his treasury and vowed that he would use the sum to sustain a war to retain his nephew's rights as king of France. After the disaster at Arras, there was no longer a place for the cardinal in the papal court, nor would there be a secure place for him in Lancastrian France when his mentor, the duke of Bedford, died two weeks later.

At seven o'clock on the evening of September 21, Isabel attended the reading of the peace treaty Burgundy signed with France in the Abbey of St. Vaast. A serious, if also cynical, atmosphere prevailed. Philip could hardly forget that it was Charles, while still the dauphin, who in 1419 had murdered his father. Although the murder was widely recognized as retaliation by the dauphin for the Burgundian assassination of his uncle, duke of Orléans, ten years earlier, Philip had responded to his father's assassination by abandoning the French for an alliance with the English. Now, however, Philip sought an alliance with the French, and needed the help of the church to annul his vow of alliance with England. Rome solved the problem with a papal decree that the earlier oath stood in the way of a general peace, promulgated war and misery, and was obviously sinful and therefore void. On this September evening, the cardinals put on the clothing Philip had provided for them—vermillion vestments embroidered in fleurs-de-lis of pearls—and holding a golden cross over the kneeling duke's head, heard him recant his vow of alliance before the high altar. Then before God and the French and Burgundian assemblies, the pragmatic duke promised never to forget how his father had been murdered and vowed to exact the punishments from Charles VII to which his delegates had agreed as part of their separate peace treaty.[3]

Isabel remained as quiet and unobtrusive at the ceremony as she did at the conference. She sat with her ladies-in-waiting in a private room belonging to one of the abbey's monks and observed both the solemn high mass and the formal ceremony that realigned the political, military, and economic futures of the three powers. Isabel was somber. Outwardly calm, she knew she had failed to achieve the three-party peace. She recognized their dependence on English trade, if France and Burgundy were to survive and flourish. She remembered Hughes de Lannoy's warnings about the potentially devastating effects of this treaty on Burgundy's merchant lifeline. As an "appanage" of France—a territorial possession reserved for princes of the royal house—Burgundy, she knew, would lose its independence and power. And she foresaw a difficult task ahead in trying to reestablish the duchy's ties with England.

Her labors at Arras had not gone unnoticed, however, and Martin Le Franc, a poet who was one of the delegates to the conference, included within his 1435 report a verse about the accomplishments of the duchess:

> Let us each bless the lady
> For her grace and her wisdom.
> Long live the lady, and bless Him
> Who gave us such a princess!
>
> Through her the horror of war is ended
> And peace once more become our concern.
> Long live the most high duchess
> Long live the lady of Burgundy.[4]

Charles VII was aware of Isabel's attempts at Arras to convince the English to accede to French demands. Although Charles in all likelihood had expected the English to refuse to his terms, and had indeed intended to shatter the Anglo-Burgundian alliance and conquer his enemies by dividing them, after the conclusion of the meetings he applauded Isabel's efforts by giving written "homage to her peace efforts during the negotiations." Charles VII also promised to direct to her personal treasury the assignment of four thousand pounds of rent money from the Vermandois in northeastern France, lands that Philip had already given to his wife but the rent from which was not certain to reach her account without the king's guarantee.[5]

Not many months passed before Philip and Isabel felt the snap of both the French and English whips as a result of Burgundy's realignment. To no one's surprise but Philip's, Charles VII refused to pay the penance imposed on him for the murder of John the Fearless, never apologized for the act, and never established the series of expiatory religious foundations that he had taken an oath to build in memory of the murdered duke. In fact, instead of making reparations, the king ordered his troops to occupy many of the towns that he had ceded to Philip—attacking those in the Somme Valley and Peronne, Montbeliard, Roye, Auxers, Mâcon, and others in the south—in an attempt to undermine ducal authority. Charles VII then encouraged the French *écorcheurs* to raid Burgundy's western frontier at every opportunity. He increased his infringement of Philip's ducal rights in the Paris Parlement by refusing to recognize the privileges due him as a prince of the royal blood—privileges that included the right to try cases within his own court in Burgundy and to refer, at his own discretion, cases to the Paris Parlement for appeal to a higher authority.

Insulted by Philip's going back on his oath of support for Henry VI, and in desperate need of funds to pursue the war on the continent against the French, the English negotiated trade agreements with Lowland merchants independently of the duke of Burgundy. The nearly empty English treasury soon profited from these new markets, by shipping both high-grade English wool for Flemish looms and English cloth for Flemish caravans to carry through the Lowlands to the Rhineland fairs. These separately negotiated treaties infuriated other Burgundians, who responded with acts of piracy against the English merchant fleets. English retaliation against the Burgundians also affected merchants from Portugal and Genoa, as well as ships of the Hansa trade association that extended from Novgorod southward, including bases in Lubeck, Cologne, Brunswick, and Danzig. A state of piracy on the high seas between all parties soon resulted in a devastating loss of profit for all.

With rumors spreading that Philip planned to retaliate with an attack on Calais that spring, the English garrison there pillaged the countryside around that port city. They hit Boulogne and St. Omer, and on May 14 they traveled south toward Gravelines, setting villages on fire, rounding up and destroying cattle, and burning local churches with the inhabitants inside. In response, Philip laid siege to Calais on July 9, but his planning was incomplete and he was unable to prevent access to the city from the sea. Frustrated with the futility of their service, Philip's unpaid militia grumbled and threatened to abandon him in the field.

Trade between England, Burgundy, Portugal, Genoa, and the Hansa states came to a standstill. There was no wool for the Flemish looms. Once more established at Ten Waele in Ghent, Isabel received daily word of the dissatisfaction among the Flemish merchants and sought the advice of Hughes de Lannoy. On July 16, Philip wrote to her and to the bailiff of Flanders, Roland d'Uutkerke, that he needed more money to sustain his men in the field against the English around Calais. On July 22, the desperate duke wrote again, pleading for money to pay his troops. On July 27, Isabel ordered one hundred letters to be sent to Flemish nobles inviting them to rejoin the siege at Calais. She wrote as well to the Burgundian admiral Jean de Hornes at Sluis to find a way to put the men on ships to attack Calais by sea—and because there were no funds to pay the men, she advanced one thousand saluts of her own. But Philip's ill-planned campaign against the English at Calais met with complete failure the next day, July 28, when his troops abandoned him before the town.

Isabel had done all she could for her lord, and now she found herself in the midst of a bristling rebellion in Flanders. Having swept back to their Flemish homes after deserting Philip before Calais, the civic militia were now armed and demanded reward for their service. Both the militia and the town leaders blamed Philip's strategies for their crises and refused to obey ducal orders. Isabel lent another twenty-four hundred livres (pounds) to defend the Flemish coast from further English attacks, and Philip rode to Artois to mobilize another army. Philip wrote to the Great Council of Ghent that it must follow Isabel's directions, and then instructed her to appear before the leaders of Ghent and those of Bruges, Ypres, and the Franc of Bruges to negotiate solutions to the crises before August 13. He needed his militia back in the field to defend Burgundy against imminent English retaliation to his action against Calais. As Philip's forces faced the French in the south and west of the duchy, Isabel hastened from Ten Waele to Bruges, where the militia still refused to disarm until its demands were met.

Isabel acted even more quickly than Philip had anticipated. On August 10, Isabel received deputies of the Four Estates of Flanders, whom she instructed to organize a defense at Bruges. On August 11, she returned to

Bruges to supervise the initial effort of the troops, and the next day she convinced a contingent of Brugeois to march to Oostburg to meet the English there. Matters refused to go well, however, and within two days that portion of the Flemish militia who also went to Sluis became embroiled in an argument with Roland d'Uutkerke. He had refused them entry into Sluis and the angry men mortally wounded the admiral of the port city, Jean de Hornes. The antagonized militia returned to the distinctly frustrated Isabel on August 26 with the new demand that d'Uutkerke be punished.

The men swarmed into the city in their battle array, filling Bruges's market square and determined to proclaim a general strike. Anticipating danger, although no physical harm to herself or her son, she arranged to smuggle the wives of Uutkerke and Hornes out of the town in her baggage train. As her procession approached the gates of Bruges, the militia challenged her. They searched each of the carts of her caravan, and throwing her bags to the ground, soon discovered the two women hidden among the cases in one of the carriages. They insulted the duchess further by pulling her from her litter and detaining her and the women for several hours. Eventually released, Isabel escaped with the two fugitives to Brussels, where she heard that Philip himself had been assaulted in Ghent on September 3 when the people rose in revolt, disarmed his bodyguard, and kept him under house arrest until he approved their requests.

All of Flanders seethed in rebellion through the winter of 1436 and all the next year. The Flemish blamed Philip for the growing struggles between merchants and artisans; they criticized his campaigns for losses in their commercial trade; and they held his policies responsible for the increasing rivalries among their towns.

As much as they mistrusted Philip, however, most of the Flemish cities held Isabel in high regard. They recognized that, as a Portuguese princess, she was familiar with the problems that plagued a maritime economy such as theirs. They trusted her judgment and shared her wish to expand Flemish trade abroad. Philip turned a deaf ear to the apologies offered by Bruges, but most of the Flemish accepted Isabel as one of their own. After the embarrassing failure of the siege of Calais, therefore,

Isabel met more and more frequently with the members of the Four Estates of Flanders on her own. And when given the right to pardon those citizens of Bruges who asked for a reprieve for their part in the riots and revolts, she did so, in a ceremony held in the central square on May 8, 1438. Meanwhile, Philip vowed not to return to Bruges unless he was in the company of a greater prince than he—a difficult condition to fulfill, given that he was widely considered the most powerful prince then alive. His vow was easier to keep because he could entrust his wife with the responsibility of maintaining a ducal presence in Flanders.

The Mediator: Center Stage

From 1438 to 1445, Isabel of Portugal took the center stage of Burgundian political action. She proved her ability to raise both money and troops whenever Philip needed them. She assumed responsibility for the government of his territories in his absence. She faced rebellious towns and bargained successfully with dissatisfied merchants and trade guilds. Relying now on Isabel's special skills, Philip the Good gave her significant powers to control the duchy's finances and involved her to a greater extent in formulating his domestic and international political strategies.

On October 25, 1437, Philip placed Isabel on the five-member Finance Review Commission for all of his possessions. Philip had no appetite for administrative tasks such as monitoring the activities of his treasury; his chief interests were leading his troops, enlarging and defending his borders, and enjoying the sumptuous life due a peer of France and the ruler of the richest dukedom in western Europe. Isabel regarded this new assignment with enthusiasm. The reports concerning the supervision of his taxes, the award and collection of loans, and the approval of the administrative costs of government would now come directly and solely to the duchess. In all but formal title, therefore, Isabel was the finance minister of Burgundy.

Devoted to her new responsibility, enjoying the opportunity to use her natural gifts for manipulating finances, and determined to provide Philip with the needed funds to defend and build a greater Burgundian state,

Isabel became oblivious to the daily difficulties faced by the inhabitants of the duchy. Neither the severe famine that spread over Philip the Good's Lowlands that year nor the waves of the dreaded plague that added fresh misery to his subjects prevented Isabel from calling in the review of accounts from each of Philip's territories. And when officials could not be summoned to her presence, she traveled to the districts herself to review the financial status of each office.

Each additional responsibility gave her more confidence, and with her success came a certain happiness. Closeting herself with the chancellor, Nicolas Rolin, she became adept at ferreting out abuses in the administration and finances of the duchy. Her ally and great friend Hughes de Lannoy advised her on matters of trade with the English—a worry for all of Flanders, Hainault, and Brabant—which she determined to improve as soon as possible. Earlier in her marriage she saw that Philip, as a reflection of his own wealth, importance, and grace, demanded beauty, opulence, and style from those who surrounded him, and Isabel now dressed in the richly fashionable clothes of Burgundy. Charles, her healthy five-year-old son, was usually by her side.

The diminutive duchess carried her additional authority with ease, and she enjoyed enhanced respect for her successful administration of the duchy's finances. However, her new authority and role apparently did not enhance her personal charm; she was considered by Philip and his courtiers to be moody, overbearing, and unreasonably jealous. As she became suspicious of Philip's dalliances, she subjected him to tirades of accusations, to which Philip responded by giving her more responsibilities to fulfill. Thus, at the same time that Isabel's work placed her at the center of Burgundian affairs, she also became increasingly isolated from the husband she wished to please.

By mid-1438, Philip was exhausted from parrying French aggressions against his southern and western borders; he worried, too, that the English would repeat their invasions of 1436 and 1437 into the Lowlands. He could no longer ignore the fact that Burgundy's trade crisis had accelerated since 1435. Although resisting Isabel's pleas to make another attempt to secure a general peace, he did recognize that some type of particular peace with

England was essential to save the Flemish cloth trade, so important to the health of his own treasury. He also agreed with Hughes de Lannoy that he must acquire an ally among the powerful French nobility who might persuade Charles VII to cease his aggressive moves against Burgundy. Philip considered either negotiating the release of the duke of Orléans, held by England since 1415, or forgiving the ransom due for René of Anjou, whom he had taken prisoner at the Battle of Bulgneville in 1431 and released in 1437. The payment of 400,000 gold crowns for René's release was still owed, accruing exorbitant daily interest of twenty pounds. There were excellent reasons to choose the latter option: René of Anjou's sister, Marie, was the queen of France, and his brother was a close and trusted adviser to Charles VII. Philip, however, chose to try for the release of Orléans, preferring to retain the bargaining power of a still-captive Anjou. He was in no position to mediate any future Anglo-French conference, as the English still considered him without honor for renouncing his oath of loyalty in 1435. Isabel, though, was ideally placed to play this role of mediator between the English and the French.

During the latter years of the 1430s, Isabel occupied herself with the two individuals who most helped and sustained her—Hughes de Lannoy and her son. From one she received the counsel she needed to pursue her goals with England, and from the other she received the unquestioning love and admiration she required as a mother. As a woman, Isabel remained isolated. She often found herself sitting among her Portuguese and Burgundian ladies, smiling at their chatter but envying their ability to lose themselves in the smaller matters of life. She would then remember the sunny land where she was doted on as her father's clever only daughter, given free rein to develop her natural abilities, and protected by five loving brothers. Now, separated from others by personality and circumstance, the forty-one-year-old princess must have cast about for companionship. As a woman she had the same needs as any of her husband's less sober company—appreciation, tenderness, understanding, and forgiveness—and searched for fulfillment. If she failed to satisfy these needs in this world, Isabel prepared a happier fate for herself in the next, and from 1437 onward she increased her contributions toward the building and support of hospitals and monasteries, the defense of the mendicant Franciscan friars against attacks from Rome, and the development of the special order of the Poor Clares to care for the sick indigents of Burgundy.

In the early summer of 1439, workmen busily prepared the site of the international conference to be held in July near Gravelines, on the continental border of England and Flemish Burgundy. The workmen had no time to enjoy the warming sun and salt-sweet breeze along the coast near Calais. They whipped the teams of horses straining to pull their loads through the marshy field between Oye-Plage and Marck on the outskirts of the port city. Their efforts turned the ground into a quagmire. The air was filled with the shouts of cursing men who hauled groaning carts heaped with canvas, thick planks, and cording. Wagons carried tapestries and richly decorated tables and chairs. Jacotin de Croix, Isabel's quartermaster, wound his way through the chaos just outside the chateau of Oye, shouting his orders, directing the carts and wagons to their proper positions.

Isabel had already arrived at St. Omer on May 29, a comfortable town only a few kilometers from Gravelines where she and Philip established their court for an extended stay. Of the many affairs Isabel had to occupy her until she traveled to Calais to meet with her uncle on June 29 to settle the preliminaries of the conference, the most important was to complete the marriage alliance arranged between France and Burgundy in 1438.

As a preliminary to the Gravelines meeting and a show of good faith in his new ally, Burgundy, the French king had agreed to send two of his daughters to Philip, allowing him to choose one of them as a bride for the duke's six-year-old. Catherine, the elder of the two and then about ten years old, had been chosen, and in early June was en route to her wedding at St. Omer. For a short time the marriage plans lulled Burgundy—and Isabel, too, it seems—into the mistaken belief that the French did intend to cooperate toward a general peace. In fact, Charles VII had no such intention. Indeed, the king remained hostile not only to England but also, fundamentally, to Burgundy—hence the peculiar state of affairs whereby a French princess was betrothed to the Burgundian heir even as French forces fought with Burgundian troops on the borders of the duchy.

Yet, while Isabel was perhaps deceived in French intentions, she was wise enough to make her own plans for an alternative course of action should the Gravelines meeting fail to bring peace. Thus, the pragmatic duchess decided that if the meeting yielded no results, she would spend August trying to negotiate with the English delegation a separate trade agreement.

Little Catherine was to arrive at St. Omer in the company of Isabel's own lady of honor, the duchess of Namur, only a few days before the marriage on June 11. Regnault de Chartres, the chancellor of France, accompanied the princess on her journey and was to perform the ceremony. The celebratory banquets, concerts, and jousting matched the brilliance of the company, and St. Omer teemed with the opulence of the Burgundian courtiers and the elegance of French nobility. The young bride and groom, however, were often led apart to their separate rooms by their governesses for pastimes more attuned to children.

Unfortunately, the dowry Catherine brought to the marriage brought further discord between France and Burgundy instead of the harmony Philip sought. When the duke abandoned his English alliance in 1435, Charles VII had ceded territory to him as part of his reward. The five lordships brought by Catherine of France as part of her dowry in 1439, however, were all located within this same territory—namely, the French border territory of the Somme River Valley. The value established within her dowry for these lordships was 120,000 ecus. But in the original agreement in 1435, provision had been made for the French king to reclaim the territory ceded to Philip for 400,000 ecus. After the marriage of the king's daughter to Philip's son, therefore, the price for the redemption of that territory had grown to 520,000 ecus. That Philip accepted the terms of Catherine's dowry indicates the duke's ambivalence between his goal to enhance his political alliance with France and his almost transparent aim to antagonize his former enemy. As a further irritant to Charles VII, the marriage contract stipulated that neither he nor his heir could redeem these territories until the full value of the dowry had been paid to Philip. For Charles, repayment was not an option: his coffers had been emptied in the long fight against the English and, moreover, his pride would not allow him to buy back territory that he regarded as already French. Thus, there remained only two ways to repossess these important towns that separated Burgundy from France: a diplomatically negotiated way out of payment of the dowry or military attack. Even while these tensions mounted between France and Burgundy, little Catherine was to live with Isabel through her adolescent years, learning from her mother-in-law the skills she would need as a duchess of Burgundy.

In the midst of these events, public and private, Isabel received a disturbing piece of news that, although it did not interfere with the wedding plans, did demand the duchess's attention. Word reached her in mid-June from the Chamber of Accounts in Lille that a large number of territorial officials were "allowing their responsibilities to go to perdition."[6] As a member of Philip the Good's finance committee, she now felt personally responsible for these lapses and was furious that Philip's income would be jeopardized. Isabel swiftly demanded from each official accused by the Lille Chamber that "by return messenger [they] present to me at St. Omer the reasons why this occurred and the necessary solutions."[7] During the first two weeks of the conference from July 6 through July 20 at St. Omer, Isabel received all of the financial records she had required of the delinquent officials. She analyzed each report and judged each performance. Given the sensitive personalities now contending at Gravelines, she may well have found relief in tackling the concrete problems of finance.

In early July, accompanied by her counselors Jean Chevrot, Jacques de Crevecoeur, and Hughes de Lannoy, Isabel traveled to a preliminary meeting with Cardinal Beaufort at Calais, where it was decided that the duchess would examine and rule on the appropriateness of each delegate's credentials. Isabel reviewed the scope of action and the breadth of authority provided within the official diplomatic instructions issued by Henry VI for each of his representatives to the conference. Cardinal Beaufort examined and ruled on the same matters in respect of the French delegates. If either mediator decided that the rank of a delegate was too low or that his instructions deviated from the agreed-upon conference agenda, that delegate would be removed or his credentials and instructions amended. Isabel was given the further responsibility of establishing not only who would attend the sessions but also the number of armed men in their company and the manner of their arrival at the meeting site. When the conference opened at nine o'clock on the morning on July 6, three hundred men armed with swords and daggers accompanied each delegation. To guarantee against any surprise attack, Isabel had sent ten scouts to explore the area for two miles toward Gravelines and Ardres, while the French certified the safety of the area two miles toward Calais.

From a distance, the flags and colorful pavilions dotting the marshy area may have looked more like blossoms blown on the summer breeze than a site for determining the fate of kingdoms. The central pavilion stood above the others, mounted on a sturdy platform to protect it from the often muddy soil surrounding the tents. The hundred-foot-long central pavilion lined with rich Flemish tapestries was filled with ornate seating arranged into two crescents about a central dais. The English delegates sat on one side; the French sat facing them on the other side. Because of the extraordinary powers given Cardinal Beaufort to act with the royal prerogative of the English king, and owing to his high position in the church and his blood ties to the royal house, Beaufort was acknowledged as the figure with the highest precedence at the conference. Any issues that could not be resolved would thus be brought to him for final decision. His seat was a chair of cloth-of-gold placed in the center of the raised dais among the delegations.

As the conference was about to begin, Isabel approached the assembly from her own nearby pavilion, and Beaufort rose from his chair to meet his niece. After embracing and kissing her, he led the duchess to the chair on his right, as the representative of Charles VII. The English, who had accepted Isabel as the most neutral figure on the list of possible mediators offered to them by the French in 1439, bowed in recognition of her role within the conference.

Philip remained in St. Omer, where he was to receive daily messengers sent by his wife carrying the latest news of each session. In this way, he was not only kept informed of developments but was also able to contribute to the conference by using the messengers to relay to Isabel instructions for the negotiations. The conference was to last a full month in spite of mistrust, rancor, accumulating heat from the summer sun, and rolling electrical storms that drifted in from the sea and lashed the tents with sheets of rain.

In the few moments before the conference was finally called to order, Isabel could congratulate herself on her success. By carefully manipulating royal pride and family jealousies, she had been able to provide the setting for the French, English, and Burgundian delegations to seat themselves together that morning before the mediators. As the flurry of shuffling papers, rustling robes, and murmuring of the delegates quieted, Isabel reflected on the value of her winter talks with her uncle Beaufort, which had established a guarantee of neutrality for the conference site during July and August. The border of this neutral zone followed the course of the River Aa from Gravelines to St. Omer in the direction of Boulogne; subjects of Henry VI and of Philip the Good could travel within the zone if they first obtained a safe-conduct or pass from the captain of Calais and the mayor of the "Staple." (The "Staple" was the standard price, amount, and assessed duty imposed on all English wool and cloth imported through the port of Calais; it was fixed and controlled by the powerful merchants of that city under the leadership of their mayor. The duty of the captain of Calais was to provide military protection to the city's inhabitants and political guidance to the Staple merchants.) Isabel could be forgiven the wisp of a smile that morning as she contemplated her recent success not only in arranging the neutral zone but also in opening discussions with the English on a resumption of trade between England and Burgundy. Even now, Hughes de Lannoy and Henri Utenhove, representing Flanders, Holland, and Zeeland, were involved in preliminary talks with the English representatives from London and the Company of the Staple at the Hague and in London.

Isabel could also congratulate herself for the successful finesse she had used to manipulate two kings into an agreement that brought their representatives to the same place on the same date. With the conference originally scheduled to commence on May 8 and with Cardinal Beaufort's cooperation, she had presented Charles VII with two choices for the location of the meeting: Cherbourg or the Marches of Calais. If the duke of Orléans, who was to be temporarily released from English custody to attend the conference, landed at Cherbourg, the French king would have to pay 26,000 nobles for his traveling expenses and a supplemental monthly sum of 12,000 nobles; but if the site of the Marches of Calais was selected for the duke of Orléans's landing and the conference site, Henry VI would pay all the expenses. Isabel favored the second option, for she saw that the Franco-Burgundian frontier location would allow Burgundy to exert greater control over the conference.

She had presented these options to both kings in early March, well before the scheduled date of May 8. The English agreed to Calais within two weeks, but there was no word from Charles VII. On April 13, she wrote again to the French king, notifying him of the English approval of the Calais site and urging him to ignore the negative views of those among his counselors who opposed the conference. Pressured by Isabel for some response, the French king acted against his council's advice, and even though aware that his ambassadors could not reach the conference site until well after the scheduled date in May—at best no earlier than May 20—Charles VII agreed to Isabel's terms. In an attempt to disguise his tardiness in responding, the king dated his acceptance March 10. Isabel, who had herself become adept at shuffling papers and dates, dated her receipt of both the French and the English documents as March 22, and they reached the English court on April 19. Both delegations prepared to travel to the Calais area in May 1439. In the absence of the French on the appointed May 8 date, however, the English agreed to postpone the meeting until July.

Now, as the conference finally began, Isabel was keen to do all she could to prevent discussion from bogging down in the rivalries and suspicions that typically accompanied Anglo-French diplomacy. The first such impediment to progress occurred during the opening session on July 6, when Isabel was forced to rule that the conference could not proceed until the diplomatic instructions carried by the English delegates were amended to omit the claim that English battle victories were evidence of God's judgment that England was entitled to the French crown. The duchess accused the English delegates not only of blatantly insulting the French by laying claim to the French crown—using the term "Charles of Valois" instead of "Our Adversary of France," as was customary—but also of having insufficient powers to settle a peace accord. The French disdained the English claim to the French throne and offered to talk only of a peace that was based on English renunciation of such a claim. Since the English delegates did not have the authority to abrogate their king's claims to the French throne, Isabel had no recourse but to demand that the English take measures to change their instructions before the conference continued. Beaufort could hardly challenge his own monarch's claim to the French throne, and thus the conference was prorogued until July 10 to give the English delegation time to travel to London and seek King Henry's instructions.

When the conference resumed on the appointed day, the French persisted in their demand that the English pay homage to the French king for their continental possessions. Cardinal Beaufort appealed to Isabel to use her influence with the French, and she invited both sides to dinner in her tent that night. After desert and wine she tried to convince the French party to alter their position enough to allow the talks to continue. She failed, though she was able to persuade both parties to accept a three-day hiatus in the conference. In the hope of finding a solution to the deadlock during these three days, Isabel met with the duke of Orléans in the company of French ambassadors near Calais. But by late the night of July 13, exhausted from her fruitless efforts to keep the negotiations open, she remarked to Orléans, "My lord, wilt thou never have peace?" No doubt yearning to return to France after his twenty-three years of English captivity, Orléans replied, "Yea, even though I die for peace."[8] Distressed by her inability to bring about any compromise with either the French or the English, Isabel left the next day for St. Omer to be by the side of her husband, who was reported (perhaps for diplomatic reasons) to be ill.

When the duchess returned from St. Omer on July 16 she brought a new plan to offer the cardinal. The next session of July 18 was a short one, but Isabel was able to present the plan to the English delegation before closing the meeting. She proposed a peace good for fifteen, twenty, or thirty years during which time Henry would refrain from using the title of king of France, and France would not claim royal sovereignty over him or demand homage for his territories in France; Henry could at any time resume the title and renew the war on one year's notice. The English delegation contemplated the offer and asked that the duchess present the terms in writing, which she did a few days later.

Although by now Isabel had come to accept that the conference was probably doomed to failure, she sought to prolong discussions, if only so that the English would remain longer at Gravelines and thus give her more time to discuss privately with them a very different type of agreement: namely, a trade agreement between England and Burgundy.

The next two sessions were held on July 22 and 25. When the English refused the written peace plan, the French prepared to leave Gravelines. To hold the conference together a little while longer, Isabel wrung a small concession from the French that was presented to the English on July 29 as a final offer: the English could keep all of Normandy except Mont St. Michel and the homage of Brittany, provided they give up their claim to the French crown.[9] Safe-conducts issued on August 2 allowed the English delegation to cross the channel with the French offer in hand and to return on September 9. Isabel remained at St. Omer with little hope for the peace but with much enthusiasm for the English return, when she planned to extend the economic talks then in session in Calais into a formal Anglo-Burgundian agreement.

When the English returned, ready formally to refuse the final French offer, they were notified that no French had been in the area since July 29. The conference was thus over, but again Isabel managed to extend the talks, this time until September 15, when, without the French king's approval, she left immediately with one hundred attendants for Calais to meet with Cardinal Beaufort and the duke of Orléans. With her stated purpose a reopening of peace talks by the next spring, she was able to prolong the negotiations for a few days more. Dining with her uncle Beaufort during this sensitive period—and with the insulted and resentful English delegation demonstrably eager to return to London—Isabel asked, with all the apparent indifference she could muster, whether the existing truce the English and the Burgundians had established for the conference site was to be continued. If it was, she inquired, would further negotiations on Anglo-Burgundian commercial relations be useful? Conscious of the economic benefits that had accrued from the two-month truce, the English agreed that further talks were indeed advisable.

The Burgundian delegation headed by Henri Utenhove in Calais reopened talks on September 18 for an *Intercursus* agreement—*intercursus* means literally a free exchange of trade—between the English and the members of the Four Estates of Flanders. The talks lasted for fourteen days, during which Isabel remained with her uncle at Calais to ensure that the talks progressed and that the English did not pack and sail home.

Encouraged by the extension of these talks between the Flemish and the English, the fishermen of Boulogne and Picardy asked Isabel to include within any new treaty a guarantee of their freedom on the seas. As theirs was as important an industry as the weaving and cloth trade in Flanders, the duchess asked her uncle to make sure that an additional article was included in the *Intercursus* discussion. This article included the requests of the fishermen of Artois, Boulogne, Pontieu, and Crotoy as well as other areas along the Somme River. Her requests granted, the agreement was concluded, reviewed, approved, and signed by all the negotiators on September 29. The truce provided for freedom of trade between England, Flanders, and Brabant for three years, but three months later, on January 21, it was in fact extended for seven years, until November 1, 1447. Beneath Isabel's signature it was noted that the *Intercursus* was "written and approved between the ambassadors and approved by the most high and all powerful lord, the king of England on one part, and by us on the other part to establish the *Intercursus* of merchandise and fishing."[10] With this substantial victory for both the cardinal and Isabel—who received from the Flemish 12,000 and 7,000 gold saluts, respectively—the English embarked for London on October 2.

The Negotiator: Isabel as Facilitator

Isabel followed her diplomatic victory of 1440 with efforts to forge a separate peace with England—based on the trade treaties already agreed on—that would be seen as an adjunct of the *Intercursus*. Even though during that year and the following one she received news of repeated English military offensives within the treaty area—ransacking towns, boarding French fishing vessels, and attacking merchant caravans—Isabel did not hesitate to begin preliminary talks with England. She did so without Philip's explicit permission, acting on the authority he had invested in her as coordinator of English trade and governor of his territories during his coming absence. Formal talks took place while she governed the Lowlands—from November 30, 1442, through the first weeks of March 1443—during Philip's preparations for the attack and conquest of Luxembourg. Rumors spread at the time that Isabel had become so powerful that Philip the Good gave free rein to her wishes, and even Pope Pius II noted that "this woman soon applied herself to increasing her power and, exploiting her husband's indulgence, she began to take everything in hand, ruling the towns, organizing armies, levying taxes on provinces and ruling everything in an arbitrary fashion."[11] In fact, Isabel did perform all these functions, but except in the case of piloting the talks with England, she acted only with Philip's specific approval.

The meetings with the English were held in Rouen, and a Perpetual Treaty of Peace—perpetual because it was based on the principle of future continuing reviews and extensions by both signatories—was announced in a letter dated May 31, 1443, by the duke of York, who had negotiated on behalf of Henry VI. Beneath the signatures on the accord it was noted that the "agreement was made with the high and powerful princess, our very dear and well-loved cousin the duchess of Burgundy and of Brabant, having the power given her by the duke of Burgundy, her husband."[12] By this document, then, Isabel reestablished peace between England and Burgundy and encouraged further development of their commerce in the North Sea.

These years carried bitter disappointment for Isabel as well as victory. The duchess was profoundly concerned over the increased aggression shown by Charles VII and his son Louis toward Burgundy after 1440. French military incursions into northern and southern Burgundy continued unabated after 1435, as Charles VII insinuated French power within Philip's imperial possessions. The French king held court in the city of Nancy in the Duchy of Lorraine—that thirty-mile stretch of land that separated Philip's northern and southern territories—and from there he challenged Philip's influence over the imperial cities of Toul, Verdun, and Metz. As a further affront, Charles VII refused to grant pardons or grant any leniency toward Flemish cases in the Paris Parlement, thus ignoring Philip the Good's special rank and refusing him the privileges customarily given to him in matters concerning his vassals.

Isabel was also disappointed by the inability of the duke of Orléans to exert influence over his uncle, Charles VII. Philip the Good had assumed that Orléans would soften the French king's antagonism toward Burgundy, hence Philip's directives to Isabel in the 1440 Gravelines conference to secure Orléans's release from the Tower of London as quickly as possible. She worked diligently to free the duke, gathering the funds for his ransom on her own. She convinced the French princes to provide sums ranging from 1,000 to 30,000 saluts, while she herself provided 15,000 nobles. She wrote letters from June to September 1440 to the nobles, clergy, and merchants of Hainault—who would profit most from more peaceful relations with France—pleading for contributions. The English demands were substantial, even by royal standards, and she needed help in providing the 80,000 ecus they required before Orléans could leave the Tower and the additional 160,000 ecus six months after his release. She finally appealed to the Estates of Burgundy for a special tax to provide the remaining amount, with which she obtained the duke's release on November 11, 1440. Unfortunately, however, it soon became clear that his influence at the French court would be minimal, and thus that her efforts to gain a well-placed advocate for Burgundy had been in vain.

Once Philip had relinquished his oath to England and renewed his alliance with the French in 1435, Charles VII and the dauphin no longer had any need to court Burgundy with favors and hypocritical promises of a friendship. By 1444, not only did Burgundy have no allies at the French court, but it also faced powerful antagonism from the Angevin faction within the court who resented Philip's increasing demands for the ransom of René of Anjou. French troops and bands of French-inspired *écorcheurs* swept Flanders, Hainault, and Picardy, extending their attacks as well into Philip's southern territories of Mâcon and the Comte of Burgundy, an imperial possession.

At Laons in 1441, the dauphin Louis confirmed Isabel's suspicions that the French had no interest in the affairs of Burgundy, apart from absorbing it into their kingdom. He gave short shrift to Isabel's pleas for relief and reparations for the suffering caused by French attacks along the duchy's borders. So obvious was the enmity of the dauphin toward Burgundian appeals for relief that many of the pro-French nobles in her company came away from the encounter far less inclined than before to sympathize with France. His cold response to Isabel convinced her that Burgundy's security rested only in an alliance with England.

Isabel's realistic outlook, however, stood in contrast to Philip's political views, which were colored by emotion. He was and would always remain a French prince of the House of Valois, even if he did pursue a crown for his imperial possessions. Unable to accept that the French really sought Burgundy's destruction, in 1445 Philip looked again to his wife's skills to negotiate terms for French reparations while also preserving peace between Burgundy and France. Although she had no hope of any better treatment by the French in 1445 than she had experienced in 1441, she obeyed Philip's commands. He directed her to travel to Reims for preliminary talks with French representatives that spring to arrange a formal meeting with the representatives of Charles VII at Chalons in the summer. Her agenda included demands that France abandon its border raids on Burgundian territory; make reparations for the destruction of Burgundian villages; and cease piracy against Burgundy's merchant ships and caravans. At her departure for Chalons that summer, Isabel received a letter that increased her pessimism about the success of her efforts with the French. The marshal of Burgundy, Thibault de Neufchâtel, informed her that "many times we have notified you of the damages done daily to your territories here by the *écorcheurs*, daily they do unimaginable things in Montbeliard." Without any ambiguity, he accused the king and the dauphin of encouraging these devastations, stating that "the king and the dauphin have secretly ordered them [his troops] to remain in Burgundy and live off the land right to the day of the opening of talks in Reims."[13]

The hostility of the French court toward Burgundy was fueled by the Angevin faction, which was led by Marie of Anjou, queen of France and sister of René of Anjou, and by his daughter Margaret, the soon-to-be queen of England. The Angevin party sought to have Philip the Good cancel his demands for the ransom of René of Anjou and encouraged the king and the dauphin to use military aggression in the northern and southern Burgundian areas to pressure the duke's embassy to concede on all points at the conference. Isabel must have entered Chalons that summer of 1445 with a heavy heart. She could not have held more than a wisp of hope for the success of any of her husband's demands, the first of which required the payment of Anjou's ransom. Next on Isabel's agenda were the resolution of cases then standing before the Paris Parlement for reparations for French attacks against Flemish merchant traffic, the ratification of the treaty of Arras by the dauphin and all French princes who had not signed that treaty in 1435, and the evacuation of the dauphin's troops from Philip's southern territory of Montbeliard.

Isabel readied herself for her visit at the French court by reading several books on etiquette for her presentation to the queen. The customs, after all, were different from the Portuguese and certainly more formal, if possible, than those of Burgundy. Thus prepared, on May 21, the duchess of Burgundy, accompanied by a grand company of noble Burgundians and several French princes, entered into the courtyard of the mansion at Chalons where the French king and queen were staying. Their horses and carriages clattered onto the paved entry with pennons and golden tassels swaying in the formal measured cadence of arrival. The velvet capes of the riders lay smoothly over the rumps of their horses, as the men swept their plumed hats to their sides waiting for the servants to hold the bridles and allow the riders to dismount. Helped from her horse while her maid of honor held her train, Isabel was approached by the duke of Bourbon, who took her hand and escorted her behind the procession of the knights and gentlemen into the mansion.

Arriving at the room where the queen was holding audience, Isabel first sent her knight of honor, the lord Créquy, to inquire if the queen wished her to enter to do her reverence. Invited into Marie of Anjou's chamber, Isabel stopped at the doorway to take her train into her own hands and to fan it out behind her as she entered into the presence of the queen of France. In the center of the room, Isabel curtsied several times before approaching the queen, who moved forward from the head of her bed to embrace the duchess and extended her hand to bid her rise. Isabel then approached Margaret, who was standing just to the side of her aunt, and after another curtsy, turned to approach the queen of Sicily, wife of René of Anjou, who sat beside Margaret. To this lady she gave only a shallow bow.

According to the diary of Alienor de Poitier, whose mother had been present at the occasion, her mother had never seen such honor bestowed on another by the French queen as that given to the duchess of Burgundy that day.[14] In spite of the respectful greeting, however, Isabel's fears were well founded. The ransom of René of Anjou quickly became a surrender instead of a concession, since Isabel was unable to negotiate any significant benefits for Burgundy in return for forgiving René's debt. The two concessions from the French that the duchess took away from Chalons—a French promise to evacuate the dauphin's troops from Montbeliard, and a letter (obtained only after Isabel had paid a French official a bribe of 6,000 gold crowns) from Charles VII to postpone cases in the Paris Parlement against the members of the Four Estates of Flanders for the nonpayment by their merchants of taxes and duties demanded by the king—were virtually insignificant, especially as the French king ignored his promises soon after Isabel returned to Burgundy. Charles VII continued to ignore Philip's request for a full ratification of the treaty of Arras. The treaty left Chalons with few additional signatures.

All in all, the negotiations were a failure for Isabel and for Burgundy. As if to demonstrate that he had not altered his policy toward Burgundy in the least, later that same July, Charles launched more armed assaults and military aggressions against Philip's western borders. And by December, the French had grown so hostile to Philip, taking every opportunity to humiliate him, that the assembly of the Order of the Golden Fleece was interrupted by an usher from the Paris Parlement who summoned Philip the Good then and there to appear before its court.

Philip was a determined ruler, but he was no diplomat. He had rashly ignored the advice of Hughes de Lannoy in 1439 that, since Burgundy had placed itself in the path of both French and English aggression by its change of alliances in Arras, the most secure course to follow was to place a friendly advocate at the French court. De Lannoy had suggested that the ideal figure to play this role was René of Anjou, but Philip had not been prepared to acquire the friendship, or at least the gratitude, of Anjou by forgiving him the ransom René owed Burgundy. In the end, Philip did indeed forgive the debt, but by then Anjou had become a bitter enemy. And despite abundant evidence to the contrary, Philip persisted in believing that in return for his loyalty to the House of Valois against England, the king and his son would eventually extend a hand of peace toward Burgundy.

Unlike Philip, Isabel had come to see that the French king regarded Burgundy's continuing existence as a challenge to his efforts to expand French territory and to centralize his authority—a process begun by Joan of Arc. Witnessing the growing influence of the pro-French courtiers who surrounded her husband, Isabel worried that, with their help, the French king might eventually absorb Burgundy. After 1441, the duchess became increasingly convinced that only an economically strong Burgundy could survive this French aggression; after 1445, she worked to underpin this strength by a firm political alliance with England. While Philip turned his attentions to the east and to his own search for recognition—perhaps a crown for the lands he held from Emperor Frederick III—he gave Isabel the responsibility for developing, guiding, and maintaining profitable trade relations with England. With this license, Isabel was to do her best to sustain the independence of Burgundy.

Notes

1. Somme, "Isabel de Portugal" (Ph.D. diss., University of Lille, France, 1985), 702.
2. Richard Vaughan, *Philip the Good: The Apogee of Burgundy* (New York: Barnes and Noble, 1970), 100; Marie Rose Thielemans, "Les Croys, conseillers des ducs de Bourgogne," *Bulletin de la Commission de l'Histoire* 142 (1959): 71–73:

   Amboise, 6 July, 1435

   Charles, by the grace of God, king of France, greetings to all those who see these letters . . . bearing in mind that this peace and reconciliation [between France and Burgundy] is more likely to be brought about by our cousin's leading confidential advisers, in whom he places trust . . . we grant and have granted by these present letters the sum of 60,000 gold saluts . . . to be divided between them as follows:

Nicolas Rolin	10,000 saluts
Lord Anthony of Croy	10,000 saluts
Lord of Charny	8,000 saluts
Philippe, lord of Tenant	8,000 saluts
The lord of Baucignes	8,000 saluts

And to Jehan, brother of the lord of Croy; Jacques, lord of Crevecoeur; Jean de Brimeu, lord of Humbercourt; and to Guy Guilbaut . . . 10,000 saluts to share between the four of them.

3. Vaughan, *Philip the Good*, 99.
4. M. le Franc, *Le Champion des Dames*, ed. A. Piaget (Paris; Lausanne: n.p, 1968), 63.
5. "In the document, Charles VII specifically states that this was because of her services in negotiating the Franco-Burgundian 'peace and reunion' at Arras." Vaughan, *Philip the Good,* 101.
6. Somme, "Isabel de Portugal," 749.
7. Somme, "Isabel de Portugal," 749.
8. In the entry for July 13 in the journal of Thomas Beckyngton, the bishop of Bath and Wells and the private secretary to Henry VI; cited in Sir Harriss Nicolas, ed., *The Journal of Thomas Beckyngton* (London: G. Eyre and Spottswood, 1835–38), entry for 13 July 1439.
9. Nicolas, *Proceedings and Ordinances of the Privy Council of England* (London: G. Eyre and Spottswood, 1834–37), 5:376–77.
10. Marie Rose Thielemans, *Bourgogne et Angleterre, 1435–1467* (Brussels: Presses Universitaires de Bruxelles, 1966), 443–53.
11. Vaughan, *Philip the Good*, 168.
12. A. Huguet, "Aspects de la guerre de cent ans en picardie maritime, 1400–1450," *Memoires de la Société des Antiquaires de Picardie* 49 (1941): 490–92.
13. U. Plancher, *Histoire générale et particulière de Bourgogne*, 4 vols. (Dijon, 1739–81), 4:141.
14. Alienor de Poitiers, *Les Honneurs de la cour,* in *Mémoire sur l'ancienne chevalrie*, ed. La Curne de Sainte-Palaye, vol. 2 (Paris, 1759), 196–201.

ENGLISH CONNECTIONS OF ISABEL OF PORTUGAL, DUCHESS OF BURGUNDY

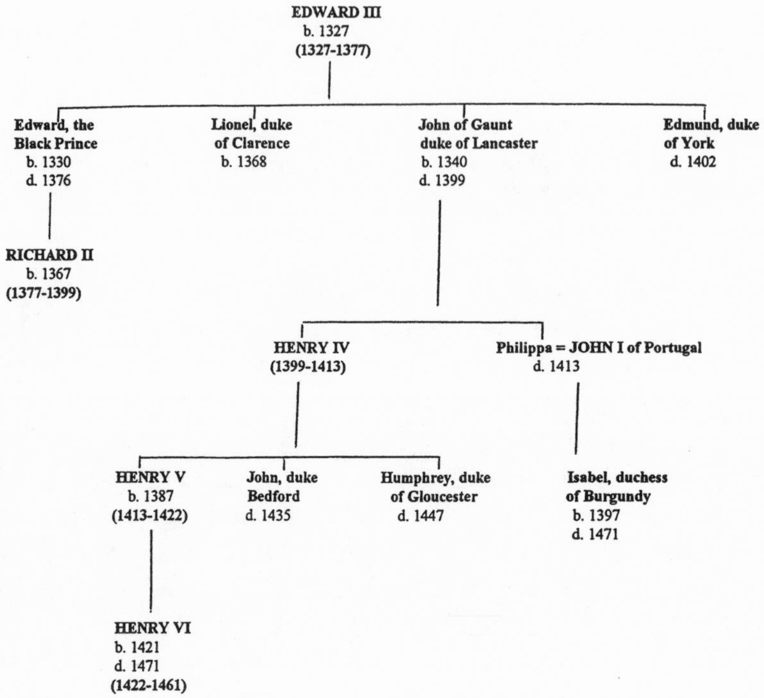

Chapter Five

Dual Challenges from France and England, 1446–1453

BY 1446 ISABEL'S DIPLOMATIC successes had given Philip the Good an opportunity to reach for power and glory beyond the borders of his territory. Her successfully extended *Intercursus* and the accompanying Perpetual Peace agreements provided Burgundy with the prospect of twelve years of profitable trade with England. As Isabel continued to work toward a firm political alliance, Philip sought to build on his dynastic dreams and searched for a crown. Since a reinvigorated France offered the duke of Burgundy no opportunity either for territorial expansion or for the crown he sought, Philip the Good looked eastward toward the Holy Roman Empire. While pursuing these goals within the empire, he seemed oblivious to the real intentions of the French king, apparently unaware that the existence of a powerful and independent Burgundy challenged an increasingly centralized France. He failed to accept the notion that the greater his duchy became, the more determined Charles VII would be to reabsorb that territory into his reinvigorated kingdom.

Philip's political aspirations were but thinly veiled by his economic maneuvers, while Isabel based her own political action on economic necessity. The duchess watched the earl of Suffolk and the duke of Somerset—favorites of the English Lancastrian queen, Margaret of Anjou, who was a sworn enemy of Burgundy—vie for power with the duke of York, by 1449 the only remaining legitimate male heir to the throne. Since York favored the economic ties with Burgundy that Isabel sought to strengthen—while the Angevin faction looked to a French alliance—the duchess was prepared to support York's political ambitions, even though these might involve wresting the crown from the Lancastrian line, to which she was herself related. As the duchess waited for the outcome of this English duel for power, she worked to develop Anglo-Burgundian trade—proposing lower prices for English wool purchased at the Staple of Calais and securing the safety of open traffic lanes through Philip's territories—but was foiled by her husband's policies prohibiting the shipment of English cloth. Of necessity then, from 1446 to 1453 the focus of Isabel's diplomacy was to find detours around the obstacles her husband placed in the way of the English alliance; Isabel's consistent aim was also to weave into that relationship the possibility of an eventual royal marriage between her son and a member of the English royal family.

Isabel spent most of 1446 in either the canal-laced town of Bruges—a short boat ride upriver from the North Sea port of Sluis, where she had frequent reports from the English court—or at Coudenberg Castle, her favorite residence in Brussels, center of Burgundian government and trade. While Isabel studied the reports of her informants in Calais and London, she also worried about the illness that confined to bed her seventeen-year-old daughter-in-law, Catherine of France. Winter in the Lowlands is cold, dark, and damp, and by February Catherine was weakened with a high fever and a persistent cough that showed signs of worsening. Isabel hoped that the spring sunshine would bring color back to her cheeks. As February passed into March, however, Catherine's color remained too pale, and she was listless and without appetite.

The young princess had been in the care of the duchess since her marriage to Isabel's son Charles in 1439 and she had followed the court in one city or another through the Lowlands ever since. She felt close to Isabel and was often seen by her side, holding her hand or leaning toward her to whisper some bit of information in confidence. The affection was returned, for Isabel had no daughter of her own and had grown fond of her son's wife. Catherine was a mature young woman, even at the age of twelve, and was considered by courtiers to be kind, charming, and intelligent, as well as fair. But the demands placed on the young princess by the many lavish entertainments, the rigid formality of Burgundian etiquette, and the extensive travel of the medieval court through the cold, blustery months of winter must have been wearing for a delicate child from the sunny Loire.

As the hesitant warmth of April began to cover the fields and waterways of Bruges, wan little Catherine accompanied the ducal court from its residence at the Princehof to the larger and bustling but equally uncomfortable castle at Ten Waele in Ghent. Duke Philip ordered that his wife and son join him there and then accompany him to Arras to witness a jousting event that would be educational for Charles. Although thirteen-year-old Charles was preoccupied by the illness of his young bride, who had also become his fast friend, he was also a boy much absorbed with armaments and the challenges of battle. Wanting to please his father, Charles put aside his concerns for his wife and instead began to anticipate the display of valor, skill, and gallantry by the knights.

Isabel encouraged her son's love of chivalry and was proud of his strength, his growing mastery in the saddle, and his courage in the ring. She approved of his ambition, satisfied that he had inherited her own Portuguese family's drive to conquer with Philip's need for glory and acclaim, but she worried about her young son's impulsiveness. For his safety, she was constantly on guard to curb him from his eagerness to display his growing prowess. With an ever failing young Catherine to supervise and a young son eager to prove himself jousting among real knights, Isabel found the month of April 1446 a difficult one.

On a misty morning in mid-April, Catherine rode close by Isabel's side in her carriage. The two women bumped and joggled toward Arras, determined to witness the joust in person and to make sure that the duke kept Charles safe from his own enthusiasms. Catherine was bundled against the cold to keep her from coughing herself into another fainting spell, and the screen in the carriage windows was pulled shut and the curtains closed. The square in Arras had been prepared for the joust with the construction of a raised tower at one end for the duke, who was to judge the contestants. The structure was covered on three sides to protect the duchess and her daughter-in-law from any chill breezes. By midday, all was ready and the citizens of Arras waited for the arrival of the ducal family.

The match began at three o'clock, as cool afternoon winds swept through the square. Charles was too involved in the excitement of the contest to notice that Catherine had been overcome by coughing and taken from the tower soon after the jousting started. Once reassured that Charles was not to participate in the joust, Isabel left with her daughter-in-law and returned to Ghent that evening. They remained at Ten Waele only until Catherine was well enough to travel and then Isabel's court left for the comforts of Coudenberg, her favorite residence at Brussels.

From the onset of Catherine's illness, on February 11, Charles had attempted to remain as close to his young wife's side as possible. He was particularly thankful for the two doctors sent her by her father, Charles VII, and had urged them to do everything in their power for her. He had visited her chambers often and played the harp for her, a gift she brought to him from France. It was to no avail: Catherine died on July 30, 1446. The death of the little princess was deeply mourned by the court. Isabel, particularly, would have felt the loss of her quiet charm and gentle ways. But for Isabel, as for Philip, the death was also a matter of state, a political matter that demanded cool and unemotional analysis and calculation. Philip turned his attention to maintaining the French alliance he worked so hard to forge; Isabel realized that the tragedy opened the prospect of finding an English bride for her son.

Isabel's Strategy in 1446

The sadness weighing down the Burgundian court at Catherine's death did not prevent Isabel from celebrating a great achievement by her envoys at Calais. On August 4, Henry Utenhove, Parent Fane, and Louis Domessent concluded a formal agreement that extended the Anglo-Burgundian

Intercursus from 1446 to 1458. She now decided to remain either in Brussels or in Hesdin to better monitor the upheavals in the English court.

Isabel spent the autumn at Coudenberg, leaving for Bruges only late in November, and received regular dispatches from her agents in England describing the increasing frustrations of the duke of York. A strong personality and an able administrator, Richard of York was also quick to anger and was impatient with the king's inability to rule effectively. Henry VI wanted peace above all, and sensitive by nature, he sought to avoid every possible confrontation. The queen was wary about the threat York's claim to the throne posed, although she was not openly hostile. York was deeply resentful when Henry VI removed him from his responsibility as lieutenant governor of Normandy—a position he had held as a popular and effective royal officer since 1440—and appointed his cousin, Edmund Beaufort, duke of Somerset, instead.

Somerset was the nephew of Cardinal Beaufort and, after Henry VI himself, was the head of the Lancastrian family. Both dukes had direct claim to the throne as descendants of Edward III—York through Edward III's second son, Lionel of Clarence, and Somerset through Edward's fourth son, John of Gaunt. Edmund Beaufort was no mere court favorite; his war record was greater even than York's and he owned more land on the continent. Somerset possessed the extensive Norman counties of Harcourt and Mortain, the seigneuries of Chanteloup in the Contentin, and many smaller properties in Normandy. In 1439 he had been appointed captain-general of the duchy of Maine, south of Normandy, which in 1446 lay within the territories of his new responsibility on the continent. He grew rich on the income from rents, duties, and taxes levied in these areas.

In Normandy, both York and Somerset were powerful landowners in the area of Normandy, and although pride was a key ingredient in their contest for the royal lieutenancy and governorship of the duchy, their personal fortunes were of equal concern to them. York's "appanages" (awarded by the king and reserved for princes of the royal house) centered on the counties of Evreux and Beaumont-le Roger as well as the seigneuries of Conches and Breteuil. Two years before, in 1444, York's second son had also been given the appanage rights to St.-Sauveur-Lendelin in the Contentin area bordering the channel. Under York's skillful administration, these territories had come to provide solid revenues. Somerset's administrative abilities were less well demonstrated, and as the Contentin region was on the French border, York anticipated more than one kind of challenge to Somerset's leadership. But as they were located on the frontier area with France, they gave the duke added concern for the efficiency of Somerset's leadership. York kept in close touch with affairs in France and maintained a stream of correspondence with the duchess Isabel from his estates in Ireland while administering that territory as royal officer for Henry VI.

Isabel was as uneasy about the appointment to France of their cousin, the duke of Somerset, as was the duke of York. If England were to have another financial fiasco on the continent, like the one involving Somerset's older brother, John, the captain-general of Gascony and France who had lost both English territory and his own life in France in 1444, the duchess realized there would surely be more delay in her negotiations with England. She worried that she would not be able to convince the Staple merchants at Calais to lower their wool prices; she also realized that in such a financial crisis the English would not agree to reparations for the damages they had caused to Burgundian merchant fleets since 1444.

Isabel had always relied on her uncle Beaufort to keep her informed of the political currents in England. Dressed in his scarlet robes trimmed in white miniver fur, Henry Beaufort, cardinal of Winchester, was imposing in manner and appearance and commanded respect. Throughout his career, the cardinal supported his Lancastrian family's claims to the dual crown, and using his considerable power and influence, he placed his relatives as close to that throne as possible.

The duchess had been fascinated with the details her uncle wrote to her about the arrest and trial of the duke of Gloucester's wife, Eleanor Cobham, a few years before. The tragedy for Eleanor and Humphrey began with the July 23 arrest of Bolingbroke, the Oxford priest and astronomer. Bolingbroke had helped the duke write his own book on astronomy, and later cast the duchess's horoscope to determine her chances of becoming queen. After his arrest, Bolingbroke confessed to having helped Eleanor consult the spirit world about the possibility of the king's early death, and she was then charged with witchcraft, heresy, and treason. Convicted three months later, the duchess submitted to the sentence imposed on her by Cardinal Beaufort; she walked barefoot and unhooded through the streets of London and was imprisoned in Kenilworth Castle and then consigned to the Isle of Man for the remainder of her days.

Isabel gave little thought to Eleanor now, except with distaste, but her trial had compromised Humphrey's reputation and perhaps threatened his safety, and he had been one of Isabel's key allies on the issue of Burgundian trade. Once the likeliest heir to the throne, he now lost power on all fronts. He had rallied great popular support for war on the continent and against the policy of ceding England's continental possessions in exchange for peace. But now the queen and her trusted advisor, the earl of Suffolk, held sway, and like the king, they favored peace on the continent at any price.

Isabel watched and waited as these contestants for power—Gloucester, York, Suffolk, and Somerset—manipulated events to gain their own ascendancy. All the power of her uncle Beaufort's wealth could not sustain either his nephew Somerset's advancement or the interests of his niece in Burgundy. In 1446, it seemed clear that the duke of Gloucester would not succeed his nephew to the throne. In the same year, Isabel's uncle, now in failing health and vulnerable to new political forces about the throne, slipped quietly from the council chamber and back to his estates to prepare for his retirement. No longer able to rely on her uncle to keep her abreast of such events, Isabel searched for other avenues to help her anticipate the fate of the duke of Gloucester and the future of his ally, the duke of York.

No economic progress was possible in Burgundy until Isabel could convince the English government at Calais to lower the price of wool sold to merchants there for shipment to the looms of Flanders, Hainault, and the Lowlands. Only an inferior quality of wool was now allocated for Burgundy, and it was twice as expensive as the finer grade available before her husband had decided to strictly enforce his prohibition of the shipment of English cloth through Burgundian territories.

Twenty years before, wool in great quantities was being shipped from England to the Low Countries, bypassing Calais under the guise of "legal exceptions" and "royal licenses" (permits). Responding to these evasions of English duty, Parliament enacted two laws in 1429, the Staple and Bullion Ordinance and the Partition Ordinance. The first of these laws raised the price of wool and requried all merchants to sell only for "cash in hand," and to deliver one-third of the wool price in bullion to the mints. The second law, the Partition Ordinance, made the regulation of merchant sales of wool at Calais even more stringent by requiring merchants to divide (or "partition") their income from wool sales in proportion to the amount of wool they had bought at the Staple and not according to the total of their sales income. Since a certain minimum contribution to the Staple was required of each merchant by the Staple, the Partition Ordinance effectively put all the smaller merchants out of business. Needing more money from the Staple sales, not less, the crown in 1430 appealed successfully to the elite group of the wealthiest and most powerful merchant Staplers to uphold the new fiscal measures. In exchange for their cooperation, the crown gave them full control over the Staple government and its trade policy.

In 1446 Philip the Good placed a heavy duty on Calais wool, under the mistaken impression that this "penalty tax" would discourage the Flemish from buying the English product and force the Staple government to lower the prices set in 1429. The duke reasoned that lower prices for English wools from the Staple, together with his prohibition against the transport of English cloth throughout Burgundian lands, would revive the failing weaving industry of Flanders.

Isabel was hopeful that she might win that reduction in the price of wool from the Staple by appealing directly to the powerful merchants instead of threatening them with a loss of sales. Isabel offered the merchants the opportunity to do more profitable business with the Flemish looms, correctly assuming that the merchants would be more likely and more able to change the Staple regulations than the royal officers with whom she had previously negotiated.

Isabel's greatest obstacle to lowering the price of wool from the Staple was the queen of England, for Margaret of Anjou was ready to nullify any measure that proved profitable to Burgundy. The duchess's greatest ally in the English court had been Cardinal Beaufort; without her uncle's influence, she was subject to the queen's implacable ire for all the years Philip had imprisoned the queen's father, René of Anjou, and for the still outstanding debt of the ransom. Margaret of Anjou's greatest loyalty was to the earl of Suffolk, who had secured her marriage at great cost. The English embassy to Charles VII, Margaret's uncle, had been prepared to pay any price to win Margaret's hand in 1444, and Charles VII had granted it only in exchange for the territories of LeMans, Maine, and Anjou—the basis of the Angevin fortune. How could Margaret ascend a throne that kept her father's legitimate possessions from him? Charles asked Suffolk. In his enthusiasm for achieving a French peace in 1445, as well as his anticipation of the immediate rewards of his success, Suffolk had been very willing to agree to the French king's terms.

In 1445, after the proxy ceremony in Tours in which Suffolk stood for Henry VI, the new queen of England began her progress through the biting wet and cold of northern France and into Paris. So ruinous was the state of the English treasury from the war with France that on reaching Rouen, the forlorn little queen had to remain there from December 12 until early April, until her new husband acquired the funds to greet his bride with appropriate ceremony.

During these three months, Margaret formed a close attachment to Suffolk and his wife, the witty marchioness Alice, granddaughter of the poet Geoffrey Chaucer. When Margaret finally landed on English soil that spring she came with a ready-made English household and very few of her French countrymen. The lovely but impoverished daughter of René of Anjou had become accustomed to forming close friendships and had not yet acquired the suspicious nature—indispensable to a queen—that would allow her to see the political and self-interested motives of those who claimed to be her friends. Once in England, therefore, Suffolk remained by her side as her friend, chief counsel, and closest adviser, a partnership that carried with it the danger of provoking the resentment of those courtiers and nobles excluded from Suffolk's patronage. As Henry VI's wife, Margaret of Anjou was naively prepared to embrace a land whose people believed that Suffolk had bought peace, and the queen, at the price of their honor on the continent.

While estimating the strengths and weaknesses of the competing factions at the English court, the somewhat isolated Isabel sought out the friendship and counsel of Anthony, the Grand Bastard of Burgundy, Philip's eldest, and most loyal and respected, illegitimate child. Unlike other courts of the time, the Burgundian court did not look down on its duke's bastards. Indeed, Isabel was close to a great number of Philip's illegitimate children. She saw to it that they were given not only the same food and drink but also the same respect as his legitimate children. They were educated at court, dressed in grey silk, and provided marriages and careers of rank. Those with exceptional talent and skill were kept close to the court, and Anthony was the best of these. He was not only a patron of the arts who collected great illuminated manuscripts but also a robust warrior who excelled in the jousting ring and later followed Philip on his crusade. He was paid 3,840 pounds each year, and rose to prominence serving not only Philip and Isabel but also their son Charles. With Hughes de Lannoy, Anthony helped Isabel develop plans that kept the merchant caravans filled and profitable for Burgundy, while London and Calais waited for Philip the Good to reconsider his prohibition against the transportation of English cloth through Burgundy.

With Hughes and Anthony by her side, Isabel studied the currents swirling about the English court, especially the tensions between Suffolk, the peacemaker, and York, who urged war on the continent and enjoyed a popularity throughout the kingdom that threatened Suffolk's leadership. Isabel was troubled then, but not surprised, when the Lancastrian faction removed York from his post as lieutenant governor in Normandy that July and appointed him to the lieutenant governorship of the more politically isolated Ireland.

Queen Margaret worked hard to obtain the territory of Maine—the real base of her family's fortune—for her father. She corresponded with the French king, promising him in a letter dated December 17, 1445, that she would do what she could to bring about the "deliverance of Maine" from English control. Henry VI followed his wife's letter with one of his own dated December 22, apologizing for the delay in the transference of Maine to France, and then signed in his own hand an agreement to surrender Le Mans and whatever else he held in Maine by April 30, 1446. This was a key negotiating point because Maine was the only newly reinforced English possession on the continent. Somerset still held personal territory in Maine, and at the queen's request, Suffolk pressed him, without success, to relinquish it. Meanwhile, with the duke of York about to depart the scene, Margaret and Suffolk sought a way to silence the duke of Gloucester. When news reached York that Somerset had flatly refused to give up his territory without guarantees of ample compensation, York accused Somerset of greed and lack of loyalty to the crown. As the two quarreled over the fate of their own possessions in Normandy and Maine, Queen Margaret and Suffolk took action to eliminate the duke of Gloucester, the most immediate and dangerous obstacle to reclaiming the Angevin fortunes. On December 14, 1446, writs were issued for a parliament to meet at Bury St. Edmunds to impeach Gloucester on grounds of treason, based on his resistance to the transfer of Maine to the French king—failure to honor the terms Suffolk had negotiated with France in 1444.

A stream of dispatches came to Isabel from her agents in London about the fate of the duke of Gloucester. Meanwhile, although Isabel kept in close correspondence with the duke of York, she hestiated to support him publicly. She needed his political talents in her negotiations with the Staple merchants, but his position had become too volatile for a formal alliance. So close to the English crown, but about to be removed from the court itself by powerful pro-French interests, he had become a dangerous ally. The political instincts of the duchess warned her that it was too early to declare her support for either the Lancastrian or Yorkist faction.

Maintaining the English Tie, 1447–1449

The duke of Gloucester and his retinue approached Bury St. Edmunds in the late morning of a stormy February 10. The ride was bitter cold and sleet stung the faces of the mounted men. Bent in their saddles and leaning against the wind, Sir John Stouton and Sir Thomas Stanley, commanding the king's household guard, were miserable dark figures whose cloaks gathered the frozen rain as they watched Gloucester's party canter toward them. The king's courtiers informed the duke that his presence was not needed in Parliament that day, and conveyed the duke's order that he proceed to his lodgings immediately, dine there, and remain within his quarters until he received further word. Within hours, the king's men entered the duke's quarters and the high constable Viscount Beaumont informed him that he was under arrest.

Gloucester, a headstrong man who did not brook opposition, was also given to overindulgence and self-gratification that had weakened his health and strength. When he was informed that a trial of impeachment was to be held against him in Parliament because of the charges of treason against him, the shock was so great that he apparently suffered a massive stroke and never revived. After receiving the last rites of the Catholic Church, Gloucester died in Bury St. Edmunds on February 23 at three o'clock in the afternoon. Like others in Burgundy, France, and England, Isabel held little doubt that some foul play had caused Gloucester's death, but there was, after all, no proof of any crime. Cardinal Beaufort himself might have been a leading suspect, but he was in seclusion at Winchester, where he died several weeks later. The transfer of Maine to France seemed even more likely, to the relief of Queen Margaret and Suffolk.

After the deaths of Gloucester and Cardinal Beaufort, and York's imminent departure for Ireland, Isabel became even more dangerously separated from political currents in England. Despite an obvious favoritism for Somerset, Margaret of Anjou showed no open hostility to the duke of York, although they were enemies. It was imperative that Isabel keep in contact with both factions. Dispatches to her agents in London increased from May 7 to May 26, as she prepared her household to remain in Bruges into midsummer.

Philip's actions during this period, however, did nothing to ease Isabel's negotiations with English suppliers of wool. Although the duke chiefly worried over formal recognition as the ruler of his imperial possessions—Brabant, Holland, and Luxembourg—he also paid close attention to Flemish merchants, who complained that they could not compete against cloth of English manufacture unless they could obtain Staple wool. In response, Philip hardened his prohibition against English cloth. His increasing seizures of English cloth, imprisonment of English and German merchants transferring the English product through Burgundian lands, and the mounting fines he enforced for transgressions against his prohibition caused the German cities to yield to his policy, and the Hansa merchants considered retaliation against the Burgundians. Meanwhile, the duke continued to negotiate with the Holy Roman Emperor for a crown; he pursued the emperor Frederick, even as the Burgundian weaving trade languished, shipments of English cloth dropped by half in 1448, and the frustrations of the English king and those of Isabel continued to grow.

Philip's policy now produced particularly dramatic results in England; the treasury of Henry VI was emptied at the moment that Cardinal Beaufort's death eliminated the English king's most reliable creditor. The duchess watched the English crisis deepen when France renewed the threat of war by attacking English territory along the Normandy border. As Philip imposed yet another 5 percent duty on wools coming from Calais, Henry VI was finally forced to borrow 200,000 marks from the wealthy Staple merchants. Duke Philip's attempt once more to squeeze the Staple merchants into lowering their wool prices—a strategy that had not worked in 1446—merely exacerbated anger on both sides of the channel. Henry VI had to place Dutch and Flemish merchants in London under royal protection that summer, as the effect of this discriminatory tax was so volatile that Burgundians were attacked in the streets, and if not killed, they were jailed and their possessions confiscated.

In reaction to the sting of this economic backlash, English representatives frequently contacted Isabel, hoping she could persuade Philip to relent. Her delegates to Calais were more warmly welcomed during this crisis than before and the Staple merchants far more open to discussion with her representatives. The Calais merchants and the Burgundian negotiators met in February and March, when vexing news reached Isabel. While the English merchants in Calais discussed with Isabel's representatives the possibility of lowering their wool prices—if she could convince the duke of Burgundy to soften his prohibitions against their product—English forces under Somerset invaded the town of Fougères, a possession of the duke of Brittany, an ally of Burgundy. Duke Philip was furious with the English action. Henry VI, with no money to finance war on the continent, turned away from the stalemate with Burgundy and decided to deal directly with the wealthy Staple merchants. They agreed to continue to supply the royal treasury, and in turn Henry VI ruled that Parliament would enforce the Staple monopoly. As a result, as suddenly as Isabel's difficulty had been exacerbated by the invasion of Fougères in late March, her opportunity to deal directly with the ruling merchants of Calais—always more open to private negotiations without the complications of supervision by a royal governor—opened the way for profitable dealing and freer trade. As these negotiations proceeded in April between Isabel's representatives and the Staple merchants, the English king paid tribute to Isabel's influence by formally demanding that his delegation immediately obtain Isabel's cooperation in solving the Calais problem.

Isabel's delegations continued to meet with the merchants of Calais in June, November, and December 1449. Isabel found the self-interest of the Calais merchants a constant hindrance, but the king, led by Queen Margaret and Suffolk, was powerless to overrule them. With the invasion of Fougères, Henry VI courted the dangerous prospect of an alliance between France, Burgundy, and Brittany. As Isabel's caravan proceeded eastward through Aerschot, Louvain, Brussels, Lens, and Arras, she received the news that on November 10 the troops of Charles VII had indeed advanced on Normandy and entered the provincial capital of Rouen. She wrote daily letters to her son from November 6 to 22, describing the capture of the Norman capital. She told him how she held her breath as York damned Somerset for his failure to field an army against the French. She explained the reason for York's fury, describing how the French had taken all of York's territorial possessions along with the whole of that province from the English.

Isabel's Wager in English Politics: 1450–1453

During 1450 Isabel grew more optimistic about her economic negotiations with England but more concerned over the increasingly volatile political climate there. As the French harassed English forces on the continent, in England itself the struggle for the crown intensified and armed retainers accompanied their lords to Parliament determined to take advantage of the crown's weakness. Meanwhile, the hardship and expense of warfare encouraged the government to look more favorably on loosening Staple regulations to stimulate trade.

Isabel watched events in Normandy with great anxiety that winter. After Somerset lost Rouen to the French on October 29, 1449, he made his escape westward to the coastal town of Caen. Encircled by the French and unable to reach the sea, he waited for English rescue. This last great English stronghold in Normandy held out for seven months, with Somerset residing within the donjon of the town's castle, a huge square structure with flanking towers that rose up from a great rock outcropping.

News reached Isabel in midsummer, however, that the French forces had laid siege to Caen itself in June. Just a few weeks later, on June 24, the siege came to an abrupt conclusion, when a round shot pierced the nursery wall of the duchess of Somerset and brough down the duke's will to resist. Having promised a ransom of five thousand golden ecus for his release, Somerset was escorted to a ship waiting in the harbor and bound for Calais. Earlier that year, English sentiment had turned murderous against Somerset's sponsor, the earl of Suffolk, whom the people held responsible for the continuing losses of English territory and honor. By the time Isabel returned to Brussels after her winter court in Bruges, therefore, her envoys in Calais informed her that the great Earl Suffolk himself had been arrested on charges of treason. Apprised of Suffolk's fate and of the violence of English sentiment against any further continental losses, Somerset chose to wait in Calais for assurances from Henry VI and Queen Margaret that he would be welcomed in England.

Henry VI attempted to pardon his chief adviser, but Parliament would not consider the king's request for leniency and found Suffolk guilty of scheming to place his own son on the throne and of "selling" the English continental possessions of Maine and Normandy to the French. On March 19 Suffolk was discharged from the court and banished from England and "all its dominions" for five years, beginning May 1 that year. The earl had only to make a safe escape from the anger of the English people to survive his sentence. But the earl's fate was sealed when the French soundly defeated the English army before the little Norman town of Formigny; thereafter, the English were determined to take their revenge on a man they held responsible for the loss of their hard-won continental possessions.

Two weeks later, thinking himself safe in a little pinnace, Suffolk sailed from Ipswich toward Calais. He came within the sight of his destination when just off the Kentish coast one of the king's great ships, the *Nicholas*, intercepted him. As his own men refused to stand by him, Suffolk was taken on board the *Nicholas* and his head was struck off on the gunwale of the ship. Suffolk's body was then taken to land and thrown out on the sands of Dover. There were no tears in England at the earl's execution, only a wave of satisfaction that justice had been done.

That one of the king's own ships was used to destroy a man whom the king had sought to save revealed the extent to which Lancastrian authority had dwindled. And that Henry Holland, captain of the *Nicholas,* was also York's son-in-law excited the suspicion that perhaps the duke's friends were responsible for Suffolk's death. Such rumors fed the blood feud between the families of York and Lancaster. Frightened and isolated, the strong-willed Queen Margaret was increasingly seen by the English as serving French interests while wearing an English crown, thereby bringing the country to the brink of military defeat. She became ever more secretive and protective of the few in whom she could place her trust, and her growing insecurities drained the remainder of Lancastrian authority.

The loss of Rouen was a painful shock for the duke of York and a personal affront to his honor. Even after Somerset formally assumed the post of lieutenant governor of Normandy, York retained the rank of captain and the responsibility of preserving Rouen for his king. Thus, according to medieval custom, when Somerset surrendered Rouen to Charles VII, he also surrendered both York's town and his honor. Thereafter, York's hatred of Somerset was implacable.

That winter there were those in France who also wondered about their own king's right to the throne. Charles VII, after all, had been disavowed by his own mother in 1422 in favor of her grandson, the son of Henry V.

Charles, however, proved adept at riding the surging wave of French morale, first set in motion by Joan of Arc in 1429. By 1450 he had almost restored France to the size it had been before Henry V's victory at Agincourt. Yet, even after Charles VII's great victory in Normandy and his ceremonial entry into Rouen in 1450, the question remained whether this man who had been disavowed by his mother and who had reigned so ignominiously when first he became king really belonged on the throne of France.

When, at Charles VII's coronation at Reims in 1429 Joan of Arc had declared him the true heir to the French crown, his fate was tied to hers. Thus, when Joan was found guilty of heresy and burned at the stake in 1431, what were the people of France to think of their king? The question had been put aside, by Charles at least, for two decades, but after his capture of Normandy he felt the time was ripe to rehabilitate the reputation of the martyred Joan and thus to allay any doubts about his own legitimacy. On February 15, 1450, the French king named Guillaume Bouille, head of the College of Beauvais in Paris and a member of the king's Great Council, to begin questioning witnesses on the legality of the trial of Joan of Arc. The resurgence of a French centralized monarchy required an undisputed kingship.

The French king paid close attention that year to the political conflict in England and was pleased as retainers of great lords swarmed into London, determined to influence the winter's Parliament. While dispatches from York brought news of these events to Isabel, she waited in Bruges with growing anxiety over the involvement of Charles VII in her husband's government of Flanders. In a fury over the denial of a request for additional taxes in Ghent that spring, Philip prepared to take revenge against his wealthiest and most important city. But as Ghent was a French possession, held by Philip as the French king's vassal, the citizens sent letters of appeal to Charles VII, hoping to preserve their self-government, now threatened by the duke of Burgundy. For his part, the French king was eager to step into the Ghent conflict to resolve its political difficulties and, by so doing, weaken the duke's authority.

As Charles maneuvered to establish the legitimacy of the Valois kingship in France, as the great lords of England dueled for the English crown, and as the duke of Burgundy and the civic aristocracy of Ghent fought for control of the city, the duchess waged her own struggle. Her efforts to maintain profitable trade between Burgundian and English lands were assisted by a number of English attempts to renew economic links with Burgundy. New officers in control of the treasury, as well as rumors of a possible attack on Calais that spring, persuaded the English government to loosen Staple regulations. By June 1451 Isabel was finally able to negotiate the sum of sixteen thousand saluts in gold with the Staple merchants as an indemnity payment to the Burgundians in return for an exemption from duty payments on cloth and wool transported into Philip's territories. There was a delay in reaching any agreement on indemnities due the English until September 20, however, when Isabel removed a final sticking point, proposing that each country could issue letters of marque (licences for piracy) against each other if redress for their complaints was not made within a reasonable time. By such intermittent small successes, Isabel was able to keep the Burgundian economy alive in spite of the increased conflict in English politics and the French threat to both England's last territorial possessions on the continent and Philip's authority in Flanders.

Matters within Burgundy remained in upheaval during the winter of 1451, however, as Philip prepared to lead a campaign against his city of Ghent. The next spring, with Philip's forces massed outside Ghent, the beleaguered city closed its gates against him. Enraged by their duke's actions, the citizen leaders beheaded all the duke's men within their walls, called a general strike against Philip's government, and sent two hundred men to the neighboring towns to help mount forces for their own defense. In response, the duke of Burgundy formally declared war on the city of Ghent and its supporters on March 30, 1452, blockaded the city, burned every village around Ghent, and hanged every prisoner.

Isabel's progress from Brussels to Bruges became a dangerous one. Her caravan filed carefully though a countryside reduced to ashes. The people were overwhelmed by starvation and suffered from a renewal of the plague. Her carts skirted the towns and villages, following the trails through the empty marshland and winding around the hills, with Ghent militia and their supporters hiding in pockets of woodland, hoping to capture the duchess. The watchful duchess and a carefully planned itinerary at last brought her caravan safely to Bruges.

Soon after reaching Bruges, Isabel received the good word that Simon de Lalaing (brother of Guillaume de Lalaing) had seized Oudenaarde, a large town and staunch ally of the rebellious Ghent. From Oudenaarde, sixteen miles up the Schelde River from Ghent, Lalaing succeeded in strangling the rebellious city's waterborne traffic, cutting off access to much-needed supplies. The Ghent militia responded by attacking Oudenaarde on April 13. On the night of Sunday, April 16, they bombarded the town so forcefully with incendiaries that Lalaing was forced to place water tanks at the street corners, and with the help of women, organized fire-watching brigades extinguished the flames as they ignited throughout the town.

With their crossbows, the Ghent militia shot messages in both Flemish and French over the walls of the town to further demoralize Lalaing. The Ghenters urged him to surrender the town and accept payment from them for his capitulation, or they would kill his two sons, whom they had now captured. He answered them with a cannonade. Lalaing withstood the siege for two more weeks, and—while Ghent decapitated the three captains in charge of the siege and named five new men in their place—the forces of Philip the Good relieved Oudenaarde and secured the remaining towns in the area. On April 28 Philip asked for assurances from Charles VII that he would not help the rebellious city of Ghent in any way. But one month later, on May 24, when the citizens of Ghent pleaded for that assistance, an enthusiastic Charles VII ordered his ambassadors to Flanders to arrange a settlement between the duke of Burgundy and his town of Ghent. The ambassadors brought another request to the table: Charles also insisted that Philip return to France the strategic border towns of the Somme Valley.

In need of funds to continue his war on Ghent, the duke suddenly dropped the prohibition on the transportation of English cloth. The ban was quickly removed in Brabant in April, and on June 11, Philip ordered his officials to restore all confiscated English cloths and promised to consult the Dutch Estates on a new ordinance. Later in June, the ban was also dropped in Holland and Zeeland. The greatest hurdle to successful negotiations with the merchants of the Staple now removed, Isabel focused on the imminent English civil conflict and on the French intervention into Burgundian affairs Philip was courting in the ongoing conflict Ghent.

While Isabel's sympathies had always remained with York, the duchess had long hesitated to offer her support openly to the duke. The English government crisis made a formal choice between Lancaster and York too risky during 1453, and the duchess waited through the spring and summer, to place her wager on the winning side. Nonetheless, it was York's diplomatic policy that held out hope for freer trade—and Burgundy's survival. Isabel and York both sought further accommodations of the Staple and the Bullion and Partition Ordinances to facilitate the participation of smaller merchants and to weaken the control of the richer elite over that government. They felt that protected sea lanes for international trade would influence the Hansa to resume their merchant traffic with both England and Burgundy. Thus, as Isabel prepared to travel to Gravelines for the series of spring journées, the economic talks with the English, her resolve to encourage the Yorkist faction finally hardened.

Once more she called Jacotin de Croix to organize her household for a caravan to Gravelines. Her quartermaster had prepared the tents and the lodgings for the earlier conference at which she had presided in 1439 and now he would be asked to prepare her household again for a similar trip. The horses and the overloaded carts found their places in the progress as Isabel entered her own carriage—unmistakenly emblazoned with the ducal insignia—in the line that traveled through the ravaged territory that lay along the North Sea coast, moving carefully to avoid bands of Ghent militia. Badly shaken by a too-close encounter with a group of Flemish soldiers, the duchess arrived at Gravelines with an agenda firmly prepared to support the Yorkist view.

In fact, her intentions were already so clear to France that Charles VII grew fearful that the duchess would encourage Burgundy to sympathize further with the English during the final stages of his conflict with them on the continent. So apprehensive were the French about Isabel's pro-Yorkist sympathies, they abruptly suspended a mission demanding redress of Philip for stolen French merchandise carried by the English into Burgundian territories. Charles was convinced that any such ill-timed reports of French complaints against the English during these Gravelines meetings would turn Isabel solidly against the French and deliver her decisively into the English camp. The duchess was by now a firm Yorkist, wanting not only to protect Burgundy from the animosity of Margaret of Anjou—who now displayed her suspicion of York's loyalty openly—but also to seek an English alliance against French intervention into Burgundy. That summer, in spite of Philip's plan to seal a French alliance through a second marriage for their son, Isabel began her negotiations for a match between Charles and Margaret, a younger daughter of the duke of York.

The year 1453 was decisive for Burgundy as well as for England and France. With the end of the ban on the transport of English cloth through Burgundy, Isabel accomplished the last of the three goals given to her by her husband—the first two having been to produce an heir and to raise funds to keep his army in the field. Philip had not before distinguished himself militarily, but the siege of Ghent gave him a decisive victory, when the city surrendered on July 17, 1453. His victory became a landmark in Burgundian history. Where earlier conflict had played out between one of his territories and another, or between one territory and the merchants of a foreign land, this was the first time that the Burgundians had united with their duke in a single cause—the defeat of the Ghenters and their allies. In that year, the patchwork duchy of scattered lands joined its duke to combat a common enemy.

With his authority more secure than ever, and no suspicion of the new danger posed to Burgundian unity by Charles VII, Philip turned eastward. After the fall of Constantinople to the Turks (only a few weeks before his victory at Gavère, July 17, 1453), Philip offered to join forces with the pope in a crusade to free Catholicism's eastern capital. Philip felt sure that victory on this scale against the Turks would at last bring the award of a crown from the Holy Roman Emperor for the territories he held within Frederick III's empire. Isabel, however, looked to the House of York for the security needed to sustain Burgundy as a significant European power.

Early that same July Henry VI became very ill, and within weeks the English king lost all touch with reality. Queen Margaret tried to keep the insanity of the king hidden from the people, but she succeeded for only three months. When on October 13 a son and heir was born to her and Henry VI, the news of the king's illness had to be discussed openly in the Great Council. The people weighed the alternatives: the forceful and popular duke of York, who made them pause with his brash resort to arms, and the wavering Lancastrians led by the French woman, Margaret of Anjou, whose loyalty to England always seemed compromised by the interests of France.

Although the birth of the heir weakened York's claims to the throne, he was still the logical choice to become protector and defender of the realm and principal councillor of the king. When the duke became the virtual regent of England, he jailed Somerset and replaced him as captain of Calais with the earl of Warwick, and civil war was now inevitable.

Charles VII also tasted victory in the summer of 1453. The city of Chastillons in Gascony fell to the French forces on July 17 and within two months all of that southwestern province—the last English continental possession except for Calais—was in the hands of the French king. With the English cleared from all of France except for that port city, and the need to move into the eastern border area of Burgundy to restore the fabric of his kingdom, Charles was more eager than ever to establish his unchallenged authority as the true king of France. He now looked to Cardinal Guillaume d'Estouteville to complete the investigation begun in 1450 into the procedural legality of Joan of Arc's trial. Although Charles VII waited two more years for the collection of testimony and learned opinion about the case to be brought to Rome, he anticipated that his patience would be rewarded with undisputed power and a great mandate to absorb the rich duchy of Burgundy into France once more.

Chapter Six

The Eclipse of Isabel, 1454–1456

THE RIHOUR PALACE IN LILLE was not Isabel's favorite residence and her mood swung back and forth between angry frustration and reluctant enthusiasm. Closeted in her solar, the large chamber on the uppermost level of the palace that captured every possible ray of the pale northern sun, she thought of Philip's plans for the immediate future. Surrounded by the gay chatter of her ladies-in-waiting, her own foreboding about Philip's blindness to the animosity of Charles VII seemed more hopeless by the contrast.

She found distraction by calling Isabella of Bourbon to her side, reviewing a lesson with her young niece. The girl was the daughter of Agnes, her husband's sister, and the duke of Bourbon, who had sent the child to Isabel's court, where the duchesss was to supervise her education. Isabel enjoyed the company of the shy young woman, but she was also a source of grave concern. Philip was very fond of his French niece, as she was not only pliant to his wishes and rather lovely to have about, but also, in the duke's eyes, ideally suited to become his son's second bride. Isabella was also conveniently within his household, under his immediate control, and could be useful in his alliance with Charles VII. The duchess had other ideas about her son's second bride, however. Isabel wanted a lady who would cement an English alliance, and was proceeding during 1454 with her own negotiations with the duke of York, who had three unmarried daughters.

In Isabel's happier moments she was proud of Philip's ambition to become the most powerful prince in Christendom, if not king of his own imperial territories. After his success in putting down the civil disturbances in Flanders, he was eager to turn his back on domestic issues and to search instead for international recognition. He filled the early winter months of 1454 with six weeks of celebrations for his victory over Ghent, manipulating his loyal knights and noble gentlemen into a fighting force. These men, Philip believed, would save the Church of Rome from further westward encroachment by the Turks, whose march toward Italy had already engulfed Constantinople in May 1453. Isabel welcomed his plans to lead a crusade; her own family had fought the Moslem invaders within their peninsular kingdom, and she dearly hoped that her husband would lead a force into the Holy Land itself. The impulse for Philip to take action became stronger in 1454, when Pope Nicolas V pleaded for help to save the church from imminent Turkish control. At the same time, Emperor Frederick III called for Philip to attend the meeting of the Imperial Diet at Regensberg on April 23, 1454. This general congress of princes of the empire, who were to discuss trade, taxes, military strategy, and the laws of succession, offered Philip a golden opportunity to solicit from an audience of his peers cooperation in mounting his crusade and acknowledgment of the legitimacy of his request for an imperial crown.

The duke's future seemed clear to both husband and wife: Philip had been given not only his holy mission but also a political venue in which to appeal for support to carry through his goals. Isabel, ever the strategist, could not help but appreciate the double value of her husband's ambition, for with the duke on a mission that took him out of Burgundy to Regensburg that spring, and later for several years on crusade, she would have an excellent opportunity to arrange an English marriage for their son.

Conflicts of Purpose, 1454

Isabel's attention was pulled in many directions during 1454, but few of her thoughts centered on Philip's plans to entertain his knights and noble gentlemen in Lille to reward them for their service to him on the field of Gavère the previous July.[1] She was fascinated instead with the news she received from London and wished their court was still at the Princehof in Bruges, where she could receive the dispatches from England more quickly.

Parliament had at last approved the duke of York's future appointment as Regent of England. Only Queen Margaret's insistence that Parliament grant her the regency instead—a demand that was a departure from her customary reluctance to assert herself in the face of strong opposition—changed the quarrel between the dukes of Somerset and York into a dynastic conflict. Each day Isabel waited impatiently for messengers from London to reveal the next step in York's career. Thoroughly convinced at last that Burgundy's interests would be best served were Richard of York to control the English throne, she continued to encourage her son Charles to value this alliance and to consider the charms of York's daughters.

Each day the duchess paced in frustration about the somber rooms of the old palace—a favorite residence of both Philip the Bold and John the Fearless—wrestling with her eagerness to return either to Bruges or to her chateau in Cassel, La Motte-au-Bois. There she could continue her work with the mendicant Franciscans, the Gray Nuns, and the Poor Clares, who concerned themselves with the care of the poor and the sick. One of the greatest lords of their court, Jean de Luxembourg, Bastard of St. Pol, was pledged to provide a building for Isabel's new order of Gray Nuns, and two other great lords, Hughes de Lannoy and Jean de la Clyte, followed his example in their own towns of Lannoy and Comines, completing three new convents for Isabel's order within the first years of its inception. The duchess was filled with enthusiasm about these projects and much preferred busying herself with them to the political complications and irritations of life at her husband's court.

Long before her marriage to Phillip the Good, Isabel had been deeply involved in the reform of religious orders in Portugal, as well as in the establishment of hospitals for pilgrims traveling through her father's kingdom to the shrine of Saint John Compostella, north of Porto along the coast of Callabria. Exercising the right granted her by Pope Eugenius IV in 1442 to appoint up to twelve ecclesiastics to a variety of Burgundian posts and assignments—a reward for Burgundian support for his papacy against Frederick III's call for a new Church Council to arbitrate between the two rival popes—she had played an active role in reviewing and encouraging the reform of the Franciscan order in Burgundy and the Lowlands. The reformed Franciscans provided the chaplains, confessors, and alms collectors for the women's orders with which Isabel was so concerned. In 1454 as in the past, Isabel was prepared to provide those Franciscan monasteries that held to their original code of poverty (the "Observants") with funds for building and repairs; for chalices, chandeliers, cruets for holy oil, and monstrances for their chapels; and for the support of numbers of individual monks and nuns.[2]

Kept from these more compelling tasks at La Motte-au-Bois by social responsibilities to her husband in Lille the winter of 1454, Isabel tried to hide her anger. As she wandered through the gloomy rooms of the Rihour Palace, she would stop to peer out the narrow windows of her private chamber but could see only the play of the pale winter sun on the stained gray stone of the Church of St. Peter and the grim facade of the Countess Hospital. Philip had recently bought a larger tract of land adjoining this property, on which he planned to extend and enlarge the Rihour, adding gardens and a wing to the old palace with larger windows that would allow more light and warmth to flood into the great rooms. Isabel could see that would be years in coming and she longed for the quiet of the forest of Nieppe that surrounded La Motte-au-Bois and the peace she found in her work there.

Isabel had been carefully adding properties to her own private estate since 1435, and by 1453 she was a woman of independent means. She wanted to leave this drafty old castle and surround herself instead with the warmth of her personal household. Now that she had taken over her own finances from the careful scrutiny of Humbert de Plaine, whom she released to serve her son's household, she would have preferred spending time poring over her accounts to fulfilling the social demands of Lille this holiday season. Isabel kept close watch over all the returns due her from her many towns and castellainies (castles and their accompanying village territories) as well as the duties collected on the transportation of goods through her private lands. She had also recently taken over the zinc and lead mines of Calamines in southern Burgundy and she was eager to learn more about the production and shipments of these metals. And she would have been keen to continue her habit of overseeing the selection and cutting of her beautiful oaks in the forest of Nieppe for Philip's ships. But Philip demanded she remain by his side this season.

She reluctantly allowed herself to be swept along by the excitement of her household over the elaborate preparations for the holiday banquets. The anticipation of visitors from all parts of Europe and dressed in all manner of styles, and the opportunities offered at such gatherings for favors to be asked and granted, piqued her political interest no less than it intrigued the young nobles and aristocrats who lived in Isabel's court. She was surrounded and frequently overwhelmed by the excitement of her wards, among whom were not only Isabella of Bourbon but also Elisabeth of Burgundy, the countess of Etampes and her daughter, Catherine and Marie of Guelders, and her own nephew and niece, Jaime and Beatriz de Coimbra, her brother's children.

Philip the Good was a grand showman, and Isabel was well aware that the theatricality of these celebrations was designed to do more than maintain his court's reputation for the splendor of its festivities. Jehan de Lannoy, squire of Boudault, and the chronicler Olivier de la Marche worked closely with Philip that winter to develop a series of three banquets, each more splendid than the one before. The excitement was designed to reach a crescendo with the third feast presented by the duke of Burgundy himself. He planned to so impress them with the power and grandeur of his court that the men would be swept up by their their enthusiasm into a force of Burgundians, Frenchmen, and imperial knights willing to follow him on his great crusade to free the Church of Rome from the Islamic captivity of the Turks.

The feasts began on January 20 when John of Cleves, a nephew of Philip the Good, hosted the first banquet in the series at the palace of Lord Valeran des Aubeaux in Lille. The event set the standard of artistry for the following two feasts, continuing late into the night before the host himself interrupted the celebration to propose an entertaining challenge to be met at Philip's banquet. As midnight approached, John of Cleves presented his family's legend, the story of Lohengrin. A knight wearing the colors of the House of Cleves sailed a beautifully detailed craft that was pulled with a golden chain attached to the golden collar of a silver swan. This Knight of the Swan was to be present at Philip's feast on February 17 and challenge all comers to a sportive joust at a tourney of love planned to precede the duke's banquet. The victor at this tourney would receive a golden swan on a golden chain from the ladies present. The fascinated guests spilled from the great banquet hall well after the midnight hour—usually, such events began in mid-afternoon and ended soon after nightfall—sated by the great assortment of dishes, enchanted by the array of entertainment, excited by the company, and eager for the next banquet in two weeks time.

The second banquet in the series was hosted by John of Burgundy, Philip's cousin, and took place in the great hall of John's castle in Lille. Long narrow tables that lined the hall sparkled with clusters of candles that complemented the low-braced torches along the walls. The tables groaned beneath the array of glazed and gilded whole fish, pastries, fruits, and flowers imported for the banquet. Dozens of dishes were served at each course, the courses punctuated by entertainments only long enough for the guests to loosen their belts and prepare themselves for the next onslaught of delicacies.

As Isabel lifted a golden plum from its web of spun sugar—a great luxury, especially in midwinter—the duchess watched torchbearers accompany the officer of John's court, dressed in his herald's coat, as he slowly entered the hall. Two chamberlains followed him, Robert Miraumont and Gauvain Quicaret, lord of Dreuil. Each was dressed in a long black robe lined in marten fur and each held a wreath of flowers. They in turn were followed by a lovely twelve-year-old girl mounted on a palfrey whose bridle, saddle, and tail were decorated in blue and gold silk, as was the rider. Three men in red and green silk walked beside the palfrey, and the company sang to the duke as they approached his chair. The young girl's braided yellow hair hung on her shoulders and her veil, shimmering with jewels, covered the face of this "Princess of Joy" until she dismounted. She bowed low, stepped up and onto the table before the duke, and knelt and kissed the chapelet of flowers given her before placing it onto the duke's head. Delighted to have been chosen to host the third banquet in such a charming manner, the duke rose and kissed the girl, signifying his acceptance of the honor. The music then resumed and the rider remounted her palfrey as the torch-lit procession left the hall.

Isabel was as impressed with the pageantry as were the other guests, and in spite of herself she looked forward to February 17, when Lannoy, Boudault, and La Marche would reveal their plans for the duke's banquet—plans that, unusually, had been kept a secret even from her. Her curiosity was heightened when she discovered that a ceremony would be staged at the conclusion of the banquet and before the festive dancing began.

Anticipation was great during the early evening hours of February 17, as Philip's guests assembled in the grand banquet chamber, which contained a window forty-six feet wide and walls covered with tapestries detailing the feats of great Burgundian heroes. Three large tables were draped with cloths of silk damask that swept to the floor. Philip's seat was at the cross table, covered with a golden canopy and trimmings marked by crests and devices. A cushion of matching fabric plumped his chair. Opposite the main table, the sculpture of a woman leaning against a column seemed almost alive in the flicker of the torchlight. A veil wrapped her hips and a hat made of precious gems arranged to resemble flowers capped her hair, which fell to her feet. Spiced wine flowed from her right breast, while a live lion, chained on a lower pedestal to guard her, paced back and forth over a blue banner lettered in gold that warned, "Do not touch my mistress." The mistress was identified as Constantinople and the lion as the lion of Flanders and the protector of Constantinople.

When the trumpets sounded the beginning of the feast, carriages and litters covered with gold and blue fabric with the Burgundian arms were lowered from the roof of the hall with the food; the company prepared for a series of courses, each of which contained twenty-eight dishes. The crowd was so great in the banqueting hall that both sides of the tables were used for seating, and movement between them was almost impossible. Many notable guests—including those who had come from across the sea and who had not been invited to the feast itself—were seated in a gallery where they sat masked, watching the event as the theater it actually was intended to be. As the banquet proceeded, music provided by twenty-eight musicians seated within a giant pie introduced each of the eight exotic interludes of entertainment. The comment made by one of the performers, "I have never seen the like,"[3] could well have been echoed by all who attended the feast.

At the conclusion of the feast the real purpose of the evening entertainment was portrayed in an elaborate ceremony. A great giant entered the hall representing the Saracen forces in the east. He carried a battle-ax in his left hand and with his right led an elephant, which represented distant lands. The tower on the back of the beast held a woman in white satin covered by a long black robe, representing the Holy Church. She approached the duke and begged for help from the "Great Duke of the West." Jean Lefevre, the king-at-arms of the Order of the Golden Fleece, entered next, carrying in his hands a live pheasant that wore a golden collar. Accompanied by two noble ladies, Iolanthe, a natural daughter of Philip, and Isabel de Neufchâtel, Lefevre addressed the duke, "Since it is and was ever customary to present a peacock or other noble bird at great feasts before the illustrious princes, lords and nobles, to the end they might swear expedient and binding oaths, now I, with these two ladies, am here to offer to you this noble pheasant; may its memory be preserved!" The duke rose, handed Lefevre a parchment, and while looking sorrowfully at the lady representing the church, he placed his hand on his breast and vowed, "I swear before God my creator, the glorious Virgin Mary, the ladies and the Pheasant, that I will do and perform diligently what I have set down in this writing."[4] The hall was silent as Lefevre read Philip's oath "to take the Cross"—to don the crusader's uniform of a red cross worn over a white jacket—if his master the king of France did the same. (In fact, Philip expected only verbal support from Charles VII, and the duke anticipated marching eastward without the personal participation of the king.) The "Church" returned thanks to the duke, invited all those knights present to follow his example, and then left the hall.

So many knights pledged to join Philip, and their oaths were so tediously long, that the duke commanded them to give their oaths in writing to Lefevre the following day.[5] Just as the company believed the evening's event over, however, the great doors of the hall swung open and torchbearers entered with musicians who played tambourines, harps, and lutes for the ball, which lasted until three o'clock the next morning.

Flushed with the success of his strategy, Philip immediately turned his attention to the logistics of his crusade. He would need a great deal of money to fund the movement of these forces. The men who pledged to lead their soldiers from all regions of Burgundy would travel to a single meeting point in the empire, and after assembling there, the crusaders would take at least six weeks to reach Belgrade, close to the enemy. Philip needed the help of the emperor and Pope Nicholas V to help him manage the complex negotiations required to carry the forces across such a great number of territorial boundaries.

There were other concerns as well. Philip intended to settle the terms of his son's betrothal to Isabella of Bourbon as quickly as possible to secure Charles's position and authority within Burgundy before his own two-year absence in the east. Once he had established a closer relationship with the French king through this Bourbon marriage, Philip hoped for Charles VII's permission to recruit men in France and to carry the king's banner into the Holy Land. Philip had already obtained a release from the pope to allow the union between the first cousins. The duke of Bourbon and his wife, Philip's sister Agnes, were initially pleased with the idea of such a match for their daughter.

With these preliminary negotiations for his son's marriage progressing successfully in early March, the duke took the first concrete steps toward raising the necessary funds for the movement of Burgundian crusaders eastward. In the midst of these efforts, the summons from Frederick III to attend the April 23 meeting of the imperial Diet at Regensburg arrived.

As Philip prepared to depart for Regensburg that March, he issued a number of proclamations that abruptly changed the atmosphere of his court from one of luxurious extravagance to one of fiscal prudence, even austerity. While setting aside ample money to guarantee the opulence of his own trip to Regensburg—sufficient to impress the German princes, and the emperor himself, with Burgundian power and prestige—he began to accumulate funds to support his expedition to evict the Turks from

Constantinople. He so severely curtailed many of the ordinary expenses of his household that his chronicler Olivier de La Marche complained that Philip had "broken the leg of the court."[6] The elaborate meals provided for his followers, the games, jousts, and concerts, and even the pensions paid to court officials were eliminated or drastically reduced.

By mid-March, the duke was well satisfied with the progress of his plans to raise money for his crusade, marry his son to a Bourbon princess, and journey through Germany toward the Regensburg Diet. His contentment did not last long, however, as he soon learned of gossip spreading through his court concerning the second marriage of his son. That the duchess Isabel was determined to find an English bride for her son, and that Charles was in agreement with his mother's choice in spite of his father's negotiations for a French bride, was a rumor shared discreetly but increasingly among Philip's courtiers. Learning of the rumor—very likely directly or indirectly from the de Croy brothers, who had their own excellent reasons to acquaint the duke with his wife's and son's scheming—that his son was being encouraged to resist his choice by one of the duke's own bastards, he summoned both young men to him. Philip insisted that although he had once sided with the enemies of France, "he had never been English at heart." He then commanded Charles to accept his decision of a French bride in spite of his mother's difference of opinion or suffer disinheritance. "As for this bastard," turning to his other son, "if I find that he counsels you to oppose my will, I will have him tied up in a sack and thrown into the sea."[7]

The duke was deeply concerned that Isabel's influence would weigh against his wishes as soon as he left for Regensburg, and he rushed the settlement of the betrothal without obtaining royal or even parental approval. Then on March 24 Philip left Lille in the hours before dawn, slipping quietly from court with thirty companions for the ride to Regensburg.

The Trip to Regensburg and the Surprise Marriage

After several days in the saddle, staying in a variety of inns where he gave the proprietors enough money to post his ducal arms over their doors, the aging duke and his party reached Ulm in Swabia. Count Ulrich of Wurttemberg greeted him warmly, and after Philip had rested for a few days, accompanied the duke to the next town, Gundzberg. The duke of Austria was eager to host the "Great Duke of the West" and he prepared an elaborate welcome. They spent several days in close discussion and elegant entertainments before Philip departed and rode for Lauingen. Three weeks of travel began to take a toll on Philip's health. He had enjoyed the comforts of splendid residences only occasionally; most of the time he had lodged at inns and eaten robust but unfamiliar dishes, and his strength had suffered. In Lauingen, Duke Louis of Bavaria and the cardinal of Augsburg not only welcomed and cared for Philip during several days of cold and fever but also saw to all of his other needs, as well as those of his company. Then, proud to be in the company of Philip the Good, the duke of Bavaria accompanied Philip into Regensburg on April 23.

The great German princes filled the town with their retinues and their self-importance. The duke of Bavaria remained close by Philip, who was still weak from travel and illness, and continued to see to his lodging and his needs for the full week of the meeting. Philip was deeply distressed to find that the emperor was absent from the diet, unable to preside over the meeting because of turmoil along his southern border in Hungary. Philip's main goal for the trip—one of only three trips he made outside his own territories—had become impossible to accomplish. Bitterly disappointed, the duke realized that the hoped-for crown had slipped further from his grasp than it had in 1442, when he and the newly crowned Frederick III had discussed such a possibility at Besançon.

As April drew to a close and the princes prepared to leave Regensburg, the duke of Bavaria persuaded the discouraged Philip to return with him through the German town of Landshut. The duchess of Bavaria and her ladies waited for him there in the company of the margrave of Brandenburg to cheer him before his return to Burgundy. Hoping to rest and regain his strength for the ride back to Burgundy, Philip remained in Landshut for ten days. Unfortunately, the company and the entertainment provided for him during his stay were interrupted by several days of illness, when the continued stress and unfamiliar diet struck him down again, this time with intestinal disorder.

Philip returned to his southern territories in early May and established himself at the salt-producing town of Salins, in the County of Burgundy. He had failed in his main goal of meeting personally with the emperor, but he had met the great and most important princes of the empire. He had established good relationships with them and in many cases laid the foundations of future alliances. He congratulated himself that his trip had enhanced the prestige of Burgundy in the strategic territories of Swabia and Bavaria. Almost as good as a crown, these friendships were essential to the success of his planned crusade and the future defense of his borders.

As Philip made his way back to his duchy, Isabel returned to Rihour Palace from La Motte-au-Bois. She was preoccupied with trade negotiations with England, and she wanted to settle matters before Philip traveled to his northern territories. Her representatives had been meeting with the English at Calais since January. They had made very little progress concerning the issue of seized goods, and in particular the return of Burgundian goods seized outside the port of La Rochelle by the English in 1453. Eager to reach a settlement, Isabel had agreed to return English goods seized by the duke in exchange. Isabel wrote letters to her son at Termonde, explaining the conflict and the status of the negotiations with the English. Then, as Philip settled his court into Salins in early May, Charles joined his mother in Lille to balance the possibility of a future conflict with England against the remaining possibility of an alliance with them—and a hoped-for peace—through an English marriage.

Philip did not remain at his court in Salins for very long before he rode to Nevers to meet with the duke and duchess of Orléans, his sister Agnes, duchess of Bourbon, and Pierre d'Amboise, representative of the duke of Bourbon, who was incapacitated with gout. Determined to finalize the betrothal by securing both royal and parental approval for the match of his son and Isabella of Bourbon, Philip immediately embarked on what would prove to be many weeks of negotiations. His demands for the lands and seigneury of the Chinon territory to be written into the marriage contract, which had been acceptable to the duke of Bourbon before

Philip's trip to Regensburg, were now rejected. The duke of Bourbon now referred to the authority of the king's decision that the duke's promise to give the lands and seigneury of Chinon to his own son, the future duke of Bourbon, took precedence over Philip's demands. On this issue Philip brooked no resistance, however, and spent many hours in tense discussions with Pierre d'Amboise. He also met for six emotionally draining hours with his sister Agnes, whose tears and pleading could not break the deadlock between her brother, her husband, and her king. Agnes was terrified that the issue would precipitate a war between them all instead of the alliance for which they hoped. Philip continued to meet with them through June and July, but to no avail. Irritated but determined to win, he left Nevers in early August for the town of Dijon to wait there until his demands were met. In an attempt to soften the disagreement between them, Agnes wrote to Philip that "I consider the thing as done, [and] I beg you to celebrate the nuptials as soon as possible, although not without me as you have promised me."[8] But Philip waited for word from the duke a while longer, and during that time he called meetings of the Three Estates of Dijon and those estates of the County of Burgundy to request financial support for his crusade. They quickly awarded their duke 60,000 livres.

Philip remained in Dijon through August and September. Meanwhile, Isabel struggled in the north with increasing Anglo-Burgundian tensions. The Calais talks threatened to break down. More and more Burgundian ships were taken by the English on a regular basis. Charles and his mother wrote letters on August 9 and 26 to Duke Philip in Dijon, warning of a probable English attack from Calais. On September 5, and then again on September 27, they asked for his directions.

By October, with the Bourbon marriage still unresolved, Charles VII grew fearful that the pro-English sentiments of the duchess of Burgundy for an English union would prevail. He was aware of Isabel's efforts during that spring and summer to negotiate for an English marriage, and although he could not accede to Philip's request to incorporate the Chinon seigneury in the marriage contract, Charles VII wrote to Philip that he was sending his bailiff of Berry to explain all the details of the dowry in full. "So pray do not postpone the marriage . . . for any cause, if by the permission of the Church and or our Holy father [for the union of first cousins] it can be lawfully completed."[9] Philip was as determined to obtain the Chinon territory as the king's bailiff was eager to experience the opulence of the Burgundian court, of which he had heard so much. Philip was in no hurry to meet with the king's messenger to discuss the details of the dowry, but he was happy to furnish the bailiff with a wealth of entertaining distractions. While he waited for an audience with the duke, the days continued to slip by. Even before the bailiff's arrival, however, the duke had sent Philippe Pot to his son Charles, carrying his orders to celebrate the marriage without delay—a marriage on the terms of the accord signed by the duke of Bourbon the previous April, which included the Chinon territories in his daughter's dowry. Philip detained the king's messenger until he had received word from Philippe Pot that the nuptials had been completed. In fact, Charles was not even aware of his father's plans and Philippe Pot's mission until the night before the ceremony, which took place October 31.

Once assured that the marriage was official, Philip invited the king's messenger to an audience and quite casually remarked that the king "had sent you hither about a matter which I am humbly grateful for his interest. . . . You know my opinion. I had no desire to dissemble. Here is a gentleman fresh from Flanders; ask him his news and note his reply." Philippe Pot laughingly responded, "By my faith, Monsieur bailiff, the greatest news that I know is that Monseigneur de Charolais [Charles] is married!" Taken aback, the bailiff stuttered, "Married! To whom?" Pleased with himself, Philippe Pot answered "To whom? Why, to his first cousin, Monseigneur's niece." Reassured of the truth of the statement, the baliff, who was after all a man of the world, recovered his aplomb and joined in the general laughter over the smooth success of Philip's sly move.[10] The delighted French bailiff left the court a few days later, highly pleased with the expensive gift of twelve silver stirrup cups.

Beside herself with frustration, Isabel found the marriage very difficult to accept and showed her resistance to poor Isabella of Bourbon by withholding the customary ceremony due the bride. This was an extraordinary lapse in court etiquette for Isabel and one that measures the distress the duchess felt at having her English liaison thwarted. Within the first week of the October 30 marriage, however, the duchess did organize a formal celebratory banquet, but all the ladies of Lille were seated together and the duchess and her new daughter-in-law were not placed in state above the rest, as the occasion demanded. Charles quietly accepted his fate, however, and leaving his bride with his mother, returned to Termonde in the Lowlands to resume his new responsibility as acting governor. The bride had already written to her parents to notify them of the marriage and no further objections were raised by them to give Chinon to Philip as he had demanded. Philip was pleased with his strategy, assuming that with this Bourbon marriage he had now repaired the French alliance of Arras, made in 1435, which had since become so tattered by military, economic, and judicial threats from Charles VII. Isabel, however, feared for the future of the duchy. Soon after, on December 8, Isabel and her daughter-in-law left Lille for Bruges.

The self-satisfied Philip faced more obstacles to his crusade, however, than those he had surmounted in securing a French bride for his son. Although the November diet in Frankfurt that same year briefly considered the issue, no solid steps were taken to organize a force against the Turks. Meanwhile, the French king declined to give any support for Philip's goals. In fact, Charles VII moved on several fronts to increase his control of the kingdom. He continued to threaten the duke's eastern borders, increased his challenge to Philip the Good's authority in Lorraine and his other neighboring imperial territories, and resolutely refused Philip the use of any French troops for the crusade.

France in Renewal—Isabel in Retreat

As the French king continued to harass Burgundy and its duke, the influence of the de Croy family at Philip's court increased. As the de Croys—Anthony, lord of Croy, his brother Jehan, lord of Chimay, and their sons Philippe, lord of Renty, and Philippe, lord of Sempy—added to their family's prestige through brilliant marriages and gifts of money and land, the duchess Isabel and her son were increasingly excluded from power and eventually from Philip's court itself. As Philip's first chamberlain and governor of Luxembourg, Anthony had greater influence at court than the chancellor, Nicolas Rolin. Anthony had acquired an even greater fortune than had Rolin, who had served the duke for over thirty years. Anthony's fortune was greatly enhanced—as was that of his brother Jehan's, the bailiff and captain general of Hainault—by gifts from the French king to recruit his persuasive powers in the renewed alliance with France. As great a lord of Picardy as Anthony, Jehan fielded an army that moved independently of Duke Philip's commands, showed no hesitation in refusing orders from the Paris Parlement—claiming immunity from its jurisdiction because Hainault was part of the empire—and successfully refuted the pope's attempts to excommunicate him in 1455. With this combination of influence and independence, Anthony and Jehan were in a position to block any pro-English strategy proposed by Isabel.

The de Croy faction succeeded in maintaining Philip's loyalty to France, even though Charles VII took no action on twenty-six articles of complaint involving French enclaves in Burgundian territory. The French king promised only to review these grievances. He limited Philip's rights in the sale and distribution of salt and ignored most of the duke's rights of jurisdiction within the Paris Parlement. Isabel's warnings of the dangers of his French strategy were ignored by the duke, but not by the de Croy family, who regarded the duchess as a growing threat to the alliance they had helped build with France at Arras in 1435.

Isabel's policies were decisively checked by the success of the French marriage and the influence of the de Croy family. The powerful brothers ruled their territories as if they were independent monarchs, and their sons were poised to inherit their fathers' positions and influence. They and the court faction that gathered around them had territorial interests in France as well as Burgundy, and they shaped Burgundian policy for their own benefit. As the year progressed and the distracted duke became more deeply involved in his failing efforts to launch a crusade and to acquire a crown for his imperial holdings, the de Croy family increased its involvement with France, hoping to benefit from its service to the king after a French victory over Burgundy.[11]

Philip bowed to the determined influence of the de Croy family during the winter of 1455–56, and his distrust of Isabel increased. The aging duke was kept isolated from Isabel, and without her by his side he was easily distracted from the significant events on his borders and at sea. He ignored the French pirates who cruised in the port of Sluis and captured English ships during the summer of 1456. He even forgave them for capturing a Burgundian vessel by mistake. In fact, the Burgundians now frequently disregarded the commercial truce Isabel had established with England and stopped the Staple merchant caravans when they passed through Burgundian land. One may suspect that with the counseling of the de Croys, the duke refused to send Isabel to smooth over the these insults—for with her probable diplomatic success would have come renewed influence with the duke—sending instead his emissary, Toison d'Or, to straighten out affairs.

In spite of the obstacles placed before her by the de Croys, Isabel persisted in her efforts to save Burgundy from the disintegration posed by Philip's present policy. The duchess understood the logic of the French king's efforts to regain the strategically valuable Somme towns he had given to Philip, and her fears mounted with each new dispatch bearing news of another French military challenge along Philip's western borders. Powerless, she understood that her only option was to keep communication open with the English ruling faction while she lived in the safe retreat of her territory of Cassel at La Motte-au-Bois.

Meanwhile, the more secure Charles VII of that period was determined to remove all doubt on his legitimacy as sovereign. Only the rehabilitation of the reputation of Joan of Arc would unequivocally confirm the divine sanction of his kingship, and he therefore was eager to bring the reexamination of Joan's trial to a speedy conclusion. Pope Calixtus III had prepared the way for this reassessment by issuing his permission to reopen the suit four months earlier, on June 11, 1455. Charles VII had championed the supreme authority of the Roman papacy against the efforts of the great Church Councils (the first of which was held in Pisa in 1409) to establish a jurisdiction superior to that of the pope. Now the Borgia pope would support the French king in turn. The king provided the setting for Jean Brehal, the General Inquisitor of France, to assure Joan's family that the church was prepared, as were the people of France, to use every means possible to give

Joan of Arc the justice denied her at her trial. As Isabel prepared for her retreat from court to La Motte-au-Bois that autumn, and Philip gathered the de Croy family ever closer into his confidence, Frenchmen crowded into Paris to hear that the way to Joan's vindication was now clear.

Joan's mother, Isabel Romée, came to Paris with her two sons, Pierre and Jean, to bring word of the pope's decision to review her daughter's trial. Those who gathered at the Cathedral of Notre Dame on the morning of November 7 soon forgot the cold fog that seeped into that great vault of ancient stone on the edge of the Seine. Many came from Orléans, where some of them had been when Joan had lifted the siege of their town. Others in the cathedral had been at Reims when Joan led the dauphin to his coronation and anointing as King Charles VII. Some of them had watched her burn at the stake in the marketplace of Rouen. Everyone watched as Isabel Romée approached the papal commissioners, who were seated before the high altar. The cathedral became silent as she unwrapped the pope's orders, which she knew would reopen the affair of her daughter's trial and execution.

Even before the pope's orders could be read aloud, the spectators who crowded the nave broke into a noisy and passionate demonstration in support of Joan's retrial, forcing the prelates to usher Isabel and her sons into the safety of the sacristy. They assured her that the long-sought retrial of her daughter would begin in Rouen in ten days, on November 17. No one asked why the church was prepared in 1455 to reexamine the verdict of the French Inquisition of a quarter of a century before.

Duke Philip, Joan's captor, still supposed himself powerful enough to threaten any decision of the church to which he was not a party, and unlike Isabel, he discounted the possibility that a retrial would bolster the French king's power and appetite for his duchy as easily as he did any danger from a possible Angevin alliance against him by Charles VII and the English queen. Philip remained unruffled, then, as the official review of Joan's earlier condemnation began and Margaret of Anjou and her husband, Henry VI, struggled to regain control of their government—which reeled in anarchy from the king's periods of insanity—while Isabel maintained constant contact with the York faction.

Out of favor with her husband because of the animosity between herself and the de Croys, Isabel frequently returned to Philip's side, still hoping to convince the aging duke of the dangers that surrounded him. The duchess also wanted to free her son Charles from the control of the de Croys so that he might offer Philip reasons to fear the French purpose and come to appreciate the advantages of English aid. Unfortunately, although Charles approved of his mother's policies, he was often too brash in proclaiming his differences with his father, and arguments between them increased during the autumn and winter of 1455–56. As the enmity between the de Croy family and Isabel and her son mounted, the duke's pro-French interests became more entrenched and English concerns faded from his policies. In the midst of this crisis, Isabel delayed but did not relinquish her plans to save Burgundy from both absorption by a revitalized France and from the challenge to its economic life from an Angevin England.

Notes

1. All material detailing the three feasts taken from Otto Cartellieri's *Court of Burgundy* (New York and London: Alfred A. Knopf, 1929), 140–53; Ruth Putnam, *Charles the Bold: Last Duke of Burgundy, 1446–1503* (New York and London: G. P. Putnam's Sons, 1908), 45–56; and Richard Vaughan, *Philip the Good: The Apogee of Burgndy* (New York: Barnes and Noble, 1970), 143–45.
2. The material pertaining to Isabel's religious functions is from LeMaîre's *Isabelle de Portugal: duchess of Bourgogne, 1397-1471* (Brussels: Biblioteque Royale Albert Ier, 1991), 69–80.
3. Cartellieri, *Court of Burgundy*, 139.
4. Cartellieri, *Court of Burgundy*, 148.
5. Vaughan, *Philip the Good*, 297–99:

   > Many of the knights and gentlemen had too much wine and their oaths were no doubt inspired by the high spirits of the celebration. Some promised not to sleep on certain days until having engaged in single combat with a Saracen. Others swore not to touch another drop of wine until they had drawn Saracen blood. When Philippe Pot swore not to wear armor on his right arm until having met in battle with the enemy, the duke protested that "it was not his wish that Sir Philippe Pot accompany him on crusade with his arm unprotected!"

6. Olivier de La Marche, *Mémoires*, ed. Beaune et d'Arbaumont, 3 vols. (Paris, 1883–84), 1:14.
7. Vaughan, *Philip the Good*, 266–67.
8. Jacques DuClercq, *Mémoires*, ed. Baron F. de Reiffenberg, 4 vols. (Brussels, 1823), 2:203.
9. *Oeuvres de Chastellain*, ed. M. Le Baron Kervyn de Lettenhove, 4 vols. (Brussels: R. Heussner, 1864), 3:20; and Vaughan, *Philip the Good*, 342 n. 1, which cites the Archives du Nord, B104, folio 39b, for letters to York during the summer and early autumn of 1454.
10. G. du Fresne de Beaucourt, *Histoire de Charles VII,* 6 vols. (Paris: Libraire de la Socitété Bibliographique, 1881–91), 5:470.
11. Vaughan, *Philip the Good*, 337 n.1; and Paul Murray Kendall, *Louis XI* (New York: W. W. Norton, 1971), 95 and 101–2.

Chapter Seven

Retreat, Reconciliation, and Renewed Challenge, 1457–1460

THROUGH EARLY 1457 Isabel continued to divide her time between her residence at La Motte-au-Bois, where she could enjoy a respite from her conflict with the de Croy family and from her dangerously strained relationship with her husband, and the ducal court, which since the previous October had been host to an important, if unexpected, guest. On October 8, 1456, none other than the dauphin Louis had arrived in Burgundy, fleeing from his father's animosity.

While at his father's court, Louis had sought acknowledgment of his authority as heir to the French crown, but King Charles had denied him that recognition at every turn. Unable to find a mission commensurate with his ambition, Louis had spent his time plotting palace upheavals, negotiating secret pacts with Italian princes, and stirring bitter factional struggles among the powerful lords who surrounded his father. In 1445 Louis had failed in a key negotiation at Chalons, where he had been charged with persuading Isabel to forgo the ransom that was owed to Burgundy by René of Anjou—a release obtained a few days later by Charles VII himself. This only confirmed the French king's resolve to limit the dauphin's independence and responsibility. Louis responded by baiting his father with devious ploys to acquire power—for instance, Louis tried to cajole his father's subjects in Armagnac to switch their loyalties to him instead of the king. If the king grew weary of these provocations, the dauphin might be banished from court for once and all. Banishment, in Louis's eyes, would be a blessing, for it would give him the freedom to forge his own path to kingship in territories distant from his father's immediate control. His relationship with his father worsened when Louis's resentment of the beautiful Agnes Sorel, the king's mistress, flared into ungovernable hatred over the pain Agnes had inflicted on his mother the queen, Marie of Anjou. In 1446, Louis ended an argument with Agnes by drawing his sword and chasing her into his father's bed, where she sought the king's protection. Even then, Charles hesitated to send Louis away, fearful of unleashing the dauphin to pursue ambitions that were almost certain to destabilize the kingdom. But by the end of 1446, Louis's troublesome meddling in both domestic and foreign affairs, combined with the birth of the king's new son, Charles, on December 28, convinced the king that the time had come to send the dauphin, now twenty-three, on a distant mission.

Louis had already been dispatched on a number of missions that Charles had found expedient—prolonged and difficult military ventures that demonstrated Louis's prowess but that failed to win him the laurels worthy of a king's heir. He had served in a campaign against the English in Normandy, and then rode south to bring order to Gascony and to regain Guienne from the English forces there. When tens of thousands of *écorcheurs,* left unemployed in the closing months of the Hundred Years War with England, threatened to ravage France in 1444, Louis had successfully gathered them into an army and led them eastward to help the German princes against the Swiss forces who refused to submit to imperial domination. On January 1, 1447, Louis led that army toward the province of Dauphiny, where his father had commanded him to establish order in this mostly lawless and abandoned territory. But suspicious of his son's methods and ultimate goals, Charles did not want Louis out of his sight for any length of time and gave him only four months to complete this charge. Now determined to prove himself an effective ruler, Louis planned to disregard the time limit and to make Dauphiny a showcase of his own successful administration.

The little province southeast of France was covered in forests and riven with valleys; to the north its high alpine slopes bordered the duchy and county of Burgundy, to the south Dauphiny bordered Savoy, in northern Italy. The territory was a gift of the Holy Roman Empire to the heir to the French throne—although by the terms of the gift the territory was never to be incorporated into France. The dauphin had taken charge of this isolated, neglected patchwork of feudal despotisms and had brought order out of chaos. In Dauphiny, Louis had found the power and authority for which he had longed and he was determined not to resubmit himself to his father's control.

In 1451, Louis provoked his father's fury yet again by marrying Charlotte, the daughter of Dauphiny's ally, the duke of Savoy, in opposition to the French king's command. The next year, Charles took his revenge on his willful son by depriving him of his annual allowance and revoking all the lands in France that he had been given. In 1453, Charles decided to end the dispute with his son once and for all and demanded that Louis return to the French court. Although a number of envoys reached Louis during the next two years with the king's order, Louis defied it, repeating each time that he wished "only to obey his father, but would not return to the French court and would surrender none of his followers."[1] In 1455, Charles forced the Italian princes to abrogate their alliances with Louis and then led French forces to within one hundred miles of Dauphiny's borders. With the king poised to enter the province and preempt the dauphin's hard-won stewardship, Louis saw that his only option was to flee. In the early hours of August 30, 1456, he left on horseback with a small group of loyal followers and made toward Burgundy, seeking the protection of his wealthy and powerful uncle, Duke Philip.

Rather than admit to the real reason for his flight, Louis dispatched a circular notifying the clergy that he had intended to join the crusade the duke had announced at the 1454 Feast of the Pheasant. In Louvain, ten miles northeast of Brussels, Louis waited there for the duke's permission to continue further into the heart of Burgundy. Isabel and her daughter-in-law, the countess of Charolais, greeted Louis in Brussels at eight o'clock on an early October evening, after Philip granted Louis's request for refuge, but not before the duke explained to the French king that he had no earlier knowledge of the dauphin's flight. The duchess, accustomed to the intricacies of Burgundian court etiquette, was taken aback by the dauphin's lack of formality. Louis, indeed, made Isabel uncomfortable for several reasons: the history of his stubborn resistance to his father's commands and the example this filial disloyalty might inspire in her own headstrong son; his disarming directness, which the duchess could not quite trust; the rumors of his political guile and the possibility that he might ally with one or another of the factions at the Burgundian court; and the likelihood that he would claim much of the duke's attention, leaving even less for his wife. The wary Isabel promised herself to watch Louis carefully, to treat him with the utmost respect as her future sovereign, and to reveal nothing of her own views.

This promise, however, went the way of many good intentions when, on January 17, 1457, the duchess ran into Louis's chamber in terror. The duke, unable to control his rage at his son's refusal to accept Philip's choice of a de Croy relative to become chamberlain of Charles's household, threatened his son with a drawn dagger. In fear for their lives, Isabel thrust Charles from the chapel vestibule where the duke had confronted them and fled with her son to the chambers of the dauphin on the floor above.

The dauphin did his best at the time to calm them and to appeal to the duke's good sense regarding the loyalty of his wife and son. But Philip, in his agitation, would hear nothing of Louis's pleas and instead, suspecting that the dauphin too was his enemy, dismissed the future Louis XI of France from his presence.

As Duke Philip grew older he had become more reliant on the members of the powerful family from the province of Picardy, the de Croys. Philip's father, John the Fearless, had looked with favor on Jehan de Croy, not least because Jehan's sister Agnes had been John's mistress. Philip had grown to manhood in the company of Jehan's sons, Anthony and Jehan, and he trusted them completely and favored them greatly. But this favoritism inspired fierce jealousies among other courtiers and had given rise to bitter factional struggles in the Burgundian court. On the afternoon of January 17, Louis had seen for himself the effects of the powerful hold that the de Croys exerted over Philip, blinding him to views other than their own. For the remainder of his stay in Burgundy, Louis, always conscious of his precarious position, decided he would do well to solicit the friendship of Anthony and Jehanne de Croy and their sons.

Isabel in Retreat

The duchess Isabel remained in Brussels for a short time after the crisis in the chapel, hoping to calm Philip and retain her influence over his economic policy with England. Swayed by the de Croys, however, the duke remained convinced that Isabel was the cause of his difficult relationship with his son and was no longer concerned for her husband's best interests, which Philip was sure lay in a closer relationship with France. The duchess, who had relinquished her large number of servants to the households of her son and daughter-in-law the year before, now seriously considered moving permanently to La Motte-au-Bois later that year.

In the midst of this tension at the court, the duchess Isabel's daughter-in-law, Isabella of Bourbon, gave birth to her first child. On February 13, the day was clear but the winter sun was unwelcome in the birthing chamber of the young countess of Charolais. The mother-to-be lay on a bed under a canopy of green silk damask that matched the material lining the walls. The windows were tightly sealed and would not be reopened for fifteen days. Her husband, Charles, had left to go hunting in the nearby woods of Nivelles as soon as the labor began. Her father-in-law ignored the entire event, asking not to be disturbed unless the newborn turned out to be a boy. As Isabelle went into hard labor later that afternoon, about to produce an heir for Burgundy, she had only her mother-in-law by her side and the dauphin of France outside her door.

According to the official court chronicler, Georges Chastellain—whose imagination was perhaps excited by the thought of the arrival of a Burgundian heir—just before the child entered the world at twilight, a great clap of thunder shook the otherwise clear skies over the castle "and was so violent, that everyone believed the whole village must have been hit and set on fire."[2] After this thunderous prelude, Isabelle of Bourbon gave birth to a girl. The delighted duchess carried the infant to the waiting dauphin, who asked that she be named Marie in honor of his own mother, Marie of Anjou, aunt of the queen of England.

The baptism took place within days of the birth. The duchess led the procession down the aisle of the Coudenberg chapel; as godfather, the dauphin followed Isabel and carried the child to the baptismal font, which was covered in green silk tapestries, as were the walls of the church. The rest of the company followed the dauphin down the aisle in order of their rank. The noblest of the court carried large white candles; notable figures from the village carried smaller ones. "Duke Philip," notes Chastellain, "chose not to attend the ceremony as it was only for a girl."[3]

Despite the ugly scene that had been played out in January, when Louis tried to intervene between the duke and the duchess, by the time of Marie's birth the dauphin was once again in Philip's good graces. In the spring, when the royal entourage could travel more comfortably, Louis's household was transported to the lovely castle of Genappe on the outskirts of Brussels, which Philip now provided for Louis's use, together with an annual allowance of 38,000 livres. Acutely conscious of his ambiguous position in Burgundy and of his dependence on the duke's favor, Louis ordered that his own followers behave with the utmost circumspection and propriety. As Louis was adamant that he would never return to France as dauphin—only as king—he was determined to please his uncle Philip in every way possible to guarantee his own security in Burgundy. Louis realized he had to allay suspicions about his own past and the circumstances of his abrupt arrival. He also had to make himself welcome among the quarrelsome factions surrounding Duke Philip. He strove to distance himself from the court as much as possible, seeking to earn a measure of Isabel's confidence without antagonizing the de Croys. He took particular care as well to court Charles, flattering the heir of Burgundy and thereby eliminating any doubts Charles harbored of the role Louis sought to play with his father, the duke. The wily Louis simultaneously flattered the powerful de Croys with his attentions, ingratiated himself with his uncle by accommodating the duke's every wish, and developed a friendship with Philip's son Charles.

A foil for the richly dressed and headstrong young Charles in both attire and temperament, the dauphin Louis was almost scandalously clad in simple gray clothes and a broad-brimmed hat with cheap, lead images of the Virgin Mary and saints tucked into its brim, a costume that he wore most of his life. There were ten years between them, but their common love of hunting created a strong bond and they spent considerable time in each other's company. There were many hours when the future king of France, dressed in a short, serviceable hunting jacket and country boots, rode beside the elaborately attired Charles, studying the personality and character of the heir to Burgundy.

While deferring to Louis in all Burgundian ceremony and delighted with his royal guest's willingness to respect the customs of the ducal court, Philip planned to impress the dauphin further with his power and prestige. The proud duke took Louis on a tour of his most prosperous territories, leaving Brussels with the dauphin on April 4 for a six-week progress through Burgundy's major industrial areas. When King Charles learned of his son's travels with Philip, he warned the duke, "You do not know the nature of the beast. You feed the wolf that will eat your lambs!"[4] But Philip refused to believe that Louis could harbor any other feelings for him than gratitude for the protection he provided, and he was cultivating the dauphin's growing respect for Burgundian power.

The duke was flattered when the rich town of Bruges impressed the dauphin—though Philip was horrified when Louis, fascinated with the waterways of the town, fell into one of the canals and nearly drowned. As Louis studied the populations, industries, and defenses of the cities of Ghent, Ypres, Boulogne, St. Omer, Aire, and Sluis, and courted the friendship of their leading citizens, Philip saw no reason to suspect Louis's motives. The duke's trust, however, was misplaced. For Louis, these travels through Burgundy gave him the opportunity to acquire strategically valuable information about the areas bordering France and to cultivate the leaders of these areas while acquainting himself with their plans and policies. Louis paid out of hand for all the services rendered him, thereby attracting a loyal cadre of followers from all levels of society. All could see Louis for the wily negotiator and diplomat that he was; the purblind Philip saw only a royal refugee, a prized guest who added to the luster of Philip's greatness.

Grown weary of her struggle to counsel caution to an unresponsive Philip, convinced that the power of the de Croys was self-serving and their pro-French policy ruinous to Burgundy, and suspicious of the modest deference of the dauphin, Isabel retreated to her residence at La Motte-au-Bois by midsummer. The simply clad sixty-year-old duchess walked often in the midst of her peaceful gardens, only a few miles from St. Omer, still anticipating that a call might come from Philip requesting her presence at court. She was not idle in the meanwhile, however. Increasingly concerned for the welfare of the sick and dying in the towns surrounding Nieppe, she brought those who were ill to her own castle, where she bathed them with her own hands, dressed them with clothing she ordered sewn for them, fed them meat and bread until they were strong enough to leave, and then provided money for their return home. She became adept at healing the needy and accomplished at teaching those skills to the nuns of the new order of Poor Clares she had established.

Unfortunately, her summer did not pass without grief. Her much-cherished nephew, Jaime de Coimbre, who had lived at her court since boyhood, died, a victim of suspected poisoning. (Suspicions were heightened when five of his attendants also died within a few days.) Philip had also loved the young man, gave him an honored role at court, and planned great things for his future. Philip made him a knight of the Golden Fleece, and arranged his marriage to the daughter of the king of Cyprus. The match extended Burgundian influence into the heart of the Mediterranean, at least until Jaime de Coimbre's untimely death.

Political Turmoil Reaches La Motte-au-Bois

Isabel's enjoyment of the peace of La Motte-au-Bois was also disturbed by increasing French hostility toward Burgundy. Charles VII's resentment of Philip's protection of his son intensified with the hospitality Philip extended to the dauphin. As Isabel had feared, Charles VII grew more assertive after the investigation into Joan of Arc's conviction had concluded that her original trial had been illegal and declared her sentence null and void. The more confident nature of French kingship was reflected in the articles from the king's embassy to the duke of Burgundy on September 4, 1457. Once more Charles VII wanted his son back in France where he could control his activities, and he commissioned two men—Richard Olivier, the bishop of Coutances, and Jean Boursier, the lord of Esternay—to travel to Philip's court with Francois Halle and Jean Le Roy to demand that the dauphin explain himself. Charles wanted to know why his son, who had asked for leave of only four months to subdue Dauphiny in 1447, now stayed away from the French court for ten years, refusing royal orders to return. He scoffed at Louis's reputed fear of his own father. If the dauphin did not provide the embassy with a detailed list of his fears and still resisted returning to his father, then the duke of Burgundy was commanded to hold Louis under a form of house arrest until the French prince agreed to return. Philip ignored the royal command. But the powerless Isabel could hear the rumblings of a possible French war precipitated by Philip's pride.

From the relative isolation of her retreat in the woodlands of Nieppe, the duchess redoubled her efforts to encourage an English alliance. As she waited for a summons from her husband to join him at court, Isabel sought to bolster her bargaining position with the duke of York by suggesting a marriage alliance between one of her nieces and one of the sons of the duke of York. Although Philip remained opposed to a political alliance with England, he did encourage his wife at this time to complete the negotiation of economic treaties with which he had earlier entrusted Isabel. Since her retirement from court, however, Philip no longer briefed her on his political strategies or asked her help on delicate missions to France or England. Until mid-1458, therefore, Isabel negotiated as an isolated figure. She tried to resolve the long-simmering disputes between English and Flemish wool and cloth merchants, but cut off from the authority of her own court she had no new offers to place on the bargaining table.

Isabel's emissaries to London became embroiled in political turmoil that winter and spring of 1458–59, however, when the duke of York returned from the Welsh borderlands. Convinced that the English queen manipulated Henry VI—and that her concern was for the welfare of

France, not of England—York returned from Wales to regain the favor of English public opinion and with that, to switch the balance of English power away from the Angevin influence that dominated Henry VI. Desperate to keep Henry VI away from the influence of the duke of York, Margaret of Anjou agreed to meet with York in February to establish a tentative peace between them for the year of 1458. Both parties planned to use this year to build their own power base: York looked beyond England's borders to win support; the queen moved to tighten her grip on the central office of government.

The truce permitted Warwick, an ally of Burgundy as well as of York, to remain head of the English navy and gave him the power to prepare and deliver an embassy to Burgundy later that spring to conclude a Yorkist-Burgundian marriage alliance. Meanwhile, York approached Charles VII for French support for his bid to break the grip of the Angevin queen and the Lancastrian faction on the reins of English power. Charles, however, would not be swayed from his alliance with the Angevin faction. Although York promised the king great territorial rewards for his support, Charles refused the offer.

As Isabel waited for dispatches from her English embassies bringing news of York's latest bid for power, she heard rumors about French ambitions that filled her with alarm. Charles VII, the rumors rightly noted, had recently sent letters to Philip suggesting that if the French armies had not been so preoccupied earlier with winning Bordeaux back from the English, they would have been turned against Burgundy. Rumors persisted throughout 1458 that French armies were preparing for an active campaign against Burgundy. Isabel knew that Louis's long sojurn with them only inflamed Charles's determination to swallow up the duchy of Burgundy, but Philip disregarded her advice, clinging to his original strategy of holding Louis hostage to Charles's territorial appetite. As logical and realistic as ever, Isabel contemplated what Louis's policy toward Burgundy would be when he wore the crown of France, and she concluded that it would be the same as his father's: to eat up the rich territory of Burgundy that sat waiting like a rich plum on France's strategic northeastern border.

Isabel studied dispatches from London through 1458–59 with as much care as did Charles VII, the dauphin Louis—who had his own network of emissaries and spies reporting to him at Genappe from many of the important courts of Europe—Duke Philip, and the de Croy brothers. To their delight or dismay, each learned that as York sought help beyond the channel and Warwick's envoys met with Burgundian representatives at Calais during May 1458 to prepare for an Anglo-Burgundian conference later that summer, Margaret of Anjou moved decisively to consolidate her position.

She convinced the weak-willed Henry VI that the duke of Buckingham—who in addition to his posts of chancellor and treasurer had assumed the role of protector of the realm after the removal of York from that post—was not working in the interests of the king. With Henry VI's permission, she replaced Buckingham as chancellor and treasurer, eliminating his role as protector, with her own man, Laurence Booth. In so doing, the queen gained the power to appoint officials in all the main branches of government. Quickly, she used this new authority to rid herself of all the Yorkist followers who occupied influential positions at court, but did not succeed in removing the powerful personal influence of the duke of York. Nevertheless, Charles VII was delighted with Margaret's strategy and quickly offered her French aid. But both Queen Margaret and King Charles still had to contend with the power of York, who continued to enjoy public acclaim.

Illness and Reconciliation

In the spring of 1458, as the French king deployed his forces to menacing positions on Burgundy's borders—threatening some Burgundian towns and overwhelming others—and as the Angevin interests in France prepared to join with Margaret's forces, Philip began to waiver in the faith he had placed in the de Croy advice and to reevaluate the benefits, especially the military benefits, of an English alliance. Apprehensive and isolated, with no one to turn to for advice save for the de Croys (who still pushed for a pro-French policy), the duke reacted to the mounting stress by throwing himself into pastimes that both absorbed his energy and endangered his health. In his early sixties Philip played hard, hunting in all weather, spending his nights in bacchanalian revelries with the de Croys at court and ending them in the arms of numerous willing women. At length, in mid-June 1458, after playing a strenuous game of tennis, Philip suffered a severe fever that required his physicians to tend to him for several days. Out of bed and eating once more, thinking himself cured, he sent Anthony de Croy to the cathedral of Notre Dame of Halle to give thanks for his recovery.

No one expected Philip's relapse on June 17, when (the victim perhaps of a serious stroke) he fell into a sudden and deep coma that lasted three days. All those who attended to him were convinced that his condition would prove fatal.

Receiving the shocking news of Philip's critical condition while on the road from Halle, Anthony turned quickly to Lille where Isabel was visiting with her son Charles. The three rode to Brussels immediately, covering the remaining seven and a half miles in just one hour. Entering the room where her husband lay on his sickbed, overwhelmed by illness, partially paralyzed, and unable to speak clearly, Isabel prostrated herself before him and through her tears lamented the wrongs between them. Philip asked her to stay to supervise his care. She accepted at once. Over the second half of 1458, Isabel used her nursing experience to good effect. She also used the time the two spent alone together to rekindle the affection between them and to regain from the duke at least a measure of the confidence he had formerly placed in her diplomatic and political judgment.

Charles VII too came near death that summer. The French king had suffered for many months with a sore on his leg that would not heal—perhaps an early symptom of diabetes or syphilis—and was consumed by a raging fever caused by the deep infection. The French king called for his son to come to him, but the dauphin would not leave Genappe and went hunting instead. The dauphin asked astrologers to foretell the exact hour of his father's death. But although the son prayed fervently for his father's demise, Charles VII was not ready to die in 1458.

The Revival of Isabel's Influence

Although York's embassy to Charles VII in May failed to secure the king's support, Warwick's embassy to Calais in May and June met with more success. In late June, as he lay recuperating from his sudden illness, the duke responded positively to the economic agenda offered by Warwick. A Burgundian embassy traveled to London and arranged for talks to be held in Bruges in August. Rumors of these Anglo-Burgundian meetings and the possibility of a joint Anglo-Burgundian attack on Normandy spread consternation in France, and the king prepared to defend the Contentin area south of Rouen from invasion.

As embassies continued to cross and recross the channel in 1458, tensions mounted and rumors of pending attacks slipped through borders. French and Burgundian armies massed along frontiers, fading into the night only to reform elsewhere. Military uncertainty was matched by diplomatic confusion, as the government of Henry VI—under the influence of the duke of York—sent a single embassy composed of both Lancastrians and Yorkists on a double commission to the courts of Burgundy and France. The delegation, led by Sir John Wenlock, former chamberlain to Queen Margaret but a Yorkist since 1454, and Louis Gallet, former master of the finances for the royal household to the courts of Burgundy and France, was charged with negotiating a truce with France and marriage settlements with either France or Burgundy. Wenlock was instructed to arrange unions of the English king's son, the prince of Wales, and the sons of York and Somerset with three eligible princesses, either of Burgundy or of Valois.

The embassy first met first with Philip in October, after the duke had regained his strength. The English proposed an alliance with Burgundy based on marriages between Marie—Philip and Isabel's granddaughter—and one of York's sons; and between the sons of the dukes of Somerset and York and the princesses of Bourbon and Guelders (nieces of Isabel). Receiving no immediate answer from Burgundy, the embassy traveled to Rouen, where the envoys met with the French king and offered a similar program of marriages to win a one-, two-, or three-year peace. They proposed that the son of the king of England be married to the daughter of Charles VII , and that the daughters of the duke of Orléans and the count of Maine wed the sons of York and Somerset. Charles thought the English terms were inappropriate for a mere truce rather than a general peace, but agreed to discuss the proposals.

Before taking return passage to England, the low-ranking English embassy, which lacked the authority to conclude either a truce or the marriage negotiations, wrote to the duke and duchess of Burgundy to inform them of the outcome of the embassy's meeting with Charles VII. They indicated that the French seemed more willing to pursue the treaty's terms than the English were to complete them, indicating clearly that England had only temporized with the French while waiting for a solid offer of alliance with Burgundy. Yorkist members of the embassy—who had secured the upper hand over the Lancastrians members—warned Philip that if a treaty were signed between France and England, passage from England to help the duke of Burgundy in case of French attack would be barred. After the embassy returned to London, the envoys sought to foster support for an alliance with Burgundy by telling their countrymen that the French king was preparing for an armed invasion of England.

Significantly, it was Isabel who answered the letter from the English envoys. She responded in early 1459 that she and her husband were both well disposed to continue the negotiations, but only when the king of England and the duke of York sent to Burgundy an embassy of the rank that befitted discussion of issues involving dynastic marriages. Isabel added that the English need not expect to hear further from Burgundy until the duke and duchess had more information on the intentions of the French king and the duke of York. Isabel was now formally involved again in direct negotiations with the English on political as well as economic issues. She was able at last to work openly to ally Burgundy with England before France launched an attack on the duchy.

As Philip waited for a response to Isabel's letter to the English that spring, he also waited for a reaction to his spring embassy led by Jehan de Croy and Simon de Lalaing to Charles VII at Montbazon. The French king, however, did not reply personally to Philip's complaints of French incursions into Burgundian territory, French piracy against Burgundian merchant shipping, and the royal neglect of Philip's ducal rights in the Paris Parlement. The king's silence had less to do with political calculation than with the fact that he was preoccupied with matters of a much more frivolous nature. The graver his illness, the more Charles neglected the duties of his reign. The king began to dress like a dandy, his tight leggings and a too-short jacket mercilessly revealing his knobby knock-knees. Since the death of his mistress Agnes Sorel in 1450, Charles had demanded the constant company of young women, and he spent more hours in the bedroom than in the council chamber.

The French king's chief legal council finally addressed the duke of Burgundy's complaints of royal injustice in a long treatise delivered at Philip's court in Brussels in the summer of 1459.[5] Why, Philip had asked, had the French king sought alliances and confederations against Burgundy with Denmark, Bern, Liège, the king of Bohemia, the emperor, and other imperial princes? Why did Charles VII continue hostilities against Burgundy on land and sea, and why were Philip's ducal rights in the Parlement perpetually denied? Philip's accusations were dismissed out of hand by the king's chief lawyers, who ignored Philip's protestations of friendship for France and instead accused the duke of disloyalty to the king. Why, they asked, was the duke of Burgundy meeting with the English, despite the fact that he had signed a treaty of peace with France at Arras, had made war against England, and had even helped Charles VII recover Paris and Normandy? Had not Philip vowed from 1435 to cherish, love, serve, honor, and obey the king of France?

In England, meanwhile, Margaret of Anjou was busy building up her forces. The queen recognized that Lancastrian England's greatest danger came not from France but from an alliance between the Yorkists and Philip of Burgundy. As Isabel worked to establish ever-closer ties to an England that she hoped would soon be in Yorkist hands, as Philip the Good and Charles VII hurled accusations at each other, and as the dauphin sat in Genappe spinning schemes from the information gathered by his web of spies and waiting for his father to die, the English queen gathered her strength to challenge the duke of York and his allies. That autumn,

Margaret of Anjou and Isabel of Burgundy faced one another across the channel, each determined to preserve the inheritance of her son.

On September 23, Margaret of Anjou acted, sending her forces to arrest the duke of York and the earl of Warwick. The men had been warned, however, and made their escapes. York fled to Ireland and his eldest son, the earl of March and future Edward IV, fled to Calais with Warwick and his father, Lord Salisbury. On November 21, the queen's men in Parliament charged those who had fled as traitors and passed a bill of attainder. Acting under the queen's directions, Parliament proceeded to extinguish their titles and confiscate their lands.

The Missed Opportunity, 1460

As the northern winter of 1460 closed in on the exiles in Calais and at Genappe, political and personal tensions increased. In Calais, York's son Edward, earl of March, prepared to return to England to reclaim his family's titles and lands. At Genappe, the dauphin grew impatient with his entanglements at the Burgundian court, with his own helplessness to act for France, and with his father's reluctance to die. And at the same time, Philip was coming to resent his role as Louis's host. Philip's luxury-loving nature made him suspicious of the dauphin's simplicity of dress and manner, and the duke was jealous of the time Louis spent in the company of his own son Charles. Urgent messages came and went from Genappe, clearly devoted to matters Louis never shared with his uncle.

Though the king of France had placed several agents at Genappe to learn about his son, Louis had an even greater number at his father's court, as well as in the households of many of the most powerful lords of France. His spies extended even into the king's own bed. Madame de Villequier (Antoinette de Mangnelais) acted as the royal mistress after the death of Agnes Sorel in 1450. When in 1458 she subsequently became the mistress of the duke of Brittany—who was often at the king's court—she continued to keep Louis informed.[6] Through this network, Louis learned how incapacitated his father had become. Indeed, according to one report Louis received, on leaving an audience with the pope, a Milanese ambassador commented that "one need not pay much attention to irritating the French, as their king is gravely ill and in peril of death."[7]

Unfortunately for both Philip and Louis, however, the successes of Margaret of Anjou and the Lancastrian forces in England had encouraged the anti-Burgundian faction at the court of Charles VII to contemplate war against Burgundy. By January 1460, relations between France and Burgundy were more strained even than they had been in 1458 and 1459. Philip did not want a war with France, for which he felt such kinship and whose forces he recognized might well take much, perhaps all, of his duchy from him. And the dauphin dared not see his future kingdom march against the duke who currently sheltered him. In the early months of 1460, in an effort to forestall open conflict between France and Burugundy, Louis sought out the Yorkist faction in England to persuade them to mount an attack on France and thus divert the French from any thoughts of attacking Burgundy.

Louis's efforts gained support from an unexpected quarter, when a diminutive papal legate named Francesco Coppini appeared at Isabel's court in Brussels. The ambitious Coppini was on a mission from the pope seeking the end of the dynastic struggle in England so that the English might help Philip launch the crusade he had announced in 1454. But Coppini had just been rebuffed by Queen Margaret. The dauphin's sources informed him that although Coppini was on a papal mission he had other orders from his patron, the duke of Milan, Francesco Sforza. Like Louis, Sforza wanted to encourage England to attack France and thus divert a French attack elsewhere—in Sforza's case, however, he sought to divert the French from attacking Naples to restore an Angevin (Queen Margaret's brother, René) to the Neapolitan crown. Louis wasted no time in approaching Coppini with his plans for the papal legate to meet with Yorkist leaders in Calais that spring. With the cooperation of Philip and Isabel, Louis immediately put Coppini in touch with the earl of Warwick and the earl of March in Calais.

To Isabel's gratification, when the earls of Warwick and March left Calais on June 23 they carried with them to England two thousand English and Burgundian fighting men, a tiny papal legate to bless the expedition, and the good wishes of the dauphin of France and the duke of Burgundy. As the Yorkist forces entered London on July 2, having met little resistance from Dover northward, the mass of people who followed them onto London Bridge was so great that thirteen men-at-arms who stumbled were trampled to death by the crowd.[8] Learning of the Yorkist advance, the royal court at Coventry moved the queen and young prince Henry toward the safety of Wales, while Henry VI joined his forces farther south to meet Warwick and the earl of March on a field in Northampton, fifty miles north of London, on July 10. Just before noon that Thursday, a great storm swept through the area as the battle began, turning the meadowland where the royal artillery was positioned into a mire and rendering the canon useless. The Yorkist forces won the day, and the king became their prisoner. The duke of York joined his son Edward to form a Yorkist-dominated government under the nominal authority of the king, whom they now held captive. Isabel was jubilant, but only momentarily. She was immediately skeptical of dispatches that declared Warwick to have secured full control of the country for the duke of York. Moreover, a Yorkist government was only one aspect of the alliance she sought. Still ahead would be difficult negotiations to secure the economic and marriage ties that would yield tangible benefits for Burgundy.

Louis had correctly anticipated that he could divert the French from attacking Burgundy and from advancing into Italy by reversing Angevin fortunes in England. But the possibility that the French would attack Burgundy still loomed; after all, Charles still coveted the duchy that had been wrenched from the French crown and that now harbored the son he could not trust. In July, therefore, conflict was impending once again. At a meeting at Villefranche on July 28, the royal council resolved to recommend to Charles VII that there was "sufficient and just cause to proceed by force of arms to ensure obedience, in all my lord of Burgundy's lands in the kingdom of France."

As the cautious Isabel had expected, the government of England was too unstable in the confusion of the king's second captivity and the return of the duke of York from Ireland to be of any help to Burgundy in autumn of 1460. With trumpets blaring, in the company of five hundred men, and with a naked sword carried before him, Richard of York entered London on October 10 displaying the arms of England as the country's chief lord. He rode directly to Parliament, which had been convened by the king at Westminster three days earlier. After Henry VI had retired to the royal chambers, York culminated his victorious progress, which had been far more royal than ducal, by placing his hand on the empty throne, which was positioned on the dais above those seated in Parliament, and claimed lawful descent to the crown through Edward III. When no cheer came from those seated in the hall of Parliament, York was asked if he wanted to see the king. He answered, "I know of no person in this realm the which oweth not to wait on me rather than I on him." The duke proceeded to take forcible possession of the king's chamber, entering the rooms and claiming them for himself, as Henry VI stood by in the empty apartments of the queen.[9] Although prudent enough to agree that Henry VI must remain on the throne until he died, York was determined to secure for himself the reins of power, and several weeks later, on November 1, the duke had himself named protector of the realm.

Margaret was not one to slip quietly away from such a challenge, and with her son close by her side in Wales, where she had sought refuge before the battle of Northampton, she busied herself rallying men to the Lancastrian cause. The great lords who had fought for Henry VI and scattered after the defeat of July 10 now reassembled behind the queen. On December 9, Margaret's forces moved eastward, destroying all Yorkist estates in their path. The Lancastrians reached the woodland surrounding York's Sandal Castle on December 21. Warwick and the duke of Norfolk had remained in London to guard the city. The earl of March had left Sandal Castle earlier in the month to recruit men in Wales for the Yorkist cause. Finding the duke of York's forces weakened by the absence of Warwick and Norfolk and their followers, the Lancastrians struck on the field of Wakefield, one mile from Sandal, on December 30. What began as a small skirmish ended in a surprising catastrophe for the Yorkist cause, with the duke of York, his son Edmund, and Warwick's father, Lord Salisbury all dead. Isabel's reserved celebrations of the Yorkist victory earlier that year now proved prophetic.

Notes

1. Paul Murray Kendall, *Louis the XI* (New York: W. W. Norton, 1971), 78.
2. *Oeuvres de Chastellain*, ed. M. Le Baron Kervyn de Lettenhove, 4 vols. (Brussels: R. Heussner, 1864), 3:297.
3. *Oeuvres de Chastellain*, 3:298.
4. *Oeuvres de Chastellain*, 3:301.
5. Richard Vaughan, *Philip the Good: The Apogee of Burgundy* (New York: Barnes and Noble, 1970), 352–53; G. du Fresne de Beaucourt, *Histoire de Charles VII,* 6 vols. (Paris: Libraire de la Socitété Bibliographique, 1881–91), 6:272–79.
6. Kendall, *Louis XI,* 93.
7. Du Fresne de Beaucourt, *Histoire de Charles VII,* 6:282.
8. James H. Ramsay, *Lancaster and York: A Century of English History, 1399–1485* (Oxford: Clarendon Press, 1892), 226.
9. Ramsay, *Lancaster and York*, 231.

Chapter Eight

The Changing Cast of Royal Players, 1461–1466

THE DUKE OF YORK'S FAMILY had welcomed the armistice with Queen Margaret and was enjoying the peaceful celebration of Christmas week when, on the morning of December 30, 1460, the Lancastrian forces of the queen launched a surprise attack. Duke Richard led his men down from his castle of Sandal, perched high on a conical hill, but was caught between the left and right flanks of the Lancastrians and was killed within the hour. Attempting to escape the carnage, York's son Edmund was overtaken only a few yards short of the bridge where his father had fallen. As some Lancastrians pleaded for the life of the seventeen-year-old, Lord Clifford stabbed the boy, swearing, "By God's blood, thy father slew mine and so will I do thee."[1]

Richard's head was cut off, adorned with a paper crown, and propped on the gates of his city of York as a warning that only Lancastrians would rule the land. But that winter, York's eldest son, Edward, earl of March, and his ally Warwick prepared to prove Queen Margaret wrong. As the forces of the great noble houses massed against one another from the Scottish border to the Thames River, almost all the peasantry and gentry of England were mere onlookers, waiting to see which side would triumph in the long struggle for power.

Isabel and the New English King

Within a few days of the tragedy at Wakefield, the duchess of York made plans to send her two younger sons to safety across the English Channel, where Isabel of Burgundy waited to receive them. In spite of her Lancastrian blood, Isabel hoped to see the earl of March triumphant, and she was pleased to welcome his brothers, ten-year-old George and eight-year-old Richard, in mid-January of 1461. She assured herself that their residence in Utrecht offered both the formality appropriate to their noble rank and the security that the children needed. The duchess had not met the young earl of March, but she had been told that he was a handsome giant of a man, with golden hair, a warm disposition, and a gift for leadership. She prayed for the young earl of March's success as fervently as she did for her own son's reconciliation with Philip. That month, Isabel had a great deal for which to pray.

Philip's illness returned just after the Christmas court. In response to the strain of constant political and domestic pressures, his entire digestive system rebelled, fomenting a series of increasingly serious ailments that were to plague him until his death five years later. As the duke lay prostrate, unable to care for himself, he called for Isabel again. The duchess came to her husband's side at once and, according to the chronicler Georges Chastellain, she and her son watched with consternation as doctors scurried in and out of his chambers and courtiers fearfully wondered what effects the duke's death would have on his faction-filled household. While servants kept continual vigil, Isabel took charge of Philip's care. So unresponsive had Philip become to the remedies applied by the physicians that Isabel and Charles dismissed them all and appealed instead to God. The duchess ordered that all of the bells of the town of Abbeville, where he had first fallen ill, be rung continuously and that the townspeople come out night and day to pray for the duke until he recovered. Isabel washed him herself and attempted to coax him to take some warm wine or broth, but Philip could not swallow any liquid for many days and his fever soared.

No one dared mention to the duke the death of Beatriz de Coimbre, Isabel's niece, for fear that the shock of this loss of one of his favorites would kill him immediately. Isabel mourned the loss of Beatriz—as she had the deaths of her two nephews, brothers of Beatriz and children of her brother Peter—to whom she had been both mother and protectress. During the long hours she spent with her ailing husband those dark winter days, she kept her sorrow to herself, but those who saw her at mass and reading her daily hours observed that she could never finish her prayers without dissolving in tears. With these deaths, Isabel was now completely cut off from her Portuguese family, and she turned to her son Charles, and to her granddaughter Marie, for the comfort and affection she had missed in her marriage to Philip.

By the end of January, when Philip was well enough to take broths and almond-flavored milk, Isabel built his strength by offering him an occasional omelet and whatever fruit was available during those winter months. As he slowly regained his health, Isabel left his side for the pleasure of a visit with her daughter-in-law, Isabelle, the countess of Charolais, and her granddaughter Marie. However, just then the dynastic struggle in England erupted once again, denying Isabel her tranquil retreat and Philip the chance of a peaceful convalescence.

Isabel's first happy weeks with her son's family at the castle of Le Quesnoy were interrupted by the news that Warwick, who was guarding both London and King Henry VI, had met the Lancastrians for a second time at St. Albans on February 17, and that there the earl had lost both the city and the king to Queen Margaret. No one knew where Warwick had fled. Camped outside London, the Lancastrians promised not to punish the city if its citizens would open their gates to the king and queen once more. But as Isabel worried that all was finally lost for the Yorkist cause, she received encouraging word that the citizens of London, infuriated with Lancastrian brutality, had armed themselves, locked their city's gates, and refused to allow Henry VI and his queen to enter the capital.

As the citizens manned London's walls, Warwick gathered more troops and joined Edward in the west. Together, Edward and Warwick led their forces to London to find that Englishmen had had enough of their French queen and her malleable king. Londoners were ready to embrace the young earl of March. Wearied by the emotional peaks and valleys of recent months, Isabel was buoyed by dispatches announcing that both the Londoners and the English Parliament had proclaimed Edward to be their lawful king on March 4. Isabel was jubilant—though she wondered how a kingdom could have two lawful monarchs.

The Parliament at Westminster solved that quandary by ruling that although York had promised that Henry VI could remain sovereign until his death, the king had broken this pledge by his support for the attack on York at Wakefield. By breaking this oath, Henry VI had forfeited his legal right to be king. Parliament ruled that with York's death, the duke's eldest son, Edward, had become the legal heir to the English throne and thus was now the constitutional monarch. The earl of March became King Edward IV. However, while Parliament had made Edward king by law, he had still to prove himself in battle if he was to remain king for long. At once, therefore, Warwick and the new king set off in pursuit of the retreating Lancastrians, catching them at Towton, a hamlet on the banks of the Humber River in the north of England, as Henry VI and Margaret pressed northward toward refuge in Scotland. The armies faced one another on opposite ridges above the Humber Valley on the morning of Palm Sunday, March 29. A few hours later, ten thousand Englishmen lay dead in the river that wound through the valley and England's new king had proved himself formidable in battle. Isabel's prayers had been answered.

The two young princes, George and Richard, left Utrecht for the Burgundian court at Brussels as soon as their brother became king. Isabel was determined that the impressionable children should carry back to London descriptions of the great power and prestige enjoyed by Burgundy, and she treated the boys to all the splendor of the Burgundian court during their three-month stay there. The duchess also overlooked no opportunity to try to persuade Edward IV of the value of an alliance with Burgundy—an endeavor that placed her in competition with the earl of Warwick, who was seeking to bolster his position and prestige by forging an alliance between England and France.

Isabel's spirits lightened in spring. The two little English princes were preparing to sail back to England, Philip had begun to recover, and a much-relieved Charles was planning to celebrate the Yorkist victory with his family at Brussels. The princes were honored at a lavish banquet Isabel prepared in early June at St. Omer, attended by the king of Cyprus, the papal legate, and the ambassadors of Persia and Georgia. The brothers of the English king were then dispatched to their older brother's care with Burgundy's best wishes. The summer appeared to be starting off rather well.

At La-Motte-au-Bois in the early summer months of 1461, however, Isabel grew uneasy as she reflected on the frequent confrontations between Philip and their son over the long-standing power of the de Croys in the ducal court. Charles's arguments with Philip threw the weakened duke into rages that threatened to estrange Charles once and for all from his father. Since Charles's permanent departure would guarantee a de Croy victory, Isabel sought to discover more about her son's activities, hoping to find something she could use to discourage any further ill-advised attacks on the duke's favorites.

The duchess left La Motte-au-Bois in midsummer to join Charles during his visit to Brussels. Isabel traveled light in July, and her carts carried only essential items—her summer clothing, a few favorite tapestries, her portable chapel, and, of course, several chests of her jewels. Perhaps the most important items she carried with her that July were several volumes she had carefully selected for Charles to read so that he might benefit from examples of great leadership from Greek and Roman times. Charles, as his mother knew well, enjoyed having the works of classical authors read to him as his musicians played after his evening meals. These volumes, she hoped, might now help to calm her hot-tempered son.

While mother and son were in Brussels, Rolande Pippe, Charles's most respected accountant, suddenly arrived at the court, in deep despair following a suicide attempt, to explain his actions. Heedless of Pippe's distress, Isabel questioned the distraught man about Charles's expenditures. But instead of gaining clues to Charles's behavior, Isabel's interrogation elicited from Pippe details about himself—in particular, the confession that he owed the treasury large sums. His honor destroyed, Pippe killed himself a few days later. He was found hanging by his belt in a well. Isabel left Brussels soon after the tragedy, depressed by the loss of a loyal and effective officer of the court, but still more distressed by her failure to discover new information about Charles. As she confessed to her intimates, she had done nothing to overcome Charles's alienation from his father, which would continue her son's powerlessness in the affairs of Burgundy for three more years.

Louis XI, New King of France

Since the beginning of the year, the illness of Charles VII had worsened. By mid-July 1461 the king's physicians concluded that he would not survive past the month of August. In his delirium, Charles VII felt himself surrounded by traitors who were loyal only to his son. The king was in large measure correct, however, for the dauphin had long been preparing for his father's death by cultivating allies among the king's courtiers and ambassadors, as well as among his father's friends and enemies abroad. Much to their dismay, the duke and duchess learned that Louis had cemented alliances with those princes in Germany who had formerly pledged support for Burgundy, and had formed strategic relationships with Francesco Sforza of Milan and several other rulers in Italy and Spain. Having spent many of his years in Dauphiny and Genappe persuading agents of Charles VII to confide their king's secrets to him, Louis had a very clear idea of which of his father's alliances and policies he would continue and which he would terminate when he became king.

Isabel's wariness of Louis increased when she learned that the dauphin had offered his support to Edward IV—while Charles VII encouraged Margaret of Anjou—and had actively encouraged the English to invade France. The duchess remained suspicious of Louis's support for her work to foster a Yorkist alliance, and she knew that his loyalties would shift again once he occupied the throne.

The news of the fatal turn in the king's illness reached Louis at Genappe on July 10. The king's council gathered at Melun one week later and decided to send a letter to Louis, which he received on July 17. The council notified the dauphin of the king's imminent death and advised the dauphin that the king's forces were poised to cross the channel but were being kept for the moment in Normandy. To be closer to the dispatchers of the latest word from his father's bedside at Melun, Louis left Genappe on July 17, the day he received the council's letter, and rode immediately for the town of Avesne. The tumor or abscess in the king's mouth resulting from an infection in his jaw bone had grown so large that he could not swallow and thus could take no nourishment for the last week of his life. Starving to death but with his mental faculties still clear, Charles realized that the end was near and requested that Louis come to him before he died and that his body be buried in St. Denis alongside his parents. Louis never came to his father, who died, aged fifty-eight, between noon and one o'clock in the afternoon on July 22, 1461.

In his haste to reach Avesne, Louis had left his wife behind in Genappe. So that she might follow him, Louis instructed her to borrow whatever carts she required from Charles's wife, the countess of Charolais, who lived nearby at Le Quesnoy. The countess promptly sent her equerry Corneille de la Barre with the carts, carriages, and wagons Margaret needed. Immediately, the new queen of France left Burgundy as her husband had done: without so much as a word of thanks to the duke, the duchess, or the countess.

Now that Louis was king, Isabel was keen to discover whether her suspicions about his intentions were well founded. Her husband, however, staunchly refused to accept the possibility of any duplicity on the new king's part, notwithstanding the revelations about Louis's secret treaties and alliances. The duke wished mightily to be convinced that Louis bore only the greatest appreciation for his uncle's support since 1456. Eager to bask in the glory that would be accorded to the new king's closest friend and principal counselor, Philip convinced himself that he had earned the position of the most important prince of the realm.

Louis XI played to his uncle's pride. Louis needed Burgundy's help to keep peace along France's northern borders, thereby giving him time to control his barons and consolidate his reign. Aware of his uncle's thirst for prestige, Louis planned to have Philip serve France as his intermediary with England to arrange an Anglo-French peace conference. Although Louis had already chosen his court long before July 22—the court was made up largely of those courtiers who had followed the dauphin in his flight to Burgundy in 1456—to please Philip, Louis awarded the post of grand-master of the royal household to Philip's own favorite, Anthony de Croy, and gave the position of receiver-general to Philip's most reliable Florentine banker, Arnoulfini. To please Charles as well, to whom Louis paid particular attention, the new king transferred to his own service Guillaume de Biche, the courtier whom Charles had been forced to dismiss as chamberlain of his household in 1457 to make room for his father's choice. Philip blindly applauded Louis's appointments, and Charles was very pleased to note the great favor Louis XI accorded de Biche, whom Charles later observed walking arm in arm with Louis XI in the streets of Paris.

In mid-August, Burgundy was well represented in the colorful cavalcade that marched with Louis from Avesne to Reims for his coronation. The three hundred nobles, knights, and squires who formed the procession of the count and countess of Charolais joined those of Philip and Isabel. The Burgundians, clad in velvet embroidered in sparkling gold and ornamented with flashing jewels, formed the most splendid element within the enormous and enthusiastic cavalcade, which entered Reims at seven o'clock the evening of August 14.

That night Louis spent in church in many hours of silent prayer, but the next day he made sure that the duke of Burgundy accompanied him to his royal anointing. The duke was also close by on August 16, when Louis was crowned in the great cathedral of Reims.

Louis became king at the age of thirty-eight. With piercing eyes, a large nose, and thin legs bowed from many hours in the saddle, he was not considered a very attractive person. Nor was he admired for his manner of dress, which did not change when he became king. Indeed, there was general astonishment when the royal party entered Paris in late August, for Philip of Burgundy so far outshone the sovereign in his attire that there was much confusion as to which of the two men was the new king. At the coronation banquet, Louis had next to nothing of value that was not a gift from Philip; even the very plate on the royal table was a ducal present. When presents were distributed in return, Philip received a lion and Charles a pelican.[2]

Louis did his best to charm the temperamental Burgundians that August and September, but nothing he did was enough to please Philip, who was stung by his exclusion from Louis's decision making, by the new king's absence at all the Paris entertainments Philip offered, and by the accounts of Louis's ridicule of the duke's richly clad courtiers and relatives. Then, toward the end of September, perhaps carried away by the frenzied atmosphere surrounding the coronation and weary of the pomp and ceremony of the company, Louis made an error in judgment. He suggested to Philip that the duke break off his talks about trade relations with Yorkist England and that Burgundy instead look only to France. Louis quickly discovered that his suggestion had been ill timed and ill conceived, for Philip flew into a rage. Louis XI wanted to undo the Anglo-Burgundian relationship, thereby diverting a possible attack on France by England while also making Burgundy more vulnerable to his own designs, but his ill-judged proposal came too close to revealing this strategy to Philip. Although the king attempted to make amends—and even broke etiquette on September 22 by riding to the Hotel d'Artois in Paris where Philip was staying to announce before an assembly of royal councillors that he owed both his life and his crown to the duke of Burgundy—Philip remained unsettled, even insulted, by Louis's attempt to exert royal power over him. Bored with the formalities and obligations of court life, Louis left Paris hurriedly the next morning. Philip and Isabel left Paris a few days later, with the duke's pride still sorely wounded and Isabel's suspicions of Louis's aims confirmed.

Isabel's Busy Retreat, 1462–1464

Remaining attentive to the strategies of the two new kings, Isabel retreated once more to her estates in Cassel in late 1461. Never willing to settle into the cloistered life preferred by most ladies of her rank after they retired from court, she ensured that she was always available to Philip should he need her advice on domestic affairs or trade negotiations. Philip did indeed call on her, especially after the winter of 1461–62, but chiefly so that she could minister to his recurring and increasingly alarming illnesses.

In February 1462, Philip summoned her again, and both mother and son rushed to Brussels, despite the winter storms, to be by Philip's side. While Charles knelt by his father's bed, pleading with him to try to swallow a bit of wine, Isabel wrung her hands in another chamber and wept with such sorrow that her waiting women feared for her own health. The chronicler Chastellain witnessed a tender moment between Philip and his son, the weak duke reaching for Charles's shoulder in response to his son's pleas for him to take some nourishment, and assuring his son that he would try to take what he could. Chastellain also observed the duke's stubborn refusal to shave off all the hair from his head—and thus hasten, or so his physicians contended, his cure—until his courtiers had undergone the same sacrifice. Even on his sickbed, the duke did not intend to suffer alone the embarrassment of a bald head. That spring, as Philip's health slowly improved, so did the self-respect of the shorn courtiers who attended him.

Meanwhile, Louis XI played his hand carefully in 1462. First, he acquired leverage for negotiations with the Yorkist king by hinting that France would aid the Lancastrian forces of Queen Margaret in Scotland. Next, Louis persuaded his uncle Philip—still weak but once again eager to regain Louis's confidence—to defer his plans for a crusade and instead to orchestrate negotiations that would eliminate the threat of war between France and England. Gratified to be offered such an honorable role, Philip was delighted to fulfill his king's request. The duke assured himself that he would fulfill his promise to the pope the following summer, and Philip threw himself into preparations for the meeting between the earl of Warwick and the French king. Once again, Philip's overweening pride made him see only the glory of the moment, and he failed to perceive that his hunger for acclaim was being manipulated by the French king. Louis ensnared Warwick, too, in his plans. Well aware of Warwick's own thirst for royal gratitude, Louis suggested that the earl should negotiate a marriage alliance between a French princess and Edward IV—negotiations that, if successful, would surely burnish Warwick's reputation with Edward yet more brightly.

Isabel was not taken in by the royal machinations. The duchess had received word that the French barons were growing restless under their new, energetic king, who did not ask for their counsel as he sought to tighten his grip on the country. Isabel saw that Louis needed peace with England, and that he needed Philip to set the stage by using his influence with the Yorkists to arrange Anglo-French negotiations. But the duchess was not going to sit idly by while the French king sought to win England away from Burgundy.

The chill of early autumn cleared the tangles of summer scrub around St. Omer, as workers prepared the site for another meeting of Englishmen and Frenchmen, similar to the one mediated by Isabel in nearby Gravelines in 1439. However, no one, not even Isabel, anticipated the arrival in Flanders of Margaret of Anjou later that September of 1463. Painfully aware that peace between Louis XI and Edward IV would mean the end of her son's chances for the English crown, the indefatigable Margaret swept down from Scotland in mid-September, resolved to prevent the St. Omer meeting by whatever means she could. Without either funds or supporters—save for the great French lord De Breze—Margaret sailed to Sluis, then bumped and joggled in a worn-out village cart to St. Pol, where she threw herself tearfully on the astounded Philip's mercy. The chivalrous Philip listened to the pleas of the exhausted Angevin queen but could do no more than send her on her way, after a few days of feasting at Bruges, with gifts of money and jewels. Philip then quickly set out to meet Louis XI in the rolling fields a mile outside the nearby village of Hesdin at midday of a brisk September 28. The French king, mounted on a "scrubby little horse"and dressed in his hunter's jacket with a horn slung over his shoulder, rode up to the side of his splendidly attired uncle. As the incongruous pair rode through Hesdin, the villagers were confused and called out, "Where's the king? Which one is he?" Confusion turned to astonishment when they learned that the king was not the man dressed in the trappings of royalty.[3]

Sensitive to the tensions Louis himself had provoked in England by hinting that he might help the Lancastrians, Isabel waited silently a few miles away at La Motte-au-Bois. She knew that Louis had used Philip to stage manage the meeting, and she was distressed that the French king had so easily persuaded the duke to relinquish his part in the coalition with Pope Pius II, the doge of Venice, and the king of Hungary to launch a new effort to retake the Holy Land from the infidels. She wanted desperately to be at the meeting in St. Omer where she would have the opportunity to counsel her husband and influence English responses to French demands.

The meeting at St. Omer was no more than moderately successful, providing Louis with only a one-year truce, not the comprehensive peace he had hoped for. Another meeting would have to be held the following year. Even so, the cunning Louis had taken the opportunity to exploit Philip's delicate pride and grand ambitions to whittle away again at Burgundian power. At the conclusion of the conference, Louis was quick to remind the duke of the gift of the Somme towns that Philip had accepted from the French king at the conference in Arras in 1435, albeit with the proviso that the king could choose to repurchase the towns in the future for an agreed-upon sum, a sum that now amounted to 400,000 livres. Philip had never expected the French king to offer the full price to regain these cities, but Louis did so. With the de Croys pressing him to accept the king's offer, and conscious that he needed money for the crusade he now planned to begin the following summer, Philip took the 400,000 livres and returned to France the towns of St. Quentin, Corbie, Amiens, Abbeville, Doullens, St. Riguier, Crevecoeur, Arleux, and Mortagne, and the county of Ponthieu, which lay along the rich valley of the Somme River between France and Burgundy.

By Christmas of 1463, Louis XI had accomplished a great deal: he had won time to establish his new rule in the kingdom; he had set the stage for a significant expansion of trade between his country and England; and in preparation for territorial expansion, he had secured much of France's northeastern border along the Somme River. During this same period, however, Philip had lost a strategically important part of his territory and endangered his profitable trade relationship with the English by encouraging England's alliance with France. Warwick had not arrived for the conference planned during the summer of 1463—sending a far less distinguished embassy in his stead and proposing follow-up talks at St. Omer in 1464—but still the king kept Philip at Hesdin on the pretense that by remaining there Philip would keep alive the chances of the English earl taking his place at the negotiating table later that summer. Would Philip be willing to remain in the king's service through 1464 and once again postpone his plans for the crusade? When the Milanese ambassador asked Louis that Christmas Day if he thought Philip would leave Hesdin to go on the crusade the following summer, Louis responded that he might indeed go as "he [Philip] was a prince who always had his own way, never sharing power with a companion or equal, and that he was not of great intellect."[4] Thus, Louis worked out a strategy to keep the duke of Burgundy in the orbit of the French court.

Isabel was unnerved during the winter months of 1463–64, as Louis stayed in Picardy, visiting his newly reacquired territories. Neither the cold winds sweeping across the low valley nor the ice storms that frosted the fields kept Louis XI from riding with his small group of followers from town to town. He slept in the houses of merchants, shopkeepers, and even peasants, determined to remain as close to the duke and duchess of Burgundy as possible to assure himself of Philip's location and, if required, to convince his uncle of the importance of his presence in the next meeting with the English. Louis was aware of Isabel's efforts to negotiate with the House of York, and he vowed never to allow any Anglo-Burgundian marriage to occur. The French king was determined instead to secure a marriage between Edward IV and Louis's sister-in-law, Bona of Savoy.

Charles was furious with his father's return of the Somme towns, and he vowed to take them back for Burgundy. Heated arguments between father and son reached such a fever pitch in October 1463 that the red-faced and fuming Charles stomped from his father's presence and rode northward toward his Gorinchem estates in Holland, where he remained until Philip decided to summon him back to court. Deeply concerned at her son's rash behavior and alert to Louis's strategies, Isabel kept herself informed about Warwick's plans for an embassy to France while intensifying her own efforts to reach agreement with Edward IV for an alliance based on trade and marriage.

In February 1464 Louis asked Philip for a second time to postpone his plans for a crusade and—quite convinced by now of his importance to the French king—Philip agreed to call a halt to all the preparations then under way. Certainly, Louis understood his uncle far better than Philip comprehended his nephew's guile, but Philip perhaps had his own reasons for acceding so readily to Louis's request—after all, as a sixty-seven-year-old man, Philip cannot have found the thought of months spent in the saddle, riding across the southern plains en route to the Holy Land, as appealing as life at court and in the beds of his mistresses. The king convinced the duke that he was needed, as Louis's leading vassal, not only to negotiate a full peace with England but also, if war broke out with England, to fight alongside France. Louis wrote to Philip, urging that "it would be scarcely honorable for him [Philip] to help . . . others to recover their kingdoms from the Turks while leaving the kingdom of France open to an attack from the English who have done more harm here than the Turks have in the lands they have conquered."[5]

When news reached Isabel that spring that Warwick had finally received permission from Edward IV to take an embassy to France to negotiate marriage, Isabel, surprisingly, was not disturbed. She had already heard the intriguing rumor that Edward IV was then conducting his own courtship in England. The rumor was borne out within a few months, for even while Warwick was traveling from London to Paris in expectation of returning home with a bride for his king and of receiving the king's great thanks for doing so, Edward IV took one of his own subjects for a bride on May 1, 1464. Edward IV's new queen was the beautiful, golden-haired Lady Elizabeth Woodville, widow of Sir John Grey, killed fighting for the Lancastrian cause on February 17, 1461. Englishmen were very disapproving of the union of their king with a woman so far beneath his royal status—from a family that had brought such turmoil to England in the struggle against Edward's reign—and Edward's Woodville in-laws were to become his nemesis. The French king and the duke of Burgundy were also distraught, and Warwick was furious. But the duchess of Burgundy was elated.

A Reversal of Policy, 1464–1466

Philip remained at Hesdin through most of 1464, waiting for Warwick to return and conclude the full peace with France. But Warwick, insulted and embittered by the king's surprising marriage, had returned directly to London and then went immediately to his own estates in the west of the country. Still, Philip waited at Hesdin. Isabel, however, lost no time in following up on this diplomatic defeat for France and moved at once to enhance the Anglo-Burgundian relationship. The duchess fired off a series of letters to her son, then still in Holland at his residence at Gorichem, urging him to intensify his own negotiations with the English king. Charles followed Isabel's advice, and soon both mother and son were actively working to reach trade agreements and marriage alliances between Burgundy and the House of York.

Louis's goals had been checked: no peace treaty with England; no marriage alliance; no opportunistic Warwick on the French side. Now, too, his own nobles were openly grumbling at his ruling without their counsel. Although Louis managed to keep his uncle at Hesdin into the summer of 1464—according to Chastellain, Louis waited daily that summer for the "terrible accident" to happen to Philip that the king's astrologers had predicted—Charles now seemed to be succeeding in his diplomatic overtures to Edward IV.[6] Louis XI decided that it was time he took action against the Burgundian heir.

In September, as the Breton Jehan de Rouville returned from England to report to Charles on the success of his mission to negotiate a coalition between himself, the duke of Brittany—a subject of France but now also an ally of Burgundy—and the English against France, Louis dispatched the bastard son of the lord of Rubempré, a relative of the de Croys. Rubempré was ordered to arrest the Breton emissary before de Rouville could reach Gorichem. Rubempré failed, but was soon found lurking about the streets of Gorichem, inquiring about Charles's daily routine. Informed of Rubempré's activities, Charles had Louis's man arrested on suspicion of spying and even of plotting to assassinate Charles. With help from such men as the Burgundian knight Oliver La March, the rumor was soon spread through the courts of Europe that Rubempré had been under orders either to capture Charles or to bring back his head to France.[7]

One suspects that Isabel's hand was behind Charles's efforts to exploit this affair to excite his father's suspicions of Louis's motives. The ploy was effective, for Philip suddenly left Hesdin on the Sunday morning of October 7, just before a planned visit that day by the king. A few weeks later, on November 5, in the security of his court at Lille and with his son by his side, Philip received an embassy from the French king led by the chancellor of France, Pierre de Morvillier. De Morvillier delivered Louis XI's demand for an explanation of the brazen harshness with which Charles had treated the French king's messenger in Holland and for the sudden departure of Philip from Hesdin. Philippe de Commynes, an eighteen-year-old page who had arrived at Philip's court three days earlier—and who would soon leave Burgundian service to assume the role of historian to the French king—captured the dramatic scenes that followed between the duke, his son, and the French ambassador.

The reception hall, de Commynes recorded, overflowed with spectators, as the French ambassador insinuated that Charles had acted as he had because he resented the fact that his pension had been discontinued by Louis. Philip replied that he would himself have arrested Rubempré under the same circumstances. De Morvillier then attacked Philip's own behavior, suggesting that the duke's abrupt departure amounted to an accusation that the king sought to harm him. Replying that he had never broken his word to anyone but ladies, Philip excused his hasty departure on the ground that he had received news that Warwick would not be arriving in Hesdin as had been planned. The ambassador continued to lay charges, accusing Charles of allying himself with the duke of Brittany, whom Louis thought guilty of treasonous ties with England. Furious, Charles attempted to respond to the charges against him, but when de Morvillier stated flatly that he had come with a commission to address the father and not the son, Philip took Charles aside and cautioned him against speaking too soon: "Think it [what you have to say] over today and tomorrow speak and spare not."[8]

Three days later, on November 8, a composed Charles knelt on a square of black velvet and stated that he had proceeded against Rubempré only because of his suspicious behavior and that no slander against the king had been intended. He asserted that his friendship with the duke of Brittany was no more than an alliance of French princes, which Louis XI should be proud to encourage among his lords, as such bonding strengthened his monarchy. He protested that he did not need the king's pension and did not care that Louis had withdrawn the payments. Finally, he stated that although Louis had at times supported Charles's enemies, Charles would never be hostile to his king. But as the banquet that followed the embassy ended, Charles held back from the company leaving the hall. Noticing this, de Commynes watched Charles carefully and heard him, in a low voice, ask de Morvillier to "recommend me very humbly to the good grace of the king. Tell him he has had me scolded here by the chancellor but that he shall repent it before a year is past."[9]

The Rubempré affair elevated Charles greatly in his father's esteem. Philip had in fact left Hesdin so hastily because he had been warned by Charles of the suspicious behavior of Louis's agent at Gorichem—and of mortal threat to both of them. The duke now voiced his own fears and suspicions about the purposes of the French king toward Burgundy, and, as Chastellain recorded, Philip henceforth listened carefully to Charles's opinions. The duke now asked himself why the de Croys had counseled him to give up the string of strategically placed towns along the Somme; and why the de Croys had worked to keep him close at hand instead of preparing for the crusade. He realized that he had waited too long and that he would never conclude his noblest venture. At last Philip realized that service to Louis brought no honor, only vulnerability and fear. Philip and Charles now shared not only an increasingly warm and close relationship but also a common enemy: their king.

Isabel was invited to participate in the Christmas celebrations at Lille. With Philip, Isabel, and Charles now in the same place and of the same mind, the political strategy of Burgundy shifted dramatically. The first formal indication of a change in Burgundian policy came soon after the holiday court when Philip appointed his son the lieutenant general of Burgundy's armed forces. Charles quickly solidified his new position with alliances at home and then with additional ties with foreign powers. Once Charles secured the loyalty of the duke of Cleves—and now further strengthened by the security of his father's confidence—Charles felt ready to move against his longtime enemies, the de Croys. The de Croys had long held the territories of Namur, Boulogne, and Luxembourg—territories to which Charles had rights of lordship as Philip's heir. In February, Charles exercised his rights and seized these lands, prompting the de Croy family to flee the duchy of Burgundy.

A few weeks later Charles fulfilled his promise to make Louis pay for the accusations he had brought against Charles and his father at Lille the previous November. In mid-March Charles joined with the disaffected French princes who had resisted Louis's forceful leadership and had formed a league against him, the "League of the Common Weal," and convinced Philip to declare war on Louis on the pretext of forcing the king to deal justly with his nobles. What Charles really wanted was the opportunity to win back the Somme towns Philip had returned to France in 1463. Formal announcement was made in the Burgundian States General on April 25 that Charles was to lead an attack on France immediately. To allay any doubt concerning his authority, Charles also demanded at that time that the Burgundian Netherlands overcome their tardiness and declare him the sole and undisputed heir of his father. In mid-May Charles set out with his main army from Le Quesnoy, where he had spent a few days with his daughter, Marie, and his wife, Isabelle. As Philip relied more and more on his Great Council to govern Burgundy and concentrated less on developing strategies for his son to follow, Isabel stepped into the void left by Philip and exerted a strong influence on her son. She encouraged his campaign against the French to regain the Somme cities that secured Burgundy's northwestern border. The duchess continued to encourage her son to maintain his ties with Yorkist England, and while never trusting France, to look instead to the German states of the empire for territorial expansion.

By early June, Burgundian forces occupied several of the Somme towns. Impressed with the revitalized Burgundy, Scotland was quick to contract an alliance with Philip and Charles. On June 4 and 15, German princes followed suit, as the duke of Bavaria and the Elector Palatine allied themselves with Burgundy. On July 16, Charles defeated Louis's forces on the field of Montlhery, a few miles south of Paris. Four days later he sent Guillaume de Torcy to describe the battle and its outcome to Isabel. De Torcy neglected to inform her, of course, that Charles had sustained a serious neck wound and had come very close to being captured. The duchess celebrated his victory, though she also harbored the bitter memory of the actions of the citizens of the town of Dinant, who on hearing an incorrect report that Charles had been defeated at Montlhery had celebrated with great enthusiasm, not only burning an effigy of Charles but also chanting that he was the bastard child of Isabel and the bishop of Liège.

The Burgundian forces camped outside the walls of the city of Paris after their July victory over Louis, but Charles could not hope to win so large a city. Prepared to take care of their own defense, Parisians had closed the city gates and firmly reinforced the walls. The siege of Paris continued for several weeks, with neither supplies nor people leaving or entering the city until late August, when Louis broke the stalemate by offering his princes a peace conference. Charles agreed to take part in the negotiations to be held in late September 1465 at Conflans, a small town on the Seine River a few miles south of Paris. Louis soon discovered that unlike the other princes with whom Charles had joined to fight against the French crown, Charles would not be bought off with promises of money or territorial awards too dispersed through France to add power to his duchy. Charles insisted on receiving the Somme territories, in addition to the castellanies of Peronne, Roye, and Montdidier and the counties of Guines and Boulogne. Louis made no attempt at Conflans to heal the breach between Charles and the de Croys; clearly, Louis calculated that the de Croys were of no further use to him, and he gave no thought to their welfare.

According to the memoirs of his chronicler Philippe de Commynes, when Louis XI was asked why he had agreed to sign, on October 4, the Treaty of Conflans, which was so harmful to France, Louis responded wryly that it was because of the pressing need to placate his princes and the threat of "the invincible power of his brother-in-law of Charolais."[10]

The duchess applauded her son's achievements and mourned with him over the death of his mostly forgotten wife. For while Charles was negotiating at Conflans, Isabelle of Bourbon, the countess of Charolais, died suddenly and alone at Les Quesnoy on September 25. Although the duchess mourned the loss of Isabelle, as she had Charles's first wife, she also sought to transform that loss into another important victory for Burgundy. Within weeks of the death of the countess of Charolais, Guillaume de Clugny, one of Charles's closest advisers, arrived in London to propose a marriage between Charles and Margaret of York, a sister of the English king.

Frantic once again to prevent an Anglo-Burgundian marriage, Louis countered the English proposal by offering Charles the hand of his eldest daughter, four-year-old Anne. But the French proposal, which included the counties of Ponthieu and Champagne and a large dowry, was refused. A few months later, in the spring of 1466, an English embassy led by Lord Scales, brother of the English queen, arrived in Burgundy to offer the hand of the king's sister Margaret to Charles, as well as to propose a marriage between Charles's daughter Marie and Edward's younger brother, George, duke of Clarence.

In 1466, Isabel, now seventy, was more important to Burgundy's survival than she had ever been. Although she had much to celebrate in Charles's victory, the de Croys' banishment, Louis's military and diplomatic defeat, and England's matrimonial overtures, her diplomacy was still essential for Burgundy's economic, territorial, and strategic growth. Her husband was increasingly ill, her impetuous son was still in need of wise counsel—as well as a wife and heir; and Louis XI was still looking hungrily toward Burgundy, convinced that the duchy was divinely ordained to be the property of France. With such serious state matters to consider, perhaps Isabel's actions that summer can be understood, if not forgiven, when her unbending dignity took its toll on the town of Dinant.

Isabel had not forgiven the citizens of Dinant who had proclaimed Charles a bastard and the son of the bishop of Liège. Although John of Heinsberg's reputation was rich in such scandals, that of the duchess of Burgundy was spotless. After the signing of the Treaty of Conflans and Charles's victory over Louis, her son entered Dinant on August 25, 1466, to restore his mother's offended pride. He sacked the town and killed every man, woman, and child inside.

Notes

1. J. H. Ramsay, *Lancaster and York, A Century of English History (1399–1485)*, 2 vols. (Oxford: Clarendon Press, 1892), 2:238.
2. *Oeuvres de Chastellain*, ed. M. Le Baron Kervyn de Lettenhove, 4 vols. (Brussels: R. Heussner, 1864), 4:52.
3. Paul Murray Kendall, *Louis XI* (New York: W. W. Norton, 1971), 121.
4. Richard Vaughan, *Philip the Good: The Apogee of Burgundy* (New York: Barnes and Noble, 1970), 369 n. 3.
5. Marie Rose Thielemans, *Bourgogne et Angleterre, 1435–1467* (Brussels: Presses Universitaires de Bruxelles, 1966), 465–69.
6. *Oeuvres de Chastellain*, 5:26.
7. Vaughan, *Philip the Good*, 375.
8. Philippe de Commynes, *Mémoires*, ed. D. Godefroy and Leglet du Fresnoy, 4 vols. (Paris, 1747), vol. 1 , chap. 1.
9. de Commynes, *Mémoires*, vol. 1 , chap. 1.
10. de Commynes, *Mémoires*, 2:500.

Chapter Nine

Madame La Grande, 1467–1470

ISABEL RELAXED in the peace of La Motte-au-Bois after months in Ghent tending her ailing husband. The duke was still recovering from an apoplectic seizure suffered in a fit of rage over the failure of his treasurers to pay the balance of wages due his men-at-arms. Philip had been unconscious for a short period, and he was still struggling to regain clarity of speech when Isabel decided to leave for her estates, perhaps earlier than planned. Philip's personality had changed as he had recuperated, and Isabel had most likely decided that her absence from his chamber would be better for them both. Philip did not seem to miss either his wife or his son; his attention was now fastened on the repair and expansion of Princehof, his residence in Bruges.

For her part, Isabel now turned her attention to the troubling dispatches describing Edward IV's simultaneous negotiations with France and Burgundy. Between writing and dispatching letters to Charles, who was in Ghent that spring, she sat quietly in her solar, attempting to fit together the perplexing pieces of this triangular, political puzzle, only parts of which she understood. Isabel knew that the highly regarded Anthony, Bastard of Burgundy, was in England, ostensibly to respond to a challenge thrown down by Lord Scales during the Englishman's visit to Philip's court the previous October. What she did not know—but what she would have been delighted to learn—was that Anthony was actually in London to arrange for talks to be held concerning a marriage between

Charles and the king's sister, Margaret. Isabel was also initially unaware as to why the earl of Warwick had traveled to France once more and was being royally entertained by Louis XI at Rouen. When she did learn the reasons for the earl's journey, she was greatly troubled: not only had Warwick been given a commission on April 8 by King Edward to negotiate with the French king on trade issues, but more perturbing still, he was also discussing with the king the possibility of two marriages: one between Edward's sister Margaret and Louis's brother-in-law Philip of Bresse; the other between Edward's brother-in-law Richard of Gloucester and Louis's youngest daughter, Jeanne.

The Death of Duke Philip the Good

As Philip recuperated in the privacy of his chambers in Princehof, he drifted away from the demands of his duchy to happier pastimes. More and more of his days were devoted to the unlikely pleasures of sharpening knives and mending glassware. Not surprisingly, his court officers feared that their duke was losing his wits.

On the evening of June 12, when he rose at six from his two-hour nap, Philip was in especially good spirits and called for his chancellor. Philip had not eaten that day, his custom being to abstain from meat, fish, and fowl on Fridays, but he felt well enough after meeting with his chancellor to take a goblet of almond milk and an omelet before chatting with some workmen. The duke then went back to bed for the night, only to suddenly waken in great difficulty at two the next morning, struggling to breathe.

Surprisingly, in spite of his chronic illnesses, there were no physicians attending Philip that night. The fact that most of his servants were also absent was even more surprising to Philip's chronicler, Chastellain, who wondered how a man who had lived such a life of privilege could have been so abandoned at the time of his final agony. The chronicler gives no explanation nor does he give us any reason for the puzzling inattention of Philip's entourage. One might almost suspect a conspiracy—after all, the duke's fondness for almond-flavored milk would have made it easy to poison him with arsenic, with its characteristic almond taste. However, although the accusations of poisoning abounded in many notable deaths of the time, no chronicler or subsequent historian mentions the possibility of Philip's having been poisoned.[1]

Chastellain recorded that Philip awoke abruptly and struggled to breathe, and his few remaining attendants tried frantically to reach into his throat to clear the phlegm that obstructed his airway. Philip's fever rose through the next day, and his violent vomiting added to the difficulty of his breathing. As Philip's suffering increased, the attendants whose services were no longer needed fled Princehof. Word was sent to Ghent on Sunday for Charles's immediate return.

Charles arrived too late to speak with his father and could only watch him struggle against death. The duke died at ten o'clock, Monday evening, June 15. Surprisingly, Isabel did not arrive for three more days, entering Bruges on Thursday, June 18. Charles was inconsolable, and he lay on his bed weeping loudly and wringing his hands in despair, bitter at the abandonment of his father in his last hours.

For the twenty-four hours following Philip's death, people filed past his body, which lay in state on his own bed in Princehof, his head capped in black velvet.[2] An autopsy completed the next day, June 17, revealed that disease affected only the spleen and the adjoining lower lobe of his lung. When Isabel arrived on Thursday, neither mother nor son could speak without tears interrupting their words. They were calmed only by the preparations for Philip's funeral. As Philip's body lay in the ducal chapel on a black-draped, six-foot bier lit by four massive candles, his wife and son ordered fifteen hundred bolts of black fabric to clothe all the servants from the least in the kitchen to the greatest lords of the court.

Deeply moved by Philip's sudden death, the people of Bruges—their numbers increased by visiting merchants and tradesmen to twenty thousand—also dressed in black and silently lined the route of the duke's cortege as it traveled toward the church of St. Donatian, Sunday, June 21. Chastellain accompanied Charles in the procession and was moved to describe the son's searing grief, as the new duke cried out loudly, "My God! Good duke, my noble and sweetest father are you really dead? Have you left us who loved and served you, now abandoned orphans?"[3]

Philip's casket was covered in richly embroidered cloth of gold and was carried by twelve counts and twelve barons. Charles and his mother walked solemnly behind the catafalque and were followed by sixteen hundred torches—four hundred each from the ducal household, the town of Bruges, the Franc of Bruges, and the artisans of the town—and behind these came the same number of noblemen, officers, and important bourgeois. A military guard of four masters-at-arms from Brabant, Flanders, Artois, and Hainault preceded the group of twenty-one bishops and abbesses who completed the procession. They slowly entered St. Donatian, which was lined completely in black except for Philip's ducal coat of arms and the symbol of his Order of the Golden Fleece. During the four-hour ceremony, the heat emanating from more than 1,400 candles was so great that it had to be released through holes cut in the windows. On Monday, June 22, Philip's heart and entrails were interred in the church; the rest of his body was to rest in the nave until Charles arranged for its transfer to the Charterhouse of Champmol at Dijon.

The Reign of the New Duke

Charles's authority, at his father's death, was in question throughout the Burgundian territories, for although Philip had given his son great freedom to govern during the last several years of his life, the duke had maintained overall control of the duchy through the administration of the Great Council. Openly encouraged by Isabel since 1464, however, and allowed to exercise his financial and administrative abilities, Charles had created his own political and financial sphere of power during that period. He had shouldered his way back into the influence of his father's court—quickly reclaiming his own lands of Picardy from de Croy control—and had successfully led the duke's forces into France in 1465. He had his own wealthy lands in Holland and had won for himself the towns of Peronne, Roye, and Montdidier from Louis XI in 1465—in addition to regaining the Somme towns, which he kept as his personal possessions—and having garrisoned them all, he now collected rich revenues from them for his treasury. Furthermore, while still the count of Charolais, Charles had gathered about himself a group of officials, courtiers, and councillors who formed the nucleus of his present administration.

Always antagonistic to Philip because he had threatened their hard-won right to self-rule, Ghent had not sent a single representative to the funeral ceremonies in Bruges. This important and unruly town was particularly disturbed by the question of the balance of power created by Philip's death. Both the wealthy merchants and the rebellious artisans who struggled against merchant control of their professions pleaded with Charles to come to Ghent to confirm that he would not abolish the city's self-rule.

On the morning of June 28, the disaffected of the town of Ghent—long resentful of the ducal support of guild merchants over their own rights as artisans and supporters of urban independence—challenged the new duke's reign. That morning, dressed all in black and accompanied by a number of courtiers, Charles entered Ghent to respond to the rebellious artisans. They saw a dark, muscular man of average height, slightly bow-legged from hard riding, with a broad back and sloping shoulders. He moved forward stiffly, keeping his eyes on the ground, his dark curly hair, dark eyes, olive complexion, round face, and heavy features unlike the aquiline appearance of his father. The Ghenters took his measure. Although both merchants and artisans had been negotiating trade and government privileges with Philip's heir for several months, they recognized a different Charles before them this morning.

The rebel leaders of Ghent must have sensed in Charles a newly somber authority, but the duke had to prove his leadership to them. The duke of Burgundy's authority was unlike that of Louis XI, whose divine right was established by anointing with holy oils at his coronation. Charles was also very unlike Philip, who found conciliation the best tool to control the patchwork of localized territories that might at any time contest his rule. But Charles, who was neither a conciliator nor a recognized monarch, now claimed a "divine right" of power over all of his father's territories.

Many of the citizens of Ghent had celebrated a local feast enthusiastically before the new duke's solemn arrival, and they unfortunately continued their celebrating that morning by tearing down the tax collector's building while Charles waited in the town hall to meet with their leaders.

The drama heated as the disorderly crowd made a number of radical demands, insisting that the duke reverse the constraints placed on them by Philip after 1453, when he had put down the town's rebellion. There was first of all the bothersome "quellote," a local tax placed on every article that entered the city. Then they demanded clemency for city officials charged with embezzlement. They stipulated that the craft-guild banners be restored, and Ghent's control over the countryside be extended. While preparing to meet with the leaders of the rebellious artisans, Charles lost his temper and struck one of their representatives across the face with his riding whip. "For God's sake, do not slap that man again," his councillor Groothouse, the governor of Holland, pleaded, "if you are ready to die, I am not. Go down, show yourself, and speak with them." Charles followed this advice, and appeared before the crowd and addressed them in Flemish; but he fled the volatile situation the following day, with his two most important possessions intact: his state treasury and his daughter, Marie.[4]

While Ghent led the resistance to Charles's reign, a series of other rebellions caught fire through all the towns of Flanders, Artois, and Brabant. The draconian response of the new duke, who did not hesitate to use military force against the rebels to burn and raze rebellious towns and execute their leaders, effectively quelled these uprisings, however, and Liège, St. Omer, and even Brussels were quickly brought under Duke Charles's command within the year. Isabel stayed particularly close to her son during this period and worked to temper his rash responses and frequent resort to force. She was joined in these attempts by the constable of France, Louis St. Pol, as well as envoys from Rome, but the Milanese ambassador reflected often in these early years that Charles was a stubborn man and only wanted war.

Having won from Louis XI at Conflans in 1465 all of the Somme towns his father had returned to the French king, Charles was content to withdraw from his new borderlands with France and concentrate on his policy of expansion into the empire. Charles had prepared himself for this strategy by following Isabel's example, establishing important diplomatic relations to protect Burgundy from French aggression. Now he could count as allies the duke of Cleves, the elector palatine, the duke of

Bavaria, Francis II of Brittany, the king of Denmark, and even Charles, the brother of Louis XI.

The duke of Burgundy found himself in a most favorable situation in the late summer of 1467. Charles enjoyed the growing unease of Louis XI, who found his strategies increasingly obstructed by conflicting factions at the English court. The earl of Warwick relied on his French allies in his plot to remove Edward of York from the throne. Recognizing Edward's need for a powerful ally—and the economic benefits such a union would bring to Burgundy as well as to England—Charles moved to solidify his alliance with the king of England.

Isabel's Last Negotiation

Louis XI's rule was weakened by the bitter dissension between the French princes and the lesser nobility. He feared Burgundian aggression and took steps to preempt the new duke's alliance with the English king, who considered Louis a usurper. That summer of 1467, the French king offered attractive proposals of his own to the English. When he had entertained Warwick's embassy of June 1467 at La Bouille, near Rouen, Philip was still alive and Charles merely his heir; now, with Philip gone and Charles a likely match for Margaret of York, Louis XI offered his brother-in-law, Philip, count of Bress, as a bridegroom for Margaret. For good measure, Louis also offered Margaret the choices of René, count of Alençon; his nephew Philibert of Savoy, the young prince of Piedmont; and even Galeazzo Sforza, the new duke of Milan. Louis enhanced the French bait by offering the hand of his younger daughter, Jeanne, to Richard of Gloucester, Edward's youngest brother—adding the secret promise to help Gloucester obtain Holland, Zeeland, and Brabant from a defeated and dismembered Burgundy. He offered to bear all the cost of Margaret's wedding and dowry, and to provide Edward IV with a substantial pension. All of this was to no avail, however, and nothing could sway the English from the Burgundian union, with its long-term political and economic benefits.

Charles's determination to proceed with the English marriage and alliance was matched by Edward IV's certainty that Warwick's pro-French policy, which foresaw the return to England of Margaret of Anjou as queen, was too politically volatile to benefit England. Although seventy years old, Isabel was vitally alert to all the factors involved in this English alliance, and quite capable of serving as Charles's most knowledgeable and trusted negotiator. When in October 1467 Edward formally agreed to the Burgundian marriage, Charles asked his mother to negotiate his marriage with Margaret, and as part of this agreement to establish terms of peace and profitable trade with England. In late December 1467, Charles and his mother prepared to welcome an English delegation to Brussels. Under the leadership of Queen Elizabeth's brothers, Lord Scales and Lord Rivers, the English discussed the agenda for the formal marriage and treaty negotiations to be held the following month.

From November 1467 to June 1468, Louis XI did all in his power to interfere with Isabel's plans. When Burgundy failed to reciprocate Edward's spirit of cooperation during the marriage negotiations—maintaining long-standing barriers of trade with the Lowland merchants and Flemish statutes protecting Burgundian interests with the English—riots broke out in both countries. Louis XI was quick to offer additional economic benefits for English trade in France. At the same time, the French king attempted to obstruct any loans Edward IV might need to meet the demands of his sister's dowry by spreading word to his financial contacts in Milan and Florence that Edward was a poor man and would not be able to meet his obligation to them. Louis provoked diversions in England that winter by encouraging a Lancaster invasion of Wales and spreading slanderous stories about Margaret's behavior, suggesting that she was not a virgin and even had a son. Failing in each of these attempts to derail Isabel's negotiations, Louis XI tried to block Guillaume de Clugny's mission to the pope to obtain the necessary dispensation for the marriage of these fourth-degree cousins. De Clugny, the papal notary of Flanders, was able to obtain the dispensation only seven months later, when his elaborate arguments and generous bribes succeeded in producing this most essential document.

Isabel based her negotiations with England on the terms of the contract for her own marriage in 1429. In talks from October to February

1468, she forged agreements between England and Burgundy on mutual defense, trade, currency exchange, fishing rights, and freedom of travel in addition to a marriage settlement far more favorable to the Burgundians—and to the new duchess—than her own marriage contract with Portugal had been. Not only did Margaret retain her rights of inheritance to the English throne but also, if she were to die within the first year of her marriage, her dowry was to remain in Burgundian hands, while Isabel's had been promised to Portugal. Finally, Isabel's strategy dictated that Edward IV provide the 200,000 crowns of this dowry in three payments, guaranteeing a financial and economic cooperation between the two families.

Based on this dowry, Charles included in his dower to Margaret the cities of Malines, Oudenaarde, and Dendermond, which provided rents and taxes guaranteed to yield 16,000 crowns each year, to be supplemented by the duke if they fell short. In addition, Isabel arranged for Margaret to receive an allowance of 22,000 livres a year for her normal expenses. Late in February 1468, as Isabel turned seventy-one, she signed and had ratified the completed treaty of marriage, trade, and alliance with England. The following month Edward IV signed and ratified the treaty in England. Two more months were to pass, however, before de Clugny returned with the required papal dispensation, and when it arrived at Westminster in late May, Edward IV proclaimed that now his sister was to marry "one of the mightiest princes of the world that beareth no crown."[5] Louis XI, meanwhile, having failed in all of his attempts to prevent this marriage uniting his enemies, ordered French ships to waylay Margaret's fleet on its way to Sluis.

The Marriage of Margaret and Charles

The marriage was not much celebrated outside Burgundy, and the chronicler Jean de Wavrin noted that the union took place in spite of the French king, the earl of Warwick, and the popular sentiments of England. The earl was so upset with the marriage that he did not attend the general council meeting at Kingston when Margaret gave her formal consent, and his refusal to help with her dowry became a serious cause for conflict between the "kingmaker" earl and Edward, the man he had fought so diligently to place on the English throne. The English merchants resisted Margaret's marriage because of the continuing restrictions on the sale of English cloth in Burgundy, and the merchants showed their anger by attacking well into the late summer months of 1468 all those merchants from Holland and Flanders who lived among them.

Surmounting all of this opposition, Margaret sailed for Sluis on the *New Ellen,* leaving Margate on June 23 in the protective company of fifteen large ships. The fleet carried the expensive cargo of clothing, jewels, horses, and equipment of the wealthy Englishmen who attended Margaret, and the well-armed ships served to protect the passengers from possible attacks by both French sailors and the pirates who hunted the channel. Although the crossing took only one night and two days, Margaret and her ladies must have spent much of the daylight hours on deck scanning the water for enemy ships and the night imagining the approach of the French or pirate sails. The wedding party arrived at Sluis harbor at six the second evening, Saturday, June 25, without incident except for a dispute over some French silks that an English ship claimed were taken in a skirmish the previous night. Margaret's wedding journey at sea was far easier than the one taken from Portugal by the dowager Isabel almost forty years before.

Trumpets and clarions greeted Margaret's arrival, and during the fanfare Simon Lalaing, one of the ducal chamberlains, boarded the *New Ellen* to greet the new bride. With Olivier la Marche, Isabel had carefully planned the details of Margaret's wedding ceremony and the receptions that followed. Charles himself had remained in the area of Sluis, Damme, and Bruges for the uncharacteristically long period of two weeks, waiting for his bride's arrival to guarantee that all the plans were carried through. By the time Margaret disembarked at six o'clock Saturday evening, the townspeople stood in their doorways holding flaming torches to light her path through town. Wearing a dark red dress trimmed in black—the colors of Burgundy—Margaret made her way along the lighted, carpeted streets of Sluis to the home of the wealthy Guy van Baenst, which had been prepared for her stay. The next day, Margaret was to meet the two most important ladies of Burgundy, the duchess Isabel and Isabel's granddaughter, the eleven-year-old Lady Marie.

These two ladies arrived at mid-morning on Sunday, June 26, and after the formalities of greeting, disappeared into the house for a private dinner. The women spent three hours together exchanging news of events in England and of current affairs that concerned them in Burgundy. There is no doubt that Marie had missed the close companionship of Isabelle of Bourbon and that she welcomed the prospect of friendship with the young woman who was about to become her stepmother. Although there are no records describing their meeting that day, that they found pleasure in each other's company for the rest of their lives is clear. Marie shared many interests with the new bride—reading, riding, hunting, falconry—and Isabel herself was later reported to have been "well pleased with the sight of this lovely lady and pleased with her manners and virtues."[6]

Never described as a beautiful woman, Margaret had fine features, and she was slim and very tall (close to six feet) with a straight carriage. She had cool, gray eyes and a small mouth, but her smile expressed warmth for those with whom she shared her wry humor, wit, and graciousness. At twenty-two, Margaret was thirteen years younger than her husband, but she had a keen intelligence and a strong will. The pair were certainly stark physical opposites, the tall, sylphlike, and fair English princess and the dark, burly duke. The following Monday, when the pair finally met at an undisclosed location, the princess had to stoop to receive the kiss of her soon-to-be husband. A week later, on July 3 between five and six o'clock in the morning, they were married in a private ceremony in the house of a wealthy merchant in the port city of Damme, a few miles downstream from Bruges. Charles left for Bruges immediately, allowing his new duchess the separate honor of her own "Joyeuse Entrée" into that city.

The bride arrived in a golden litter that was covered in crimson cloth and drawn by a matching pair of splendid white horses. She was dressed in "white cloth of gold trimmed with white ermine and a cloak of crimson" for her entry into that important city, with a regal bearing that impressed the burgers and merchants who crowded the streets in greeting. Any aloofness

Margaret might have suggested was dispelled, however, as she lifted her hand and acknowledged the citizens of Bruges, oblivious to the wind and rain that threatened to sweep away the golden coronet perched on top of her now damp, shoulder-length hair. Escorted by Lord Scales and Lord Ravenstein, an important half-brother of Charles, she was followed by many of the great lords of England and Burgundy, who were in turn followed by the Knights of the Golden Fleece. Several other groups joined in the procession: self-important and dour black-cloaked city magistrates and burghers contrasted with over ninety elegantly clad bishops; and the seven merchant associations made a magnificent show, Spanish, Hansards, Genoese, Florentines, Lombards, and natives of other northern Italian states, each dressed in the colors of their "nations." The arms of England and Burgundy fluttered everywhere along the route, with the mottoes chosen by the duke and the new duchess appended: the lion, the lily, and the leopard rode the breeze over "Je l'ay emprins" (I have undertaken it) for Charles and "Bien en aviengne" (May good come of it) for Margaret.

As the now thoroughly soaked Lord Scales and Lord Ravenstein escorted Margaret toward Princehof, the great processions entered the courtyard of the castle's main gateway, where red and white wine flowed freely from the bows of sculpted archers. As Margaret rode through the stormy, grey courtyard toward the ducal residence, she was both pleased and startled to see mead spurt from the breast of a golden pelican perched on an artificial tree. Quite weary, however, from many days of formalities and processionals preceding her arrival in Bruges, and cold and wet from the storm that swept her entry through the town, Margaret must have welcomed the opportunity to rest in a room prepared particularly for her in a tower of Princehof. As she placed her head on the silken pillow, she may not have even noticed the walls decorated with daisies, or smiled at the tapestries illustrating wifely chastity, which hung on all the walls of her chamber.[7]

In spite of the rain, Bruges had decorated with torches the many canals that wound through the town and placed pennants and flowers on each of the 525 bridges. Preparations had been made throughout the city for nine days of formal celebrations. While the aristocracy dined that night in the banqueting hall that was draped in blue and white—the high table in purple, black, and gold—and lit by an ingenious system of candelabra and mirrors, the townspeople prepared the marketplace for the Tournament of the Golden Tree. When the duke made his appearance there the next day, he wore a golden gown encrusted in diamonds, pearls, and great jewels and a splendid crown, and he rode a richly ornamented horse covered in a tapestry fabric hung with golden bells. For his wedding celebration, Charles had been transformed from a soldier to a knight who might well have stepped out of one of his tapestries.

Isabel, Margaret, and the Policy of Charles the Bold

Charles left Bruges immediately after the wedding celebrations and Margaret journeyed alone with Marie to the great towns of her new territories in Flanders, Brabant, and Hainault. She applied the intelligence and court experience she had gained in England to impress both the citizens and their leadership in such towns as Ursel, Ghent, Dendermonde, Asse, Brussels, Oudenaarde, and Courtrai. Although Louis XI had not been successful in preventing this marriage, the French king's antagonism toward Margaret was clear, and he began a careful campaign to neutralize the threat it presented to France. His opposition promised that Margaret would soon be exposed to a larger theater of politics than the domestic quarrels of the English aristocracy with which she was familiar.

The dowager duchess Isabel also left Bruges shortly after the wedding celebrations for the quiet privacy of her estate at La Motte-au-Bois. At peace in the shade of her beloved forest, she expressed pleasure in her new daughter-in law's progresses throughout Burgundy and was satisfied that both Margaret and Marie were comfortably situated in Brussels for the month of August. As these ladies spent their days at Coudenberg, alternately reading and hunting in the adjoining parkland forest of Soignes, Isabel was occupied with the strategies of Charles and Louis XI. She was aware that her son's larger plan to expand Burgundian territory into the empire held more promise in 1468 than when pursued by his father all the years before, as the duchy now benefited from the firm

English alliance she had worked so long to obtain. Isabel had no doubt that Louis XI threatened Burgundy's western frontier, however, and she approved of her son's military opposition to the French forces that gathered south of the Somme River. But never an advocate of battle to solve diplomatic issues, Isabel hoped for a peaceful settlement between France and Burgundy that would allow Charles to turn eastward to pursue the crown so long sought by his father.

From August to October, French and Burgundian forces postured on the frontier, but neither attacked. Isabel therefore hoped that a diplomatic solution might still be reached eventually. At the moment, a standoff was the best that could be hoped for. Charles wished to husband his forces and wanted a French guarantee that his eastern borders would be secure from French aggression when he moved into the empire; Louis did not want to engage a Burgundy firmly backed by a strong English alliance while France faced a simultaneous danger of attack by Charles's ally, Duke Francis II of Brittany. Finally, a meeting between Charles and Louis XI was arranged on October 15 in the town of Peronne in Picardy, where Louis agreed to sign a treaty of friendship with the new duke and Charles promised to pay homage to Louis XI for his French holdings. In turn, Charles exacted 100,000 crowns in reparations from Louis for the damages inflicted earlier by French troops along the Somme. If Louis did not honor any of the terms of the treaty, the territories dependent on the French crown in Burgundy would relinquish French jurisdiction. When the Treaty of Peronne was formally announced in Paris on November 19, 1468, Charles was free to turn his full attention toward the Rhineland and in particular to Lorraine—which would connect his northern and southern territories—while Louis XI became more determined than ever to break the Anglo-Burgundian bond.

The autumn had ended well for Isabel. She was eager to congratulate her son during the Christmas season celebrations planned at Hesdin, and also eager to greet her new daughter-in-law and enjoy the gaiety of her twelve-year-old granddaughter. But intensely involved in state business, Charles could not join his ladies that December. The duke of Burgundy demanded the submission of the proud city of Ghent, stripping the leaders of their hard-won self-government and imposing a long list of punishments for their open rebellion against his accession to the duchy in July. Convinced that obedience to ducal rule was a divinely ordained duty, he dealt with Ghent brutally—just as in Liège, where he had punished the rebellion on October 9, massacring the populace and burning much of the town, and then ordering the leaders tied back to back and thrown from the highest towers. Charles's reputation for harshness and brutality preceded him into the Rhineland. Soon after these bloody events in Dinant, Ghent, and Liège, Charles took the opportunity given him by Duke Sigismund of Austria in early 1469 to purchase the upper Rhineland territory of the Alsace, and the German princes became alarmed that they too might fall prey to the duke's brutality along with his ambitions.

Isabel's political strategies proved too subtle for a man of Charles's temperament. Despite her earlier recommendation, he remained unaware of the German princes' resistance to his role in the empire, while Louis XI did not. The French king encouraged their alliance with the Swiss cantons against Burgundy in the south and east. Charles now turned his attention from the unstable situation in the east toward England, where he hoped to help Edward IV lure the embittered Warwick back into the Yorkist court. But the Burgundian marriage had so embarrassed the earl that the cost would be high. To heal the wounded Warwick and to please his proud brother-in-law, Edward IV arranged for the earl to lead a prestigious embassy to present Charles with the Order of the Garter. This was a great honor for Charles, but it was also a dangerous one for him to accept: a liege-man of the French king, as Charles was, was forbidden to become the knight of a foreign power. Louis XI learned of the offer and was pleased that once again Charles's pride had played into his hands.

Warwick arrived at La Motte-au-Bois in early April to meet first with the dowager duchess Isabel. As the earl had a personality much like her son's—ambitious, direct, impatient, and proud—Warwick's company pleased the great lady, now seventy-two. Warwick spent several days with Isabel, mining her political acumen, enjoying walks in her gardens, and relishing the sumptuous dining and entertainments she had arranged to detain him with her for that period. She too studied the earl, and acutely aware of diplomatic dangers, arrived ahead of the earl at Hesdin later in April, to warn Charles that the glory of accepting an English knighthood could bring charges of treason.

Warwick concealed his resentment of the Burgundians and used his time in the Low Countries to advantage. He met with the Lancastrian exiles, Edmund Beaufort, duke of Somerset, and Henry Holland, duke of Exeter, who had been given protection by a Burgundy striving to maintain a measure of neutrality, but who asked to distance themselves from Bruges during the wedding of Margaret and Charles. Warwick convinced his former enemies that insurrection might now succeed in returning their estates and inheritance.

The earl plotted to remove Edward IV, the English king responsible for his failure, and to establish a new, more malleable man to wear the crown. His plan was to marry his oldest daughter, Isabel, to the younger brother of Edward IV, George, duke of Clarence, and place him on the English throne. England would join with France to defeat Burgundy, and Warwick's own wealth and influence, increased by the partition and absorption of several of Charles's Lowland territories, would predominate near the throne.

On returning to England, however, Warwick learned that Edward IV forbade the marriage between his daughter, Isabel Neville, and the king's brother, the duke of Clarence. After a very curt reception for the French embassy that had accompanied Warwick to Edward's court, Edward demanded that the earl explain these marriage plans, which reeked of secret arrangements with the French. Warwick, however, avoided answering Edward's summons directly, and managed to reconcile with Edward, allaying the king's suspicions of the Neville family's intentions until the following summer, when, on July 11, Clarence married the earl's daughter.

Within days of the marriage, Warwick and Clarence declared against the king's bad government and declared war on him. Throughout the summer, men from the north and west of England joined Warwick's fight to remove Edward from the throne and, with him, the hated Woodville family. As Warwick and his new son-in-law moved to take charge of the government in London, Edward faced the choice of remaining in his capital as a prisoner or escaping to the continent. He fled England with his youngest brother, Richard, duke of Gloucester, and a few hundred supporters on September 29. He reached the safety of the Lowlands possessions of Charles of Burgundy a few days later.

The duchess of Burgundy remained relatively close to Charles during these first two years of his rule. During this time she was able to influence her son to use economic pressure instead of military force to help restore Edward to his throne. Charles threatened the merchants of London with a loss of all trade rights with Burgundy unless they immediately declared their loyalty to Edward IV. When the merchants joined the Lancastrian movement to restore Henry VI to the throne—providing no support for Warwick's aim to replace Henry VI with the duke of Clarence—the earl was forced to withdraw his son-in-law's claim to the throne and to sail immediately with his family to the safety of Calais in early April 1470. Warwick was refused entry into Calais because of his treason against Edward IV, but Louis XI welcomed the earl.

In his pleasure at the manifest weakness of the English monarchy—and the greater likelihood of removing Charles from power—Louis offered Warwick the same terms given the Englishman in 1467: Louis would give Holland, Brabant, and Zeeland to Warwick if he supported an Anglo-French invasion to dismantle Burgundy. Warwick spent the following summer under French protection, attacking the Burgundian navy and merchant fleets whenever possible, harassing their convoys and capturing nearly one hundred of their ships.

Furious with this French support of Warwick's piracy, Charles was in no mood to receive the ambassadors Louis XI sent to his court. Chastellain describes in tones of wonder, and one suspects wry humor as well, how in preparation to receive the French envoys Charles had his dais raised an additional five inches, placing upon it his canopied throne, draped with golden cloth and trailing black velvet that flowed down a long flight of steps and extended over the entire audience chamber, "offering a regal presence not assumed by any emperor nor king." Charles did not restrain his contempt for Louis XI when Jacques Spontin of the Paris Parlement and Guyot Pot, bailiff of Vermandois, appeared before him on

July 15, 1470, to offer French compensation for Burgundy's naval and merchant losses. Chastellain heard Charles taking a page from Isabel's own philosophy, telling the Frenchmen, "Among us Portuguese there is a custom that when anyone we have reckoned among our friends makes friends with our enemies, we commend them to all the hundred thousand devils in Hell." All those about Charles were quite astounded by the manner in which he addressed the envoys of the king.

But Louis XI was not impressed by Charles's anger. The French king had enough arrows in his quiver to bring down Charles of Burgundy: the German princes and neighboring Swiss cantons ready to unite against Charles; the duke's own reputation for brutality, which made him unfit to rule; and Charles's treasonous acceptance of an English knighthood. When the French king finally won over Francis II of Brittany, a crucial ally of Burgundy who had threatened the security of the French king's northwestern frontier, Louis XI was prepared to act to destroy both Edward IV and Charles of Burgundy. That summer he supported Warwick's plan to marry the earl's younger daughter to Queen Margaret of Anjou's son—with the proviso that if Henry VI had no further children, the English crown would be given to Warwick's other son-in-law, the duke of Clarence—if Margaret agreed to accept Warwick as an ally in an invasion of England that France was willing to support.

The marriage was contracted in early August, and as good as his word, Louis XI traveled to Honfleur to meet with Warwick and to provide him with the necessary men, money, and ships to back a Lancastrian invasion of England. With the imminent destruction of the English Yorkists—and with Burgundy weakened by the removal of that English support—Louis XI planned to announce his annulment of the treaty of Peronne, bring charges of treason against the duke of Burgundy, and to declare all Burgundian lands forfeit to the king of France.

As Charles of Burgundy kept Edward IV informed of all of Warwick's activities during the summer and fall of 1470, the duchess Margaret wrote desperate letters from Brussels to both of her brothers—the duke of Clarence in Paris and the inexplicably nonchalant English king Edward—

attempting to prevent the coming rebellion. She followed these attempts with long gossipy letters to Isabel, keeping the dowager duchess apprised of the unfolding crises and probably eager for any suggestions the experienced Isabel might offer her. Meanwhile, the mother of both men, Cicely, duchess of York, had also attempted to bring peace between the brothers, but nothing these ladies did cooled the forward movement of rebellion, and Warwick sailed with an English fleet toward English shores on September 29, 1470. Within a few days a coalition of Warwick's followers and the Lancastrian faction—representing a decided majority of the nation—accepted Henry VI as their legal king. On October 2 Edward IV escaped from the north of England, where he had ridden just as Warwick landed in the south. Edward reached Lynn on the Channel coast, and on October 3 sailed toward the Low Countries where he was met by Gruuthuyse, the governor of Holland, and taken to the Hague.

When the chronicler de Commynes returned to Calais after Edward IV's expulsion from England, he was amazed how quickly the loyalties of men change. The Yorkist symbol of the white rose was nowhere to be seen, the "ragged staff" of Warwick's household having replaced it throughout the city. Men who had been suspect were now held in highest regard. Chastellain disagrees with de Commynes, however, noting that Edward IV had "stout-hearted followers who never laid aside their roses."[8]

On October 8, one week after Warwick's landing in England, Louis XI brought his charges against the duke of Burgundy and on November 13 the French announced their treaty with Warwick to reinstate the Lancastrian kingship. A few weeks later, on December 3, Louis declared war on Burgundy and pronounced all sections of the treaty of Peronne null and void. As Charles joined his mother, wife, and daughter at Hesdin in 1470 for Isabel's last Christmas, each member of the family realized that Louis XI had left them with no alternatives. Duke Charles could no longer maintain any pretense of cautious neutrality between England and France. Although Edward IV was now an embarrassment and Margaret's ties to England were now devalued, Charles had to back the exiled king completely in his effort to regain the English throne.

Notes

1. The chronicler "leaves up to God the judgement of such a great man whose vices might have outweighed his virtues." *Oeuvres de Chastellain*, ed. M. Le Baron Kervyn de Lettenhove, 4 vols. (Brussels: R. Heussner, 1864), 5:227–29.
2. Vaughan, *Charles the Bold*, 1–2; *Oeuvres de Chastellain*, 5:227–35.
3. *Oeuvres de Chastellain*, 5:233.
4. Ruth Putnam, *Charles the Bold: Last Duke of Burgundy, 1433–1477* (New York and London: G. P. Putnam's Sons, 1908), 170–80.
5. Christine Weightman, *Margaret of York, Duchess of Burgundy, 1446–1503* (New York: St. Martin's Press, 1998), 41.
6. Weightman, *Margaret of York*, 51.
7. Weightman, *Margaret of York*, 52–55.
8. *Oeuvres de Chastellain*, 6:488.

Chapter Ten

The Death of Isabel: Danger for Burgundy, 1471

Isabel, the French War, and the English Dilemma

NEARLY SEVENTY-FOUR, Madame la Grande was tired of the demands of court life. She dared not, however, stay away from the Christmas celebrations at Hesdin in 1470. Louis XI's December 3 declaration of war on Burgundy had placed Charles in a political dilemma, and Isabel was determined to help her son find a solution that would strengthen Burgundy and ensure its future. Louis XI's support that winter of Warwick's campaign to replace both Henry VI and Edward IV with yet another candidate for the English crown—the earl's own son-in-law, Edward, Prince of Wales—forced Charles to make a formal choice between the royal contenders. Charles must either fully support Edward IV's attempt to regain his crown or allow Warwick's campaign to proceed unopposed, with the French king's encouragement. Louis IX had, in effect, called on the duke of Burgundy to reveal which side he was on in the dynastic struggle in England.

As Isabel ordered her caravan readied for the uncomfortable trip northward across the wet, windy fields leading to Hesdin, she worried about the new pressures Charles faced because of the presence in Burgundy of his brother-in-law, Edward, the English king who waited patiently in The Hague for the duke of Burgundy to decide his fate. Ever pragmatic, Isabel had always maintained a position of apparent neutrality in regard to English affairs—reluctant to support either side openly for fear of damaging Burgundy's economic relations with England, while discreetly supporting the faction most likely to succeed. She now wanted to ensure that Charles would carry on her struggle to secure Burgundy's economic future. She must use this time with Charles to make sure that he would not show his hand until the outcome of the dispute was clearer.

Comfortably accommodated and splendidly entertained since his arrival in The Hague, Edward was nevertheless growing increasingly impatient as Christmas approached. While providing Edward with every courtesy, Charles had not granted the English king a formal presence at the Burgundian court, in keeping with the appearance of Burgundian neutrality. The strategy allowed Isabel to use the holiday season at Hesdin to good advantage. Although she earnestly supported her daughter-in-law's pleas that Edward be given help in his bid to regain the English crown, she advised restraint, and reminded Charles of the merchants of Holland and Flanders.

Finally, a few days after Christmas, the eagerly awaited summons to meet with his brother-in-law arrived at The Hague and Edward wasted no time responding to the call. Racing both his companions and his caravan of supplies, Edward's horse cleared the marshy lowlands quickly, as the king made his way south toward the small and blustery winter post of Ostcamp, near Bruges. Isabel also hurried back across the wintry fields well before the new year, as Charles had asked his mother to prepare her residence for this important meeting. Because Isabel's retreat at La Motte-au-Bois was not an official residence of Burgundy, her estate was an ideal location in which to draw up a strategy to reclaim the Yorkist crown.

When Edward arrived at Isabel's residence on January 2, he was no doubt surprised at the simplicity of La Motte, the very private nature of the meeting, and the perplexing coolness of his brother-in-law. During the two-day visit—which included two Lancastrian dukes, Somerset and Exeter, to give the appearance of continuing Burgundian neutrality—Edward must have been both puzzled and annoyed by Charles's refusal to declare his support for the Yorkists. The duke of Burgundy seemed more attentive to Somerset and Exeter, especially when they asserted that Warwick was now their enemy as well as Burgundy's. They argued that the "kingmaker" earl had not only stripped them of their estates and inheritance in 1461 but also now strove to replace Henry VI with the king's son—who was now married to the earl's youngest daughter—to increase his own influence and power in England. Edward's consternation lasted only one day, however, as he was soon informed in secret that Charles only appeared to favor the Lancastrians and was in fact prepared to support Edward's return to England.

Soon after leaving La Motte in early January, Charles sent an embassy to assure the Calais government of Burgundy's intention to maintain alliance with England. In a more compelling message, however, his ambassadors also warned the Calais government not to endanger their town's safety by welcoming Warwick's soldiers, who were about to cross the channel to join French forces against the Burgundians.

Having thus sought to counter Warwick's plans in Calais, Charles then proceeded to upset the earl's ambitions in England. Aware that English merchants desperately needed to keep the Anglo-Burgundian alliance alive, Charles threatened that they would lose this Lowland trade unless they threw their support behind Edward's kingship. Where once Warwick had pulled the strings, making and unmaking kings, he was now a puppet in the contest between Louis XI and the duke of Burgundy.

Having declared to the English in Calais that he thought of himself as "more Lancastrian than the Lancastrians in England," the duke of Burgundy was secretly arranging for the funds, men, and supplies Edward of York needed to reclaim the English crown. Charles discreetly arranged for his brother-in-law to receive the enormous sum of 5,175,00 French francs, to sail on the *Anthony* (a ship belonging to the brother-in-law of one of the admirals of the duchy) with a fleet of thirty-six vessels (fifteen hired from the league of Hansa merchants), and to lead a secretly recruited force of about two thousand Flemings, who were to accompany Edward during his first two weeks in England. But still eager to project an image of neutrality,

Charles also prepared a proclamation to be issued on Edward's departure, forbidding his subjects to take part in the Yorkist attempt to regain the English crown. Satisfied that his strategy provided him with allies on both sides of the English struggle, the duke of Burgundy prepared to lead his troops westward into Picardy to face Louis XI.

Edward had left La Motte for Hesdin soon after Charles's departure in early January, eager for the opportunity to meet with his sister Margaret, for the first time since his arrival in Burgundy. They had much to discuss concerning Edward's return to England, as well as the balance of Margaret's unpaid dowry, and he remained with Margaret until January 13. As Isabel's important guests left her in the quiet of her retreat once more, it must have been gratifying to the dowager duchess that her strategies were still proving beneficial to Burgundy. Although overwhelmed with weariness from the strain of state matters, Isabel was almost joyful. Only the concern she felt for the outcome of her son's contest with the French king—not too far from the woods of Nieppe—filled her with apprehension.

Louis XI had planned a spring offensive against Burgundy to give Warwick time to organize his men in England and return with them to Calais. But learning that on January 13 the count of St. Pol, constable of France and formerly a close friend of Charles of Burgundy, had persuaded St. Quentin, the most fortified town of the Somme, to allow royal troops to garrison within its walls, Louis XI advanced quickly into Picardy. By January 26, seasoned French troops were garrisoned in towns all along the Burgundian border in Picardy. On February 3, the French king learned that his grand master of arms, the count of Dammartin, had persuaded Amiens, the second largest city of the Somme, to open its town's gates to royal forces. Now the French king controlled both the eastern and western ends of the Somme. His troops were ordered to wait in their garrisons along fifteen miles of the left bank of the river.

As Charles of Burgundy led his troops across the Somme toward Amiens in mid-February, Louis still waited for Warwick's men to sweep down from Calais, forming the second pincer of the attack that the earl and the king had planned. But Warwick never appeared in France, as Edward's forces had landed at the mouth of the Humber River in the northeast of England and the progress of his advance toward the town of York consumed all of the earl's attention.

As Louis XI's forces continued their fruitless wait for Warwick to appear, Charles's ten-day march was unopposed all the way to the walls of Amiens where he met twenty-five thousand of the best French troops, commanded by the Constable of France and the count of Dammartin. The duke of Burgundy attacked Amiens, placing the town under a two-week siege that battered the towns defenses, killed much of the population, and severely depleted Louis's forces before both leaders agreed to negotiate a truce. The chronicler de Commynes, who witnessed the struggle, noted Charles's exasperation when the battered town refused to surrender; for his part, Louis was determined not to wager his power on a single military action and was open to any face-saving means of withdrawing from the confrontation with Burgundy. Thus, when on March 12, Charles sent the king a conciliatory note in his own hand, Louis received it gladly. Charles wrote, sincerely it seems, of his indignation at the treachery that both he and the king suffered. Charles informed Louis that the king's own brother resented that he was no longer heir to the French throne since the birth of Louis's son, and was therefore restoring old alliances to regain his former power. Charles added that the count of St. Pol was seeking to emulate Warwick's strategy—attempting to hold the balance between two powers, Burgundy and France—to increase his own influence. Burgundy and France, Charles declared, had both been manipulated by men they trusted into a renewal of a war for the profit of others. Charles's note brought the desired effect, and on April 4 Louis XI and Charles of Burgundy agreed to a three-month truce to last through June 1471.

Isabel and the Lancastrian Inheritance

Waiting impatiently for the latest news of events in England and in Picardy, Isabel kept in close contact with Margaret during the critical days of late March and early April. Margaret wrote Isabel detailed accounts of

Edward's landing and his reunion with their brother Clarence. Margaret must have been thankful that her entreaties and those of her mother and sisters seemed to have prevailed and that instead of fighting, the brothers had once again joined forces. The duchess described for Isabel how the brothers' armies had faced one another near Banbury, fifty miles northwest of London, but that at the moment of confrontation, Clarence had ridden out alone, ahead of his men, and fallen on his knees before Edward, who had lifted him up, embraced him, and gladly acknowledged Clarence's cry, "Long live King Edward!" Margaret did not realize that their reconciliation probably had less to do with the pleading letters from the women in their family than with Clarence's decision that it was better to be the brother than the brother-in-law of a king.

Isabel also learned that although Clarence had failed in his attempt to persuade Warwick to join forces with Edward and accept him as the rightful king, Edward's strength grew in number as he marched eastward toward London. Edward's purse was filled with funds provided by Duke Charles and he used the money wisely, buying the services of adherents and strengthening his army as he approached London toward the middle of March. Warwick prepared to defend the capital, but his efforts were undercut by the disgruntled merchant population, who refused him their support. The puppet government that the earl managed for Henry VI offered the merchants nothing, neither profitable exchange with the French nor open trade with the Lowlands. Charles of Burgundy, however, promised them a return to the favorable rate of exchange with Holland and Flanders if they supported Edward of York. On April 11, Edward encountered only weak Lancastrian resistance when he marched into London. Warwick fled, leaving the merchants to look forward to more prosperous times.

As the restless truce between her son and Louis XI settled over the Somme area in early April, Isabel turned her full attention to the reports out of England. London settled down somewhat uneasily under Yorkist control, as Edward IV prepared to face the familiar challenge of defeating the forces of Henry VI on the battlefield to solidify his claim to wear the English crown. Isabel steeled herself for the inevitable clash. Whatever the outcome, she would assess it coolly and somehow find advantage in it for Burgundy.

The suspense drained the dowager of her usual energy, as a full week passed and then another without any news from Margaret. Charles was preoccupied with negotiations for the return of the cities of St. Quentin and Amiens from French occupation. Margaret was overwhelmed with the responsibilities of securing funds to keep Burgundian forces supplied. Isabel herself was often distracted by the outbreaks of plague in Champagne, which were increasing and spreading northward toward Picardy that spring. More and more people were appearing at her gate, pleading for help and bringing tales of the sickness that now reached many villages to the south. Despite these alarming tales, Isabel was in no mood to flee; she remained at La Motte-au-Bois, determined to wait for news from Margaret about the fates of Edward of York and her cousins Warwick and Henry VI.

Eventually, Isabel was to learn that after taking London, Edward had almost immediately set off in pursuit of the Lancastrian forces. Edward, who had brought King Henry with him, caught up with Warwick's men on April 13 on the St. Albans road near the town of Barnet, twelve miles northwest of London. Warwick's men were both tired and hungry. That night the Lancastrians camped on a hill covered by woods and scrub.

In the darkest hours before dawn, Edward moved his men along the low ground, positioning them within five hundred yards of the Lancastrian forces. Answering the trumpet's call to arms at daybreak on Easter morning, both armies found themselves blanketed in heavy ground fog. The men soon realized that their lines no longer faced each other, but extended beyond each other's positions at opposite ends. In the heat of battle, the Lancastrians soon doubled back on themselves, and one thousand men lost their lives in the first hour. Warwick was unable to marshal his forces for an attack on the center of Edward's line, and the earl and his brother were both killed while their army scattered in confusion. Henry VI, still a prisoner of Edward, forlornly returned to confinement in the Tower of London.

The dispatch that reached Isabel describing this Yorkist victory at Barnet field also contained details of Edward's disrespectful treatment of the corpse of her cousin, Warwick. Distressed by the news, Isabel asked Margaret for an explanation. Margaret responded that Edward had "heard that nobody in the city believed that Warwick and his brother were dead so he [Edward] had their bodies brought to St. Paul's where they were laid out and uncovered from the chest upwards in the sight of everybody." In late April, weary from the burdens of managing her woodland residence, Madame la Grande prepared to travel to Aire, some forty miles north. She would wait there instead for news of the fates of Henry VI and his son, Edward.

As Isabel's caravan rolled northward across the fields of Picardy toward Aire, another tragedy had already begun to unfold as Margaret of Anjou—ignorant of the events that had occurred on Barnet field—sailed to England with her son, Edward. The English queen had been keeping her son by her side, carefully protected at her uncle Louis XI's court, while Warwick prepared England to install the young prince on the throne in place of his father, Henry VI. Margaret and her son had prepared to board ship in France in late March, but a series of storms in the channel had thwarted them time after time. Finally, in late April, when the storms abated, Margaret and the young prince were able to sail to England. By then, however, they were too late to help Warwick.

Within days of their landing at Weymouth—and in spite of their belated discovery that Warwick had died on April 13—Queen Margaret's army moved northward. They met the Yorkist forces at Tewksbury, on the Severn River near the border with Wales, on May 4. Unable to prevent her son from joining the Lancastrians, Margaret and her ladies rushed to the protection of a nearby abbey. The Lancastrians turned at bay to meet Edward IV's challenge. But outnumbered and without Warwick's leadership, Margaret's forces were overwhelmed. As the Lancastrians scattered in disarray, the young prince attempted to escape by riding toward the safety of a nearby town. But the nineteen-year-old heir to the crown was captured by York's men, and while pleading with his brother-in-law Clarence for his life he was executed, with Edward's approval, on the spot. His mother was taken prisoner and returned to London, where she was imprisoned. Two weeks later Henry VI was found suffocated in his Tower cell. Word of the royal deaths reached Isabel along with rumors of Edward IV's complicity in the murders.

Isabel would surely have been joyful that the outcome at Tewksbury guaranteed Burgundian economic survival; on the other hand, though, she must have been distressed by the eradication of her own Lancastrian line. Familiar with the capricious demands of politics and the bitter rules of war, Isabel accepted victories and defeats with an equanimity that came from the practice of finding the success that hid in every loss. Nonetheless, she must have needed time to weigh the results of the great triangular struggle between France, Burgundy, and England in which she had played so active a part for forty years, and she retired for several days into the privacy and solitude of her chambers, taking no part in the court celebrations honoring the Yorkist triumph.

Isabel was pleased to reflect that Louis XI would now have to acknowledge that the Yorkist victory had destroyed his plan to dismember Burgundy, and she rightly anticipated that the king of France would be on the defensive. Louis's own allies, including his brother, Charles, his sister, Yolande, and the duke of Brittany, now turned readily to Isabel's son, to whom they pledged their money and military support against the French king. As the pleasant days of May slipped easily into June, she again seemed to improve. She became more involved and energetic than she had been for many months before, calling repeatedly for her legal and financial advisers, with whom she closeted herself for hours.

Isabel had controlled her own finances for twenty years, and she now began to put her estate in order for the future. She made plans to distribute her wealth to the many religious houses she had reformed and still supported; she made provisions for the several houses she had established for the care of the sick; she provided a large sum for her granddaughter, Marie, and prepared the papers that transferred her estate in La Motte-au-Bois to her daughter-in-law, Margaret. Most important, she wanted to guarantee the future power of the duchy by providing Burgundy with that elusive prize her husband had struggled to so long to win: legal claim to a royal crown. In early June, Isabel prepared to transfer her right of inheritance as the senior surviving member of the House of Lancaster to Charles of Burgundy.

The dowager's exertions quite probably led to a bout of serious illness later in June, which alarmed Charles and brought him to her side at Aire. But even before her son's return to the field in July to fight the French, Isabel felt well enough to undertake the official transfer to Charles of her claim to the English throne. All through the late summer and autumn of 1471, Edward IV's expressions of gratitude to the duke of Burgundy for his support were as enthusiastic as were his guarantees of their firm trade alliance. The English king's appreciation would no doubt have been less effusive if Edward had been aware of the claim to his throne that Charles would make public later that year.

The Death of Isabel of Burgundy

Isabel remained secluded at Aire all that summer, as the plague raged through Picardy, Brabant, Flanders, and Hainault. As her health continued to fail, concern for Charles diminished any peace of mind. She husbanded her strength, however, hoping each day to hear details of her son's campaigns in France. But no word came from her daughter-in-law, for Margaret was busy traveling from her residence at Le Crotoy, near the frontier, to neighboring towns to raise funds, collect supplies, and recruit men for her husband's army. There were no summer visits to allay Isabel's fears.

The Burgundians suffered many defeats in the campaign that summer. Perhaps Charles's most remarkable failure—as recorded by the chronicler Commynes, who witnessed many of the battles—was the duke's attack on Beauvais, where he spent three weeks besieging the town and losing more than three thousand men before finally breaking camp on July 22. As Charles resumed his march to Normandy through the richest and most fertile areas of France, from Rouen to the walls of Dieppe, his army stripped the countryside and razed all the villages in its path. Charles reached the right bank of the Seine by mid-August and established camp there to wait for his ally Duke Francis of Brittany to join him in an attack on Paris. But Louis XI had made certain that this meeting would never occur. As the Burgundians waited near Paris, they realized the growing danger of their position. For two weeks Charles's forces were harassed by French troops, who always refused combat yet hovered about the Burgundians, challenging them in whatever direction they chose to move, first appearing ahead of them and then racing to assume the defense of strong emplacements before the Burgundian troops could reach these positions.

Frustrated by the wait for his ally and by the French tactics, Charles learned that the French were also attacking the unprotected borders of Flanders and Hainault from positions in Dauphiny and Champagne. In early September the irate duke reluctantly abandoned his position on the Seine and began his march homeward. As Isabel waited to receive word that her son still lived, his army burned more than two thousand towns, villages, and castles on its return to Picardy, earning for the duke the name of "Charles the Terrible." But Charles had also added much to his military reputation by penetrating deeply into strongly fortified enemy territory with comparatively few losses and had returned his army whole, without any appearance of a hasty retreat.

When Charles finally came to visit his mother on October 14, he was alarmed by her condition. Her strength had ebbed during the summer months, and he remained with her at Aire until negotiations with Louis XI called him away, at which point he advised his wife and daughter to come to Aire to take his place. From October 21 onward, either Charles, Margaret, or Marie was to be found by Isabel's side. On November 11, Charles decided that the time had come to notarize the legal transfer of inheritance to the English throne from his mother to himself and made his proclamation public. The next day, November 12, Duke Charles issued a formal "ordonnance of state," declaring Burgundy independent of the French crown.

From mid-November to mid-December Isabel's condition worsened. For the final few days of her life, Isabel could take no nourishment, and her family watched helplessly as the tiny duchess slowly faded away. On December 17 Isabel lay back in the arms of her distraught son, and closing her eyes, Madame la Grande slipped away from this life with a quiet sigh.

Too distressed at his mother's death to orchestrate the first days of mourning, Charles let Count Ravenstein make the necessary arrangements. On December 18, the day after her death, the notables of the court and the town filled her chamber to pay their last respects to Isabel, who lay on her bed dressed in the robes of the Order of the Cordeliers (Foresters) she had founded. That night an autopsy was performed and her body was embalmed. She lay in state at Aire until December 29. Then, without Charles, who was still too distressed to lead the sorrowful cortege, Ravenstein escorted Isabel's body to Arques, St. Omer, and finally to St. Bertin on December 31.

Charles joined Ravenstein at St. Bertin on January 2 and accompanied his mother's body to Therouanne and finally to Gosnay on January 4, where she was interred for two years. On January 4, 1474, Charles traveled with the bodies of both his mother and father, from Gosnay and Mons, respectively, on a four-day progress southward to Dijon. They remained at the ducal residence in Dijon for one month while the tombs they had planned for placement in the Chartreuse de Champmol in that city were prepared. Philip the Good and Isabel of Burgundy were interred in the Chartreuse (the word means charterhouse, or monk's residence) on February 11, 1474. There they lay undisturbed until 1793, when in the violence of the French Revolution, the Chartreuse was destroyed. Nothing remains except the tomb of the duke and the doorway to the chapel.

Epilogue

DURING THE FORTY-ONE YEARS that she was duchess of Burgundy, Isabel parlayed the economic power of the duchy's northern territories into political power, enabling the duchy to play an influential role as both a broker and a player in the struggles between England and France and among the German princes of the empire. Isabel's close familial and political relationships with Portuguese and English royalty bore considerable weight in the courts of Europe and enhanced her effectiveness in both domestic and foreign negotiations. After her death, Burgundy lost first its influence and then its independence within a relatively short span of years.

After Isabel's death in 1471, a five-year series of truces with France allowed Charles to concentrate on territorial expansion. With a healthy and energetic Edward IV on the English throne, Charles decided not to press—but also not to forget—his legitimate claim to the Lancastrian crown. Instead, Charles organized his armies to move eastward to the Rhine and into the empire. By 1475 he had gained control of northern Alsace and of considerable lands on the east bank of the Rhine. These territorial gains encouraged the duke to dream, as his father had done, of uniting the northern and southern portions of Burgundy into a single, uninterrupted domain that would extend between France and the empire and run from the North Sea to the Mediterranean. This territory would be known as "Lotharingia," the name given to the ninth-century middle kingdom of Charlemagne's legacy. But two forces stood in the way of Charles's dream: one was Louis XI, the French king; the other was the League of Constance, a union of Swiss cantons and concerned German princes.

Louis XI did his best to strengthen imperial opposition to Charles's plans, cultivating the German princes' fears of Charles's ambition and brutality, encouraging Emperor Frederick III's natural distrust of an expansionist Burgundy, and giving the Swiss rich rewards for participating in the League of Constance. Meanwhile, with Isabel gone from the scene, Louis found it easy to lure Edward IV away from his alliance with Burgundy. Louis also waged a psychological war against the duke of Burgundy, spreading rumors to the effect that Charles lacked the character and financial strength to govern.

Preoccupied with military conquest, Charles was oblivious or least dangerously inattentive to Louis's machinations, and continued to extend his truce agreements with the French. During this period Louis XI so undermined the duke's credit that the Medici bankers not only refused to lend Charles any more money but also were prepared to call in his current debts. Having compromised Charles's financial status, the French king proceeded to choke Charles's Lowland trade and industry, crippling his economic base by blocking Burgundian trade routes and supporting piracy against his merchant vessels. As industrialized Holland, Zeeland, and Flanders were deprived of their normal food supply and smarted under the French embargo on French wine and wheat, their resentment of Charles grew. By 1476 Louis's continuing propaganda campaign against the duke's cruelties in Dinant and Liège had fueled a frenzy of fear against Charles's rule among German townsmen, convincing them that the duke was far more interested in war than in peace.

By 1476, as Charles swept through Lorraine to reclaim the capital of Nancy—without first attempting to subdue the surrounding towns that had slipped from his control while he campaigned farther south—he placed himself in great danger. Although his captains repeatedly begged him to retire from the field, where three men of the German and Swiss forces challenged his every two, he refused that advice. His chronic inability to acknowledge or correct a mistake in his own judgment led him to his ruin. Completely overwhelmed by the Swiss and German forces, the Burgundian army was put to rout outside the city of Nancy on January 5, 1477, Charles with them. Two days later, those searching the battlefield found the forty-four-year-old duke's body, naked, pierced with Swiss pikes, his head cleaved in two, identifiable only by his long nails and battle scars. Charles's dream of forging his duchy into a permanent middle kingdom died with him.

Before his death, however, Charles had arranged the engagement of his daughter, Marie, to Maximilian, the son of the Holy Roman Emperor, Frederick III. Charles's widow, now the dowager duchess Margaret of York, who had always cherished Marie as a daughter, was a great help to the heiress in the confusing months after Charles's death. Margaret's experience in her brother's court, where she had managed to avoid becoming a pawn in the games of others while helping to orchestrate her own marriage to the richest duke in Christendom, was invaluable in counseling Marie about the offers of marriage that now flooded into Ghent. Among those suitors Marie turned down were Edward IV's recently widowed brother, George, duke of Clarence; Louis XI's son, Charles, the dauphin; and the English queen's brother. Marie married Maximilian on August 18, 1477, in Ghent.

After the ducal marriage, Margaret of York moved quickly to obtain military aid from her brother, Edward IV, for besieged Burgundy. With this English support, Marie and Maximilian were able to withstand French military aggression along the borders of the weakened duchy. Resisting Louis XI's attempts to buy her loyalty with the promise of a French pension and his personal protection, Margaret then sailed to London to negotiate a resumption of the Anglo-Burgundian alliance that had ruptured during the years of Charles's eastern campaigns and to revitalize Lowland trade with England.

Margaret's efforts gained only a little time for Marie and Maximilian to bolster their defenses against French attacks. Repeated French inroads into Burgundian territory continued to dissipate the duchy's strength. In 1482, the weakened Burgundy sustained a tragic and mortal blow. While hunting in the parkland surrounding Bruges, Marie was thrown from her horse and broke her back. She died a few days later, on March 27. Within months, Burgundy was carved up between the empire and France. By July, Flanders made it known to Louis XI that the Flemish wanted peace with France irrespective of Maximilian's wishes. On December 23 the Three Estates of the Lowlands signed the Treaty of Arras with Louis XI securing that peace. Since Edward IV had extended the Anglo-French truce in 1477, he was unable to send Maximilian help to defend his territories against the French. Thus, the French acquired the Burgundian Lowlands, the duchy of Burgundy, Picardy, and the county of Boulogne. In addition, Mary's three-year-old daughter, Margaret of Austria, was betrothed to the dauphin of France and brought in her dowry the counties of Burgundy and Artois. The remainder of the great duchy that Charles had sought to build fell back into the control of the empire.

The tangible evidence of Isabel of Portugal's accomplishments has all but disappeared. Most of her letters and personal documents no longer exist; all of her residences have been destroyed; her tomb has been emptied. But this diminutive princess left a clear imprint on the history of Burgundy.

Talent and experience in finance enabled Isabel to reconstitute the state treasury system, build a personal fortune in trade and land, and develop and maintain a delicate series of Anglo-Burgundian trade treaties and alliances that sustained Burgundy's economic welfare. Although always a faithful ambassador for her husband's policies, she held firmly if sometimes only privately to her pro-English policy. She also rarely wavered from her strategy of maintaining contact with Burgundy's present and potential foes rather than pressing blindly ahead or resorting to war in an effort to secure Burgundy's goals.

There is a fascinating dichotomy—or, rather, a series of dichotomies—in Isabel's personality, which the researcher may uncover beneath her usually inscrutable demeanor. The Portuguese princess who became a duchess in the luxurious Burgundian court brought with her a stern sense of discipline and duty and an austere view of life. Although she enjoyed the richness of court life, she always remained an advocate of the poor. Her contemporaries saw her as both compassionate and haughty. An intelligent and level-headed diplomat and administrator, she was also capable of passionate anger and cruelty, fierce jealousy, and a dominating pride. When her reputation was called into question, she demanded the ultimate punishment, such as the one she called down on the town of Dinant, whose citizens had cast aspersions on her character and her son's legitimacy. These conflicts within her character reveal a woman with less assurance than her public image suggests.

Yet, in an age when men dominated virtually all fields of public life, Isabel possessed a commanding presence. Records note how quickly and humbly great officers of the Burgundian court responded to her summons and how assiduously ambassadors sought her opinions and her influence. Without Isabel, Burgundy would not have enjoyed many years of peaceful and profitable trade with England. Nor would it have obtained the formidable influence it exerted in the contest between England and France. Although her negotiations with France did not always yield the results Philip wanted, her conferences with Charles VII gained valuable time for Burgundy, enabling Philip to readjust his strategies in the Paris Parlement, in the conference room, and on the battlefield. After Isabel's death, Burgundy quickly fell apart, disintegrating into a patchwork of territories, some claimed by France, some by the Holy Roman Empire.

An active participant in diplomacy at the highest levels, an entrepreneur shrewdly investing in businesses and land who achieved substantial independent wealth, a patron of scholarship, and a reformer of religious orders: Isabel was the model of the aristocratic woman emerging from medieval shadows into the light of the Renaissance.

Index

Abbey of St. Vaast, 74–75, 78
Agnes, duchess of Bourbon, 22, 1265, 1343, 136–37
Aire, 214
Albergati, cardinal, 77
Alice, marchioness of Suffolk, 111
Alienor de Poitier, 99
Alsace, 201
Amiens, 211, 213
André de Chalonja, 24
Angevins, 96–98, 111, 161
Anglo-Burgundian relations, 157–58, 203; and cloth trade, 84–85, 109–10; Edward and, 208–9; Gravelines conference, 83–94; Isabel and, 94–100, 104, 137; treaties, 72–83, 106–7
Anglo-French relations, 112–13, 203; Gravelines conference, 83–94; issues in, 91–93; marriage and, 193–95; treaties, 72–83
Anglo-Portuguese relations, 8–9
Anne, duchess of Bedford, 22
Anne of France, 184
Anne of York, 10
Anthony, Grand Bastard of Burgundy, 58, 61–62, 112, 187–88
Anthony of Brabant, 22
Antoinette de Magnelais, 160
Arnoulfini, banker, 172
Arras, treaty of, 72–83, 98, 139, 222
Augsburg, cardinal of, 135
Auxonne, 66

Barnet, 213
Basel, 12
Baudoin de Lannoy, 24
Baudricourt, Robert, governor of Vaucouleurs, 38
Bavaria, duchess of, 135
Bavaria, duke of, 183, 192–93
Beatriz de Coimbra, 129, 167
Beaufort, Edmund, duke of Somerset, 103, 107–8, 113, 116–18, 202, 208–9
Beaufort, Henry, cardinal of Winchester, 56, 58–61, 69, 108–9, 114; at Arras, 76–77; and Gravelines, 88–90, 92–93
Beaufort, John, captain-general, 108

Beaulieu, 49
Beauvais, 216
Berry, bailiff of France, 137–38
Bona of Savoy, 177
Bonne of Artois, 22, 68, 71n18
Booth, Laurence, 155
Boulogne, 16, 80, 183
Bourbon, duke of, 73, 125, 133, 136–37
Bourges, 39
Bouvignes, 49
Brabant, 53–54
Brehal, Jean, 142
Brittany, 93
Bruges, 51, 68, 82, 104, 152, 189–90, 198–99
Brussels, 1–5, 16–19, 53–54, 104, 150, 170
Bulgneville, battle of, 85
Burgundian-French relations, 37, 48, 69, 133, 205, 213, 216–17; after death of Isabel, 219–22; conflict in, 152–55; Gravelines conference, 83–94; Isabel and, 95–99; Louis and, 170–73; marriage of Isabel and Philip and, 8–9; marriage plans and, 86–88; Philip and, 9–12, 103–6; treaties, 72–83
Burgundian-Portuguese relations, 27–28, 44n1
Burgundy, *xvi;* after death of Isabel, 219–22; court of, 19, 57, 73; dukes of, 22; independence of, 217; Joan of Arc and, 41–43; nobles of, 48, 73, 100n2; under Philip the Good, *21;* strategy of, 181–82. *See also* Anglo-Burgundian relations

Calais, 80, 91, 116, 137
Calixtus III, pope, 141
Catherine of Austria, 22
Catherine of France, 22, 86–88, 104–6
Catherine of Guise, 22
Catholic Church, 35, 78, 127–28, 132; and Joan of Arc, 56, 60–61, 141
Cauchon, Pierre, bishop of Beauvais, 55–56, 61
Chalons, 66, 68
Charles the Bold, duke of Burgundy, 14–19, 22, 84; birth of, 65–69; character of, 15, 105; conflict with Philip, 1–5, 16–19, 134, 148, 169, 177; as duke, 190–93, 199–205; and England, 11, 179, 207–10; marriages proposed for, 10, 106; marriage to Catherine, 86–88, 104–6; marriage to Isabel, 125, 134, 137–39, 182–84; marriage to Margaret, 9, 123, 184, 187–88, 193–99; as military leader, 217; relationship with Isabel, 10–11, 84, 105, 143, 169; relationship with Louis, 14–15, 150, 172–73, 179–83, 200, 203–5, 210–11, 220–21; relationship with Philip, 14–16, 174, 189
Charles V, king of France, 11, 22
Charles VII, king of France: and Burgundy, 11–13, 48, 100n2, 152–53; character of, 40; death of, 170–71; and Ghent, 121; goals of, 10; and Isabel, 79, 91, 98–99; Joan of Arc and, 9, 36–44, 55; and marriage of Charles the Bold, 137–38; as military leader, 124; murder of John the Fearless, 11, 76, 79–80; and Philip, 80, 133, 158–59; relationship with Louis, 145–46, 153, 156; right to throne, 118–19, 141
Charles VIII, king of France, 221–22
Charlotte of Savoy, 148, 172
Charny, Seigneur de, 101n2

Chastellain, Georges, 12, 149–50, 166, 174, 179, 188–89, 203, 205
Chaucer, Geoffrey, 111
Cicely, duchess of York, 166, 205
cloth trade, 50–51, 55, 109–10, 120–22; conflict and, 79–81, 84–85, 94, 114–15; in Ghent, 48–54; negotiations on, 90, 93–94, 120, 136, 153
Commynes, Philippe de, 180–81, 183, 205, 211, 216
Compiègne, 37, 43–44, 53, 55
Constantinople, 123
Coppini, Francesco, papal legate, 161–62, 169
Coudenberg, 54, 57–58, 63, 69, 104, 106, 150, 199
Crevecoeur, Jacques, Seigneur de, 20n11, 73–74, 88, 101n2
Le Crotoy, 216
de Croy family, 5; and Charles, 10, 15, 18–19; and France, 12–13, 20n11, 139–141; and Isabel, 145; and Philip, 10, 18–19, 134, 139–141, 148–49, 155, 181; territories of, 16, 182
de Croy, Agnes, 148
de Croy, Anthony, 1–2, 16, 62, 172; and France, 20n11, 48, 73–74, 101n2, 139
de Croy, Jehan, 16, 73–74, 101n2, 139, 148, 158
de Croy, Philippe, Seigneur de Renty, 25, 139
de Croy, Philippe, Seigneur de Sempy, 1–2, 13, 16, 18–19, 139
crusades, 25, 123, 126, 143n5, 147–48, 176, 178; feasts for, 129–33, 147; logistics of, 132–33, 137
Cyprus, cardinal of, 74–75
Cyprus, king of, 153, 170
Dauphiny, 15, 146–47, 217
Denmark, 12, 193
Deschamps, Paul, 50
Dijon, 65–69, 137
Dinant, 49, 183–84
Domessent, Louis, 106

écorcheurs (bandits), 12, 49, 80, 96–97, 146
Edmund of York, 164–65
Edward III, king of England, 102
Edward IV, king of England, 160, 194, 220; in Burgundy, 207–10; character of, 166; Isabel and, 166–70; marriage of, 178; and Wars of the Roses, 161–62, 165–66, 205, 211–14; and Warwick, 179, 195–96, 201–2, 213
Edward, the Black Prince, 102
Edward, king of Portugal, 24, 27–28, 30
Edward, Prince of Wales, 207, 214
Eleanor of Aragon, 24–25
Eleanor of Portugal, 14
Elector Palatine, 182, 192
Elisabeth of Burgundy, 129
English politics: Isabel and, 9–10, 32, 94–100, 102, 113–24, 127, 166–70, 211–16; Joan of Arc and, 36, 40–42, 44, 55–56, 59–60. *See also* Anglo-; Wars of the Roses
Estates, 70n4; of Dijon, 67, 69, 137; of Flanders, 51–52, 81–82, 94; of Lowlands, 222
Eugenius IV, pope, 128–29

Feast of the Pheasant, 129–33, 147
Fernando, prince of Portugal, 27, 29, 31–33
Flanders, 50, 81–83, 94, 110, 114–15, 217

Fougères, 115–16
France, *xvi;* Joan of Arc and, 9, 61; morale of, 9, 61, 139–43. *See also* Anglo-French relations; Burgundian-French relations
Franciscans, 85, 127–28
Francis II, duke of Brittany, 116, 160, 179–180, 193, 204, 215–16
Franc of Bruges, 51
Frederick III of Holy Roman Empire, 14, 115, 126, 128, 133, 220

Gascony, 124
Gauvain Quicaret, Seigneur de Dreuil, 131
Genappe, 16, 150
George, duke of Clarence, 166, 168, 184, 202–4, 212, 221
Georges de la Trémoille, 39–40, 48, 65
German states, 146, 170, 182–83, 201, 204, 220
Ghent, 48–54, 61–65, 119–21, 123, 191–92, 200–201
Gorinchem, 177, 179
Gravelines, 86, 88–94, 122
Gray Nuns, 127
Grey, John, 178
Groothouse, governor of Holland, 192
Guelders, duchess of, 64
Guelders, duke of, 74
Guilbaut, Guy, 20n11, 73–74, 101n2
guilds, 50–51, 67, 192
Guillaume de Clugny, 184, 194–95
Guillaume de Lalaing, 50–51, 62
Guy van Baenst, 196

Hainault, 16, 96, 140, 217
Hanseatic League, 80, 122, 209
Henry of Burgundy, 27
Henry III, king of Castile, 28
Henry IV, king of England, 28, 102
Henry V, king of England, 9, 23, 39, 102
Henry VI, king of England, 9, 102, 155, 167–68, 205, 213–15; and Burgundy, 116; and France, 39, 42, 55–56; insanity of, 124, 142; and Wars of the Roses, 107, 117–18, 163
Henry of England (son of Henry VI), 124, 162
Henry the Navigator, prince of Portugal, 27, 29–32
Holland, Henry, duke of Exeter, 118, 202, 208–9
Holy Roman Empire, 9, 11–12, 103, 123–24
Hughes de Lannoy, 76, 78, 81, 84–85, 88, 90, 99, 112, 127
Humphrey, duke of Gloucester, 102, 108–9, 113–14
Hundred Years War, 72–83, 146

Intercursus agreement, 94, 106–7
Iolanthe of Burgundy, 132
Isabel of Bourbon, 10, 22, 147, 149–50, 172, 182; death of, 183–84; marriage to Charles, 126, 133–34, 137–39
Isabel of Burgundy: as administrator, 52–53, 62–63, 65, 83; background of, 8–11, 27–32; character of, 3, 84, 95, 222–23; charity of, 29, 64, 68–69, 85–86, 127–28, 152, 213, 215; and Charles, 1–5, 10–11, 16–19, 84, 105, 143, 169, 199–205; and court of Burgundy, 19, 57; death of, 207–18; education of, 27, 29–30; and English politics, 9–10, 32, 94–100, 102, 113–24, 127, 166–70, 211–16; and financial issues, 52–53, 62, 128–29,

215; later life of, 187–206; and marriage of Charles and Margaret, 193–95, 197; marriage to Philip, 23–27, 32–37; as mother, 62–64; as negotiator, 2–5, 10, 48–54, 72–100, 158, 173–74, 195; and Philip, 1–5, 7–8, 15–18, 57–59, 84, 125–26, 140–41, 155–56, 166–67, 187; withdrawal of, 125–52
Isabel of Neufchâtel, 132

Jacotin de Croix, 86, 122
Jacques de Villiers, 47–48
Jaime de Coimbra, 129, 152
Jean Boursier, Seigneur d'Esternay, 153
Jean de Brimeu, Seigneur d'Humbercourt, 20n11, 73–74, 101n2
Jean de Heinsberg, bishop of Liège, 49, 58, 183–84
Jean de Luxembourg, count of Ligny, 44, 47, 49, 54–56, 60, 64, 127
Jean de Thoisy, bishop of Liège, 62
Jeanne de Bethune, countess of Ligny, 54–55
Jeanne of France, 188, 193
Jeanne de Harcourt, countess of Namur, 36–37, 58, 87
Jeanne, Lady of Luxembourg, 54–55
Joan of Arc, 36–44; capture of, 44, 47, 49, 54–55, 59; confession of, 59–60; execution of, 42, 61; and French morale, 9, 61; rehabilitation of, 119, 124, 141–42, 152–53; trial of, 56–57, 59–61
John, duke of Bedford, 38, 42, 57, 77–78, 102
John, duke of Berry, 22
John of Burgundy, 130
John, duke of Burgundy (the Fearless), 11, 22, 76, 79–80, 148
John, duke of Cleves, 37, 74, 129–30, 182, 192
John of Gaunt, duke of Lancaster, 8, 27–28, 102, 107
John I, king of Portugal, 8, 23, 26–28, 102
John II, king of France, 22
John, prince of Portugal, 27, 29, 32
Josse of Burgundy, 64
Juana (the Mad) of Castile, 22

Ladislas, king of Bohemia, 12
Lancastrians, 9, 107, 118, 124, 167, 204, 211–16. *See also* Henry VI; Margaret of Anjou
Lancelot de la Viefville, 62
Lang, Andrew, 46n11
League of the Common Weal, 182–83
League of Constance, 220
letters of marque, 120
Liège, 49, 62, 201
Lille, 88, 125, 127–28
Lionel, duke of Clarence, 102, 107
Lisieux, bishop of, 12
Lohengrin, 130
London, 203, 212
Lorraine, 12, 95
Louis, duke of Anjou, 22
Louis, duke of Bavaria, 135
Louis de Chalon, prince of Orange, 48
Louis XI, king of France, 147, 149, 170–74, 176, 179, 215; and Burgundy, 96–97, 151–52, 154–55; character of, 15, 148, 151, 172–73; and Charles the Bold, 14–15, 150, 172–73, 179–83, 200, 203–5, 210–11, 220–21; and Charles VII,

145–46, 153, 156; and marriage of Charles, 193–95, 199; and Philip, 4–6, 12–13, 16–19, 147–48, 150–51, 160, 171–72, 175–78, 181
Louis de Luxembourg, 56
Louis St. Pol, constable of France, 64, 192, 210–11
Lowlands, 57–65, 80, 222
Luxembourg, 12, 16, 54, 182
Luxembourg, Jean de. *See* Jean de Luxembourg

Mâcon, 67–68
Maine, 112–13, 117
Margaret of Anjou, 9, 12, 97, 99, 103–4, 111–12;
and France, 118, 175; and Henry, 124, 142, 167–68; and Wars of the Roses, 109, 114, 116, 127, 155, 159–60, 162–64, 204–5, 217
Margaret of Austria, 222
Margaret of Flanders, 22
Margaret of York, 9, 22, 123, 184, 187–88, 193–95, 216, 221–22; and Charles, 195–205; and Isabel, 210–12, 215
Maria of Cleves, 22
Maria of Savoy, 22
Marie of Anjou, 85, 97–99, 146
Marie of Burgundy, 22, 149–50, 167, 182, 184, 192, 197, 215, 221–22
Marie of Burgundy, duchess of Cleves, 58
Maximilian of Holy Roman Empire, 22, 221–22
Medici bankers, 52, 220
Metz, 12, 95
Michelle of France, 22, 71n18
Milanese ambassador, 160–61, 177, 192
Mont St. Michel, 93
La Motte-au-Bois, 8, 152–55, 173–74, 187, 199, 208–9, 213

Namur, 16, 49, 182
Nancy, 12, 95, 220
Neville, Richard. *See* Warwick
Nicolas V, pope, 126
Nieppe, 129, 152
Normandy, 93, 107, 117

Oliver La March, 179–81
Olivier de la Marche, 12, 129
Order of the Cordeliers, 218
Order of the Garter, 48, 204
Order of the Golden Fleece, 35–36, 132, 152, 190, 198
Orléans, duchess of, 136
Orléans, duke of, 75, 78, 85, 90–92, 95–96, 136

pageantry: Feast of the Pheasant, 129–33; Isabel's entry to Arras, 74; Isabel's entry to Brabant, 54; Isabel's entry to Burgundy, 26–27; marriage of Isabel and Philip, 33–36; marriage of Margaret and Charles, 197–99
Partition Ordinance, 110
Peronne, treaty of, 200, 204–5
Peter, prince of Portugal, 24, 27, 29–31, 167
Philibert of Savoy, 193
Philip St. Pol, duke of Brabant, 53
Philip of Bresse, 188, 193
Philip the Bold, duke of Burgundy, 11, 22
Philip the Good, duke of Burgundy, 6–8, 11–14, 22; and Brabant, 53–54;

character of, 3, 13, 83; and Charles the Bold, 1–5, 14–19, 134, 148, 169, 174, 177, 189; and Charles VII, 12–13, 80, 133, 158–59; and cloth trade, 110, 121–22; death of, 188–90; and England, 76–77, 114–15; and France, 9–13, 97, 99–100, 103–6, 140, 154, 177; and Gravelines, 89–90; illness of, 155–56, 166–67, 187; and Isabel, 15–16, 57–59, 84, 125–26, 140–41, 166–67, 187; Joan of Arc and, 41–44, 47, 49, 55, 142; and Louis, 4–6, 12–13, 16, 147–48, 150–51, 160, 171–72, 175–78, 181; and marriage of Charles, 137–38; marriage to Isabel, 23–27, 32–37; as military leader, 66–69, 81–82, 84–85, 119–21, 123; mistresses and illegitimate children of, 58, 84, 112, 132, 134, 156, 187, 198; and pageantry, 129–33
Philip of Castile (the Handsome), 22
Philip, count of Nevers, 22, 71n18
Philippa of Portugal, 8, 28–29, 102
Picardy, 41, 140, 148
Pierre d'Amboise, 136–37
piracy, 11–12, 80, 120, 141, 203
Pius II, pope, 95, 176
plague, 69, 84, 213, 216
Poor Clares, 86, 127, 152
Poperinge, 77–78
Portugal: and Burgundy, 27–28, 44n1 and England, 8–9
Pot, Philippe, 7, 16, 138, 143n5
Poulegny, Bertrand de, 38
pourpoints, jackets, 57

quellote, 192

Ravenstein, lord, 198, 217–18
Regnault de Chartres, chancellor of France, 87
René of Anjou, 85, 96–100, 145, 161
René, duke of Bar, 38
Richard II, king of England, 102
Richard III, king of England, 188, 193, 203
Richard, duke of Gloucester, 166, 168
Richard, duke of York, 95, 104, 107–8, 113–14, 116, 118, 127; death of, 164–65; Isabel and, 122–23; and Wars of the Roses, 154–55, 160, 163
Rolin, Nicolas, 12, 65, 67, 74–75, 84, 140; and France, 20n11, 73–74, 101n2; son of, 2
Roubaix, Jean, Seigneur de, 24–25, 33, 62

St. Albans, battle of, 9
St. Croix, cardinal of, 74–75
St. Omer, 80, 86, 169, 175–78
St. Quentin, 210, 213
Salisbury, lord, 160, 164
Sandal Castle, 163
Savoy, duke of, 12, 147
Sforza, Francesco, duke of Milan, 161, 170
Sforza, Galeazzo, duke of Milan, 193
Sicily, queen of, 99
Sigismund, duke of Austria, 201
Sigismund of Holy Roman Empire, 53
Simon de Lalaing, 121, 158, 196
Somerset, duchess of, 117
Somerset, Edmund, duke of, 103, 107–8, 113, 116–18, 202, 208–9
Somme towns, 87, 121, 176–77, 181–83, 210
Sorel, Agnes, 146, 159

Staple, 90, 110, 120, 141
Staple and Bullion Ordinance, 110
Stouton, John, 113–14
Suffolk, earl of, 103, 109, 111–13, 116–18
Swiss cantons, 12, 146, 201, 204, 220

Ten Waele, 49–50, 54, 63, 81
Termonde, 5, 16
Thibault de Neufchâtel, marshal of Burgundy, 97
Toison d'Or, 141
Toul, 12, 95
Turks, 123, 126

Ulrich, count of Wurttemberg, 58, 134–35
Utenhove, Henri, 90, 94, 106

Valeran des Aubeaux, 129
Valois, House of, 11
Venice, 176
Verdun, 12, 95

Wars of the Roses, 116–24, 153–54, 159–63, 165–67, 203–4, 211–16; beginning of, 9–10, 103–4, 107–8, 113–16
Warwick, Richard Neville, earl of, 124, 154–55, 157, 201–2; and Edward, 179, 195–96, 202, 213; and France, 174, 178, 188, 193, 203, 209–11; and Wars of the Roses, 160–62, 165–68

Yolande of France, 215
Yorkists, 9, 159, 161, 167, 177, 203, 205. *See also* Edward IV; Richard, duke of York

Zedelaire, Guillaume le, 62

About the Author

Aline S. Taylor, former editor of three academic journals, including *Medievalia et Humanistica* and *Progress of Medieval and Renaissance Studies in the United States and Canada*, and professor of history, is currently a reader and researcher at the Huntington Library in California, where she specializes in sixteenth-century political history. She is the author of *The French Baron of Pentagouet: Baron St. Castin and the Struggle for Empire in Early New England.*